Ruth Davidson's Conservatives

Ruth Davidson's Conservatives

The Scottish Tory Party, 2011–19

Edited by
DAVID TORRANCE

EDINBURGH
University Press

Edinburgh University Press is one of the leading university presses in the UK. We publish academic books and journals in our selected subject areas across the humanities and social sciences, combining cutting-edge scholarship with high editorial and production values to produce academic works of lasting importance. For more information visit our website: edinburghuniversitypress.com

Edinburgh University Press Ltd
The Tun – Holyrood Road, 12(2f) Jackson's Entry, Edinburgh EH8 8PJ

Typeset in 10/13 Giovanni by
IDSUK (DataConnection) Ltd, and
printed and bound in Great Britain.

A CIP record for this book is available from the British Library

ISBN 978 1 4744 5562 6 (hardback)
ISBN 978 1 4744 5563 3 (paperback)
ISBN 978 1 4744 5564 0 (webready PDF)
ISBN 978 1 4744 5565 7 (epub)

CONTENTS

TABLES

NOTES ON THE CONTRIBUTORS

Alan Convery is senior lecturer in politics at the University of Edinburgh. He is the author of *The Territorial Conservative Party: Devolution and Party Change in Scotland and Wales* (2016) and is the lead editor of the *British Journal of Politics and International Relations*.

Mark Diffley is a social researcher, political pollster and consultant based in Edinburgh. He worked as Director of Ipsos MORI Scotland for ten years before launching his own company, Mark Diffley Consultancy and Research, in 2017. During his career, Mark has worked with and advised parties and campaigns from across the political divide, notably leading the UK Government's polling during the 2014 independence referendum and, currently, advising Progress Scotland on its polling and research activity.

Jonathan Evershed is a postdoctoral research fellow at University College Cork, where he works on the Economic and Social Research Council project 'Between Two Unions: The Constitutional Future of the Islands after Brexit'. He specialises in the study of the politics and culture of Unionism and Loyalism in Northern Ireland and his first monograph, *Ghosts of the Somme: Commemoration and Culture War in Northern Ireland*, was published in 2018.

Paris Gourtsoyannis has been Westminster correspondent of the *Scotsman* since 2016, covering the aftermath of the EU referendum and the 2017 general election. Prior to that, he worked on the Scottish edition of *The Times*, the *Edinburgh Evening News* and *Holyrood* magazine, where his first assignment was Ruth Davidson's leadership campaign launch in 2011. He graduated from the University of Edinburgh in 2010.

Dr Gerry Hassan is a writer, commentator and Senior Research Fellow at Dundee University. He has written and edited more than two dozen books on Scotland, the UK, social change and the future of society, politics and ideas. His most recent publications include *The People's Flag and the Union Jack: An Alternative History of Britain and the Labour Party* as well as the collections *Scotland the Brave? Twenty Years of Change and the Future of the Nation and The Story of the Scottish Parliament: The First Two Decades Explained*.

Richard Hayton is associate professor of politics at the University of Leeds. He has published widely on British politics and the Conservative Party, and is founding editor of the New Perspectives on the Right book series hosted by Manchester University Press.

Chrysa Lamprinakou is a research associate at the University of Strathclyde. She was previously a postdoctoral researcher at the Parliamentary Candidates UK (PCUK) research programme, hosted by University College London and Birkbeck, University of London. She has also taught at University College London and Brunel University. Her research and teaching areas are British politics, elections, candidates and elected officials.

Murray Stewart Leith is Professor of Political Science at the University of the West of Scotland. He researches national identity, nationalism and politics and lectures widely on Scotland, the broader United Kingdom and the United States. His most recent works focus on the nature and identity of Scots both at home and abroad and the evolving diaspora policy of the Scottish Government. His latest co-authored work, *Scotland: The New State of an Old Nation*, will be published in 2020.

Neil McGarvey is a senior teaching fellow in the School of Government and Public Policy at the University of Strathclyde, Glasgow. He is the co-author (with Paul Cairney) of *Scottish Politics* (2008, 2013, new edition in draft) and has published widely in the fields of Scottish politics, local government and public administration.

David Patrick works as a postdoctoral research fellow with the International Studies Group (University of the Free State, South Africa). He was awarded his PhD in history from the University of Sheffield in 2013, and his first monograph, *Reporting Genocide: Media, Mass Violence and Human Rights*, was published in 2018. His current research interests include media coverage of the 2014 independence referendum and sociological components related to professional boxing in the twentieth century.

Anthony Salamone is Managing Director of European Merchants, the Scottish political insight firm which he founded in Edinburgh. A political scientist and analyst, his interests focus on EU politics and institutions, Scottish politics, British politics and international relations. He has degrees from the University of Edinburgh and the London School of Economics, and is completing a PhD in British and European politics at Edinburgh. He is a Members of the Edinburgh Europa Institute.

Jennifer Thomson is a lecturer in comparative politics at the University of Bath. She is the author of *Political Institutions and Abortion Law: Explaining Policy Resistance* (2018) which looks at the case study of abortion law in Northern Ireland. She has published many articles in journals including *International Studies Review, International Political Science Review* and the *British Journal of Politics and International Relations*.

Lauren Toner graduated from the University of Strathclyde with a dissertation on the Scottish Conservative Party. She is currently an MSc student of political research, an undergraduate tutor and will begin her PhD in 2020. Her previous employment includes both the private and public sector, most recently at the Scottish Parliament.

David Torrance was for many years a freelance journalist, writer and broadcaster, as well as author or editor of more than a dozen books on Scottish politics. Since 2018, he has kept his opinions to himself as a constitutional researcher at the House of Commons Library.

INTRODUCTORY NOTE

This volume was originally conceived as a study of the Scottish Conservative revival after the 2016 Holyrood elections. Following the resignation of Ruth Davidson as party leader in August 2019, it became an analysis of the Scottish Conservatives during the period of her leadership, 2011–19. It therefore does not include analysis of the December 2019 UK general election.

ONE

'Ruth Davidson's Conservatives', 2011–19

David Torrance

Introduction

Reflecting on her election as leader of the Scottish Conservative Party seven years after the event, Ruth Davidson said she had 'no intention' of seeking to replace Annabel Goldie after the 2011 Holyrood election. 'I was the youngest member of our parliamentary group and the only new face,' Davidson wrote in 2018. 'I needed to learn my trade before I could even think about taking on any sort of leadership role.'

But then, by Davidson's account, Murdo Fraser announced his plan to create a completely new centre-right party in Scotland. 'The idea that a new party with a new name – but essentially the same people and policies – would suddenly succeed where the current model had failed struck me as illogical,' said Davidson. 'To me, we would look like Tories who were ashamed to be Tory. And I wasn't.'

> After a long talk with a senior member of the Scottish party, I was persuaded to stand for the leadership ... I [became] the youngest party leader of a major political party anywhere in the UK, as well as the least experienced. I had no idea how to lead, and on the horizon I had the single biggest and most important vote in my lifetime – on the very existence of the United Kingdom. (Davidson 2018a: 11–13)

Murdo Fraser offered his own reflection on the 2011 leadership election in 2019. When Davidson had defeated him, he admitted, he 'didn't believe that the party was capable of revival'. 'I underestimated her,' added Fraser, but with 'a combination of energy, charisma, and a great deal of effort, she took the Scottish Conservatives from political irrelevance to being the second force in Scottish politics.'

In this, she was substantially assisted by the SNP's drive for independence, and the way in which the 2014 referendum changed Scottish politics for a generation: dividing us into a country of unionists or nationalists. By making the Conservatives the party of the Union, we were able to garner the votes of many of those who would not in the past have considered supporting us. (*Scotsman*, 3 September 2019)

There was a degree of post hoc analysis in these accounts, not least because Davidson's path to the leadership had been more premeditated than a spontaneous response to Fraser's candidacy,[1] but both were correct in identifying the 2014 independence referendum as a critical juncture in Scottish Conservative – and therefore Ruth Davidson's – fortunes.

The original intention of this volume was to examine the revival of the Scottish Conservative Party under Davidson's leadership. Her resignation in August 2019 prompted a rethink. Happily, it did not radically alter the content of chapters already written, while those in progress simply required an alteration of tenses. Ironically, the Scottish Tory leader's resignation provided the book with a more definite conclusion than it would otherwise have enjoyed, particularly during a period of political and constitutional uncertainty. *Ruth Davidson's Conservatives* is, therefore, a study of the Scottish Conservative Party and its leader between 2011 and 2019.

Teething Troubles

The party leadership election of 2011 generated a lot of media interest, particularly Murdo Fraser's declaration that there was 'no future for the Scottish Conservative and Unionist Party in its current form' (*Guardian*, 5 September 2011). His proposal for a completely new centre-right party won support from a majority of Scottish Conservative MSPs (Members of the Scottish Parliament) and party grandee Sir Malcolm Rifkind. Ruth Davidson, therefore, ended up being the 'continuity' candidate, her five-point plan to revitalise the party (including comprehensive policy reviews) winning support from two MSPs and another party grandee, Lord Forsyth. As Convery observed, in the absence of any major ideological or policy differences beyond the constitution, issues of personality became more prominent: 'Who would most likely lead the Scottish Conservatives to electoral success?' (Convery 2014b: 319).

Davidson won the contest by 2,983 votes to second-placed Fraser's 2,417, but began her tenure in a position similar to that later experienced by UK Labour leader Jeremy Corbyn, sustained by a party membership mandate but lacking significant support among parliamentary colleagues. In her first Scottish conference speech as leader, she claimed the party could once again be the voice and choice of the 'Scottish mainstream'. To that end, Davidson announced a rebranding exercise, with a new logo to replace David Cameron's doodled tree. This was unveiled towards the end of 2012, an eight-pronged cross that she said was 'distinctly Scottish but with colours which clearly reflect our pride in the United Kingdom' (*Scotsman*, 24 November 2012). This owed something to the party's history, the old Scottish Unionist Party logo having featured a combination of the Union and Saltire flags (Torrance 2017).

Davidson was deemed to have performed well enough at the weekly First Minister's Questions, although without landing too many blows on the (admittedly more experienced) Alex Salmond. At local government elections in May 2012, her party continued its electoral decline, losing 28 councillors compared with 21 gains in 2007. Davidson appeared unable to set out, as promised, a precise strategy for a Conservative revival north of the border, prompting 'internal muttering' about her leadership and even talk that Murdo Fraser would 'launch a coup' (private information).

When it came to domestic policy, Ruth Davidson also failed to innovate, instead observing during the 2012 UK Conservative Party conference that a 'corrosive sense of entitlement' in Scotland meant that only 12 per cent of Scottish households paid more in taxes than they received via public services (*Daily Mail*, 8 October 2012). There were noises about freeing schools from local authority control (and 'vouchers', a policy that dated back to the late 1980s), halting wind farms and strengthening non-custodial sentences, but as Magnus Gardham commented, 'it was traditional Tory fare and entirely predictable' (*Herald*, 10 November 2012).

After a year as Scottish Conservative leader, Davidson had little to show in terms of policy development, strategic direction or opinion polls. Writing in his diary, the *Telegraph* columnist Alan Cochrane declared the Scottish Conservative leader 'absolutely awful':

> She is totally and utterly useless and so are her team. They haven't a bloody clue but she is the problem – big problem. Not up to the job, as Attlee would say, and I suspect that some hacks will start asking questions. [David] Mundell said he knew she wasn't cutting the mustard . . . But he claims they've got someone lined up to help her. Christ, they need it. They're all just bairns in her office and I suspect the Tory MSPs ain't helping her. (Cochrane 2014: 85)

Pulling Together

'We were at our lowest ebb, we had our least number of political representatives, least amount of money, the least amount of direction,' Davidson said of the pre-2014 Scottish Conservative Party, 'we were considered a joke, and actually the referendum helped us pull together as a party' (BBC Scotland 2019). Similarly, in 2012, David Cameron predicted that the forthcoming fight for the Union would imbue the Scottish Conservatives with renewed vigour, just as resistance to Irish Home Rule had a century before (Torrance 2012). Both were correct, although it proved a slow burner.

The party's 'Conservative Friends of the Union' campaign, however, indicated the existence of a 'unionist' vote beyond Scottish Tory supporters, attracting 50,000 offers of support and money by November 2012 (*Telegraph*, 5 November 2012).[2] But there was a problem. During the leadership election, Davidson had declared that the Calman Commission's recommendations for the partial devolution of fiscal and welfare powers to Holyrood were to be a 'line in the sand'. This, however, was washed away by the Prime Minister in February 2012. 'When the referendum is over,' Cameron told business leaders, 'I am open to looking at how the devolution settlement can be improved further' (*Scotsman*, 17 February 2012).

Convery criticised such 'ad hoc' constitutional policy-making (Convery 2014a), although the Prime Minister's pledge compelled Davidson to respond. She began to pivot with a Burn's Night speech in January 2013, during which she ruminated on Scottish Conservative decline:

> Uncomfortable though it may be to admit, too many of our fellow Scots whose values we share simply don't trust our motives. When it comes to Westminster elections they see us as London's party in Scotland not Scotland's party in London. When it comes to elections to the Scottish Parliament, they want to vote for a party that will put Scotland first, and too few truly believe that of us. We need to prove to them beyond all reasonable doubt we do indeed put Scotland first, and that we are single-mindedly determined to do so in the future. (*Telegraph*, 25 January 2013)

A key part of Davidson's leadership strategy thus became establishing distance between *her* party on the periphery and David Cameron's party at the centre. 'Ruth and I were immediate political soulmates,' recalled Cameron in his memoirs. 'I was so proud of how much our party had changed, and excited about what we could achieve with Ruth at the helm in Scotland' (Cameron 2019: 316). A few months later, Davidson established a working group to make good on the Prime Minister's promise of further powers, to be chaired by UK party grandee Lord Strathclyde.

Convery urged the party finally to begin formulating a Conservative vision for devolution 'from first principles' rather than being 'swept along in the pro-devolution tide without a compass by a mixture of guilt and expediency' (Convery 2014a). Murdo Fraser, who had proposed greater fiscal accountability as well as a new party in 2011, was quick to note the irony, although he concluded it was 'still too early to herald a new dawn', a reminder that Davidson did not enjoy unequivocal support from her Holyrood colleagues. Even Lord Forsyth, an early backer of Davidson's leadership, said her plan for greater fiscal devolution was 'a bit like a suicide mission' that would hit Conservative supporters 'extremely hard in the pocket' (*Scotsman*, 27 May 2013).

Davidson's biographer viewed the 2013 Scottish Conservative spring conference as 'the point at which she tackled internal critics and delivered a fundamental change to the party that would make it electable again' (Liddle 2018: 148). Scottish Government legislation to legalise same-sex marriage later that year also helped the Scottish Conservatives to 'modernise' in the same way Cameron had with similar legislation in England and Wales, with Davidson's speech in that debate widely praised. Initially reluctant to talk about her private life (she had broken up with a long-term partner in March 2013), Davidson's sexuality, as charted by Jennifer Thomson in Chapter 6, increasingly came to the fore.

Lord Ashcroft analysed Scottish Conservative prospects in a report, *Cameron's Caledonian Conundrum*, published in October 2013. Based on a 10,000-sample poll, focus groups and follow-up surveys, it found what many Scottish Tories had long believed, that there were 'potential Tories at large in Scotland'. As well as a small 'Tory Core', Ashcroft identified a group of what he called 'Reluctant Cameroons', one in six of the Scottish electorate who liked Cameron and trusted his party on the economy but would not readily vote Conservative. Finally, another one in ten constituted the 'Willing to Listen' group, those currently leaning towards Labour despite preferring Cameron as Prime Minister.

Ashcroft identified three drawbacks for the potential Conservative vote in Scotland: first, people doubted the Conservatives were 'on their side'; second, they did not feel the party cared much for Scotland or for devolution; and third, they considered the Conservatives to be irrelevant in Scottish elections. At the same time, he found swing voters had 'a generally positive view' of Ruth Davidson, remembering, for example, that she had been asked for proof-of-age identification while trying to buy beer at a concert at Glasgow's Hampden Park.

When it came to policy, Ashcroft found that many of those open to voting Conservative felt Holyrood's job was 'to wave the flag and hand out the money'; therefore, advocating greater fiscal responsibility could be to the party's 'political advantage' in that the Scottish Tories would then assume the role of making sure 'the books were balanced', thus solving the problem of perceived relevancy *and* lack of enthusiasm for devolution. 'As long as voters think the Scottish Parliament exists to sign the cheques,' concluded Ashcroft, 'while the fiscal prudence happens elsewhere, the Conservatives will seem redundant' (Ashcroft 2013).

The Scottish Conservatives had clearly reached the same conclusion. Indeed, even before Lord Strathclyde published his recommendations, David Cameron told the 2014 Scottish Tory conference that giving Holyrood 'greater responsibility for raising more of the money it spends' was 'what Ruth believes – and I believe it too'. In a Q&A session with members of the Strathclyde Commission, only one questioner was (politely) opposed to the idea of devolving more powers, an indication – according to party strategists – that most Scottish Tories had learned to stop worrying and love devolution (*Herald*, 17 March 2014). Having been, as Convery put it, 'anti-devolutionists' (until 1999), 'willing participants' (1999–2009) and then 'half-hearted supporters of further powers' (2009–14), the party was finally working its way towards a 'definitive answer' (Convery 2016b: 4). More generally, Davidson declared that Scotland's referendum debate was 'revitalizing' the Conservatives (ConservativeHome, 14 March 2014), although she could only have been referring to activists rather than its poll ratings.[3]

The Commission on the Future Governance of Scotland reported in May 2014, recommending, as expected, the full devolution of income tax and some additional welfare powers (Scottish Conservative Party 2014b). Notably, it made no mention of reforming or abolishing the Barnett formula, which Davidson had earlier declared to be 'in its death throes' (BBC News online, 26 March 2013). Nevertheless, Convery viewed the Strathclyde Commission as significant in two ways: first, the Scottish Conservatives appeared to have 'found a path through the competing ideological demands of their Conservatism and Unionism' and, second, for the first time since the 1970s they had 'something authentically Tory and positive to say about devolution'. Even more strikingly, the party had managed to 'outbid' Scottish Labour when it came to further devolution (Convery 2014c).

Davidson said she relished the opportunity to 'marry these vital Conservative instincts' of responsibility and accountability, Holyrood's ability to spend but not (necessarily) tax having proved 'a licence to avoid difficult decisions and blame others' (*Scotland on Sunday*, 1 June 2014). This move came just months before the independence referendum and eventually dovetailed with similar commitments from Davidson's 'Better Together' colleagues. The Scottish Conservative leader, as David Patrick notes in Chapter 7, was actually a rather marginal figure in that long campaign, although she at least enjoyed greater party coherence than Scottish Labour and the Liberal Democrats, with only a tiny fringe of Conservatives pledging support for independence.[4]

It later emerged that Davidson had been unhappy with her UK party colleagues in the later stages of the referendum campaign (or at least wanted that to be the perception). She thought the Prime Minister, Ed Miliband and Nick Clegg deciding to 'chuck PMQs and dash to Scotland' was a 'gimmick', while she was reportedly 'f***ing furious' with Cameron over the so-called 'Vow' (a cross-party commitment to grant Scotland more autonomy). 'I wish,' Davidson remembered saying, 'people would just hold their effing nerve' (Liddle 2018; BBC Scotland, 19 March 2019). Two days before the Smith Commission (formed after the referendum to make good on the Vow) published its report, the Scottish Tory leader apparently told Andrew Dunlop, Cameron's adviser on Scotland, that the UK Government would 'have to suck it up' and deliver whatever Lord Smith recommended (Pike 2015: 197).

'Poster girl for a Tory revival'

With the Union apparently secure, Ruth Davidson made an audacious bid to occupy 'the centre-ground of Scottish politics'. She also framed Nicola Sturgeon, about to succeed Alex Salmond, as, improbably, the 'most Left-wing First Minister Scotland has ever known', as well as a referendum 'denier' determined to 'put the country back through what we've just finished' (*Scottish Daily Mail*, 1 October 2014).

Davidson thus viewed the referendum as having aligned her party with the 'silent majority' of unionist Scots, from which she clearly expected to derive electoral benefits. When Salmond formally resigned as First Minister in November 2014, the Scottish Conservative leader nominated herself as his successor, feeling the need to offer 'an alternative vision of Scotland'. This hinted at a developing strategy of presenting the Scottish political arena as Sturgeon versus Davidson.

But over the next six months, the polls did not budge, although John Curtice detected a modest rise in Scottish Conservative support between 2012 and 2014 (Liddle 2018: 166). Undeterred, Davidson predicted that thousands of 'Tartan Tories' were 'coming back home', attracted by what she called the 'best-regimented, best-organised, best-resourced and best-recruited' campaign in twenty years (*Scottish Daily Express*, 26 April 2015). According to Pike, Davidson had no objection to the UK party's demonisation of the Scottish National Party (SNP) during the 2015 general election, having herself referred to 'Alex Salmond pulling the strings in Westminster' (Pike 2015: 215).

It was at this stage that Davidson began to attract a small group of media cheerleaders, although what Bale (2010) called a Conservative

'Party in the media' did not exist to anything like the same degree as in England. 'Fearless, fiery and funny . . . Ruth's the poster girl for a Tory revival,' proclaimed the *Scottish Daily Mail*, although its author, Chris Deerin, noted a weak 'talent pool' beyond Davidson, Murdo Fraser and Eddie Barnes, her 'canny, street-smart' Director of Strategy and Communications. Deerin also attempted to extract a political philosophy from the Scottish Conservative leader. 'The reason I'm a Tory is because I believe people make better decisions about their lives than the state,' said Davidson:

> I believe hard work should be rewarded, that aspiration and opportunity shouldn't be dirty words, that a pound in the pocket is better spent by the person who earned it rather than by some nameless, faceless government official . . . It doesn't matter where you're from, it's what you do and where you're going that counts. Responsibility, hard work, just reward, helping those at the bottom and clearing a path for others to explore even greater horizons. (*Scottish Daily Mail*, 9 April 2015)

This was an orthodox blend of Thatcherite and Cameronian tropes, and indeed, beyond setting herself against SNP-style universalism (on, for example, prescription charges and tuition fees), the Scottish Conservatives remained policy 'lite' almost four years into Davidson's leadership. 'We've been promised a Conservative revival in every election for a decade,' one sceptical Conservative told Pike ahead of the 2015 election, 'Ruth Davidson's biggest problem is she's a Tory' (Pike 2015: 288).

On polling day, Davidson worried that her sole MP (Member of Parliament) in Scotland (and Scottish party chairman), David Mundell, would be swept away by the SNP tsunami (Pike 2015: 265). Mundell held on, but the party garnered its lowest-ever share of the vote. 'The persistence of an anti-Conservative mood amongst a significant part of the Scottish electorate,' concluded Mitchell, 'remains important' (Mitchell 2015: 100). Davidson put a brave face on the result, arguing that hers was the only pro-UK party to increase its vote, although the SNP said it was the worst Conservative performance (14.9 per cent) in Scotland in more than 150 years (*Sunday Herald*, 10 May 2015).

The party's strategy of trying to 'cleave away' 'No' voters from other unionist parties in places like Perthshire had failed. '[Ruth] was excellent – genuine and conducts herself well,' one voter told Lord Ashcroft. 'But I could never vote for her policies' (Liddle 2018: 187). 'It was clear from focus groups they were still voting for the SNP on the basis of competence,' said one senior Scottish Conservative official. 'And in that election, the SNP suddenly became relevant.' At the same time, it had become clear, post-2014, that there existed 'a clear unionist feeling, a desire to stop the SNP', something the party was conscious it had to 'harness'. After the election, therefore, the party 'modelled' 'No' voters in parts of Scotland with growing numbers of Conservative voters. They identified 'fashionable followers', those (generally younger) voters attracted by Davidson, and 'credibility voters', strong unionists who wanted to vote Tory but did not think there was any point. 'Both were latent voters,' noted the party official, 'and we had to motivate them' (interview, 26 May 2016).

In the autumn of 2015, some commentators began to speculate that the Conservatives *could* become the principal opposition party at Holyrood following the 2016 Scottish election, largely on account of Scottish Labour, which had lost all but one of its MPs at the 2015 election, 'suffering something of the stigma that's surrounded the Tories for years' (*Scotland on Sunday*, 3 October 2015). Davidson had predicted such a shift shortly before the 2015 general election,[5] and a November 2015 poll found Scottish Labour just two points ahead of the Conservatives in voting intentions for Holyrood the following year (MailOnline, 18 November 2015).

Initially, the Scottish Conservatives attempted to build on this modest momentum by presenting themselves as the 'real alternative' to the SNP (*Daily Record*, 7 December 2015). But this approach 'didn't work', recalled the senior party official, being seen as neither 'credible nor desirable'. Instead, party strategists began to adopt a more 'realistic' analysis of what they might hope to achieve in May 2016, and 'that was coming in second place'. A YouGov poll in February 2016 put the party at nearly 20 per cent on the regional list vote, while instead of canvassing in the traditional fashion, activists asked voters 'who would best stand up to Nicola Sturgeon'. They were surprised when people 'volunteered Ruth Davidson', even echoing party messaging in expressing the need for a 'strong opposition'.

In early 2016, the Scottish Conservatives also began to push a line about Labour and the Liberal Democrats being 'soft' on independence, and indeed the constitutional question began to drown out everything else. 'We didn't go on policy,' recalled the source, 'because we didn't need to', although there was some focus on fiscal policy given the Scottish Government's new responsibility for setting the Scottish rate of income tax and related concern among some voters as to the consequences.[6] 'We then reinforced that,' recalled the party official, 'that gave us confidence' (interview, 26 May 2016). As Mark Diffley argues in Chapter 2, the Scottish Conservative revival was sudden rather than gradual.

'One good election doesn't make a revival'

In preparation for the 2016 Holyrood election, Ruth Davidson also over-saw what was depicted as a gentle 'changing of the guard' but which was, in reality, more like 'Murder on the Orient Express'. One Conservative MSP 'tried to bargain a knighthood or peerage for stepping down, but was firmly told, "No chance"' (Pike 2015: 287). In all, seven of the party's 15 serving MSPs were intending to stand down, which allowed the party to bring forward some new faces, most prominent of which was the constitutional academic Adam Tomkins, formerly a left-wing republican.

In March 2016, Davidson declared herself 'ready to serve' as opposition leader in the Scottish Parliament, while the backdrop at her party's pre-election conference declared in large blue letters: 'Ruth Davidson for a Strong Opposition'.' For the next 62 days, declared David Cameron at the same gathering, 'we're going to fight to become the official opposition' (*Financial Times*, 6 March 2016). This novel pitch was calibrated to make voting Conservative feel like less of a commitment. 'I've not asked the country to put me into Government in this campaign,' Davidson explained to reporters during the campaign. 'I fully accept that there are people who are not ready to see me as the First Minister of Scotland – but they do want me to do a job for them, and that's to be the opposition leader' (*Independent*, 4 May 2016).

For once, electoral reality matched expectations. On polling day, the Scottish Conservatives pushed Kezia Dugdale's Scottish Labour Party into second place at Holyrood, winning 31 MSPs (24 of them new), including Ruth Davidson in Edinburgh Central, a significant urban (and constituency) gain. The Scottish Tory leader's stock rose inexorably; David Cameron tweeted his congratulations and Ladbrokes cut the odds on Davidson succeeding him as UK Conservative leader from 50/1 to 33/1 (*Daily Record*, 6 May 2016). The SNP, deprived of an overall majority, attempted to play down the Scottish Conservative result, arguing that the party's vote share was still lower than that in 1987.[7]

Thereafter Davidson ditched the colourful photocalls with which she had become associated during the election campaign, conscious of the need to adopt a more 'serious' demeanour now she was leader of Scotland's largest opposition party. She also continued to claim the political centre ground, declaring herself 'a John Major Conservative', while acknowledging that the Scottish Conservatives were still 'on probation'. 'These are very mobile votes and they can be taken elsewhere pretty quickly,' she told the *Telegraph*. 'One good election doesn't make a revival.' Local government elections in 2017, she added, would ensure that result was 'built on stone and not sand' (*Telegraph*, 7 May 2016).

The sense of elation did not last long, not least because of an imminent referendum on the UK's membership of the European Union. Even before it took place on 23 June 2016, journalists were being briefed that should Boris Johnson become UK Conservative leader (as looked likely in the event of a Leave vote) then the Scottish Conservatives would 'break away . . . under a new name', a variation on an old theme (Torrance 2012) but one later rebutted by Davidson. She went head to head with Johnson during one of the EU campaign's highest-profile debates at Wembley Stadium, comparing his 'brazen chauvinistic style' to that of Alex Salmond, 'this time repeated for a UK audience' (*Telegraph*, 20 June 2016).

Initially, the majority Leave vote looked as if it might cause serious damage to Davidson's standing. 'We thought, after all these years [the party's recovery has] lasted six weeks; it was never meant to be, the misery will continue,' recalled a senior party official. A 'crisis' meeting was quickly convened, at which it was assumed support for independence would 'go way ahead, that we were in for a bumpy ride'. With two words, however, Nicola Sturgeon – who said another independence referendum was 'highly likely' – provided a 'shot in the arm for unionism . . . it meant we had something to say; it gave us something to get through the rest of 2016 and into 2017' (interview, 11 February 2019). 'The 1.6 million votes cast in this referendum in favour of Remain,' cautioned Davidson, 'do not wipe away the two million votes that we cast less than two years ago' (Liddle 2018: 247).

Thereafter, as Anthony Salamone argues in Chapter 11, the Scottish Conservative Party was required to factor Brexit into its recovery strategy, albeit reluctantly. Davidson called Theresa May, who succeeded Cameron as UK party leader and thus Prime Minister, a 'proper grown up . . . best placed to navigate the stormy waters ahead'. She spoke of the UK remaining part of the EU Single Market and Customs Union and thus retaining reciprocal freedom of movement, telling the 2016 UK Conservative Party conference that 'immigrants should be made to feel welcome in the UK' (*Telegraph*, 5 October 2016).

This pragmatic Brexit stance would prove unsustainable, but in the wake of the Holyrood elections and EU referendum, Davidson had 'arrived on the UK's political stage' (*Independent*, 23 June 2016) and enjoyed the sort of limelight experienced by Nicola Sturgeon a year earlier. News of her engagement to partner Jennifer Wilson had made UK front pages while, visiting London on 13 July, she was appointed to the Privy Council and entertained members of the Commons Lobby ('Labour's still fumbling with its flies' was one line, 'while the Tories are enjoying a post-coital cigarette after withdrawing our massive Johnson'), fuelling speculation of a move to Westminster and ascension to the UK party leadership (*Independent*, 13 July 2016).[8] By September, Ipsos MORI found that Davidson's 'satisfaction' rating with voters was at +31 per cent, 17 points ahead of Nicola Sturgeon (+14 per cent) (MailOnline, 15 September 2016).

Policy development, however, continued to take a back seat. In October 2016, Davidson expressed opposition to grammar schools in Scotland and joined UK colleagues in urging a general extension of the franchise to 16- and 17-year-olds (Davidson et al. 2016), but otherwise the resurgent Scottish Conservative Party did not seem terribly interested in ideas. Convery believed this was due to the dominance of the constitutional question, meaning the Scottish party had not experienced the same 'difficult debates about modernisation' experienced by the UK party, instead preferring 'familiar and comfortable themes' (Convery 2016b).[9] 'Like so many politicians who have emerged from the world of media, she is stronger on presentation than substance,' was Mitchell's view. 'It is clear what the Tories oppose but not what they support' (Mitchell 2016).

In Davidson's own words, she was attempting to get 'back to proper, old-fashioned, blue-collar Toryism that somehow, somewhere, half our party forgot' (Davidson 2015). But then she had become leader just as an existential battle over the future of the United Kingdom got under way. That had not changed after 2014 and now, following the EU referendum, the party's priority was opposing a second referendum, a largely manufactured 'threat' in 2015 but now, in the wake of Brexit, the defining issue of Scottish politics.

'We said no. We meant it'

The 2017 Scottish Conservative Party spring conference – the first since 1998 to be held in Glasgow – found Ruth Davidson on pugilistic form. She spoke of her party as a 'government in waiting', ready to 'demand a politics that no longer obsesses over the colour of a flag, but rather focuses on the content of our lives'. But the main message was clear:

> This party – the Scottish Conservative and Unionist Party – will never waver in our determination to stand up for the decision we made as a country. We will fight you every step of the way. We said no. We meant it. Are you listening, Nicola? No. Second. Referendum. (*Financial Times*, 4 March 2017)

At First Minister's Questions, Davidson bellowed 'sit down!' at the First Minister during a highly charged debate on a second referendum, but she refused to say if the UK Government should block a Section 30 order, necessary to hold another referendum. In 2015 she had conceded a 'mandate to hold one' should the SNP win 'an outright majority' with a clear pledge, as in 2011. 'In the longer term, Westminster saying "No you cannae" will not play well in Scotland,' Davidson observed, 'and I think that it would damage the unionist cause' (*Guardian*, 12 June 2015).

This condition – a single-party SNP overall majority – had not been met in 2016, so when Nicola Sturgeon asked for a Section 30 order at the end of March 2017, Theresa May's 'now is not the time' response was deliberately nuanced, 'oscillating between flexibility and principle' (Hassan 2018: 141). Shortly afterwards, the Scottish Conservatives launched a financial appeal and online petition (against a second referendum). 'We got 120,000 signatures in 24 hours and money like we'd never had before,' recalled a senior party official. 'We could feel the momentum.' At the same time, the party's local government candidates and councillors were unhappy about the campaign 'being all about Ruth and the constitution' (interview, 11 February 2019), a novel departure in local campaigning analysed by Lauren Toner, Chrysa Lamprinakou and Neil McGarvey in Chapter 5. Nevertheless, Sturgeon's S30 order request gave the Scottish Tory local government campaign a boost, as did the Prime Minister's decision on 18 April (backed by two thirds of MPs) to hold a 'snap' general election on 8 June 2017.

The announcement also helped distract from problems on the policy front, the UK Government's so-called 'rape clause' having become a feature of the campaign. Initially Davidson defended the policy, then tried to blame the Scottish Government for not reversing it, before finally mounting another defence. Although media talk of the row having 'halted the Scottish Tory revival in Scotland' represented wishful thinking rather than serious analysis (*Sunday Herald*, 16 April 2017), it highlighted an ongoing problem for Davidson in being forced to defend UK party policy with which she did not necessarily agree. She did, however, make some, largely tactical, policy decisions, making clear her support for free prescription charges in Scotland, something she had previously opposed. As Henderson and Mitchell observed, Davidson's 'communication skills failed her when she was forced to defend Conservative policies' (Henderson and Mitchell 2018: 117).

Thereafter the Scottish Conservatives rolled two separate campaigns – local and general – into one, with the pithy and consistently uttered line 'we said no, we meant it', as used in Davidson's March 2017 conference speech. Whereas in the rest of the UK elections were fought on the basis of Brexit, in Scotland discourse was framed by the Yes/No cleavage of 2014. As James Mitchell observed, they had 'essentially become a single-issue party', with independence being as important to the Conservatives as it was to the SNP, just in opposition rather than support (*Observer*, 29 April 2017). This was ironic, for anti-Toryism was almost built into the DNA of both the SNP and the wider independence movement, yet it was precisely the push for another referendum that had acted as the catalyst for a Conservative – or rather unionist – revival.

Although reductive, this anti-independence messaging had a number of advantages beyond campaign literature, not least the ability to appeal to 'unionist' voters who might not otherwise countenance voting for the 'eff-ing Tories', a dynamic also aided by the fact that, following the Holyrood elections of 2016, doing so would no longer be seen as a 'wasted' vote. On 6 May 2017, almost 20 years since the Scottish Conservative Party lost all its MPs in Scotland, it gained 164 additional councillors, even in parts of Pais-ley and Glasgow hitherto considered 'no-go' areas. The media, meanwhile, made much of a Tory win in Ravenscraig, 25 years after its eponymous steelworks had shut down.[10]

Davidson moved swiftly to maintain momentum. 'We will speak up for the millions of Scots who have had enough of the uncertainty and division of the last few years,' she promised. 'We will stand up for everyone who doesn't want a second referendum on independence' (*Daily Record*, 6 May 2017). The party had already decided to target 12 Scottish constituencies in the forthcoming general election, something the pollster John Curtice believed could credibly 'threaten the SNP's vice-like grip on Scottish rep-resentation in Westminster' (MailOnline, 23 April 2017). Davidson spoke of a 'titanic battle' to oust Angus Robertson, the SNP's Westminster leader (*Scotsman*, 2 May 2017), whose Moray constituency had come within a whisker of voting 'Leave' in June 2016.

Lending further credibility to such ambitions was the ferocity of the SNP's response. 'The more Tory MPs there are, the heavier the price Scotland will pay,' warned Nicola Sturgeon darkly. 'The bigger the Tory majority, the more they will think they can do anything to Scotland and get away with it' (*Daily Record*, 24 April 2017). Alex Salmond, whose Gordon constituency was also being targeted, said a continuing Scottish Tory revival would 'drag Scotland back into the dark', ushering in a new era of Thatcherism, a 'social desert' in place of the welfare state, and even threaten the existence and powers of the Scottish Parliament (*Sunday Herald*, 14 May 2017).

In a speech to the George Orwell Foundation in London, Davidson accused the SNP – which was marking a decade in devolved government – of pursuing 'Orwellian' nationalism, taking advantage of the celebrated author's (arguably questionable) differentiation between 'patriotism' and 'nationalism'. Although she acknowledged that all parties in Scotland had claimed a monopoly of the national mood at one time or another, Davidson suggested the 'modern SNP' had 'made this technique their own' (*Scotsman*, 15 May 2017). The Scottish

Conservatives also depicted UK Labour leader Jeremy Corbyn as a 'clear and present danger' to the future of the United Kingdom, highlighting examples of where he had 'failed' to stand up for the Union (*Telegraph*, 24 April 2017).

Scottish Conservative strategists, meanwhile, targeted two groups of voters: middle-class unionists who had stopped voting for the party because of the 'stigma' and perceived wastefulness, and also 'Yes-Leavers', small 'c' Conservatives who had voted 'Yes' in 2014 but 'Leave' in 2016. In the North East of Scotland, strategists detected a feeling that Nicola Sturgeon did not 'represent' the area in the same way her predecessor had, while in the Central Belt the main drivers of increasing Conservative support were (1) 'hatred of Nicola Sturgeon', (2) opposition to 'indyref2' and (3) a perception that Ruth Davidson 'was alright'. 'People didn't change their vote because of Ruth personally,' recalled a senior party official, 'but she made the journey easier for them – she was the key that opened the door' (interview, 11 February 2019).

Indeed, the Scottish Conservative Party leader continued to enjoy a UK-wide profile. 'I have an internal barometer, telling me if I have done well or badly,' she told the *Daily Mail*'s Jan Moir. 'If anyone is gushing about me, my head won't be turned. If anyone is critical, I won't be upset. I just get on with it.' This, added Davidson, made her 'very Presbyterian' and 'very Scottish'. The same interview highlighted Davidson's skill in telling stories which emphasised her relatively 'normal' background, in this case the fact her wedding had been postponed due to spending 'a small fortune' on vet bills. 'Next month she will stand on the brink of history,' gushed Moir, 'a one-woman blockade on the road to the People's Republic of Sturgeonistan' (*Daily Mail*, 27 May 2017).

Focus groups generally concurred, with voters recognising Davidson as 'more of a Scottish Conservative, as opposed to an English Conservative in Scotland' (quoted by Hassan 2018: 139). More to the point, for the first time in decades the Scottish Conservatives 'had an issue which allowed them to unapologetically speak for a majority of voters and which genuinely represented what they stood for' (Hassan 2018: 133), 'Davidson's verve and enthusiasm' serving to highlight 'the incompetence of the broader Conservative campaign' (Tonge et al. 2018: 2). The Scottish Conservative leadership also resisted 'significant' efforts by Downing Street, especially Fiona Hill (a Scottish ex-journalist), to 'make the election in Scotland all about Theresa May' and her mantra 'strong and stable' (private information; *Guardian*, 19 December 2017).

Campaign material, therefore, focused on Ruth Davidson at the expense of her party and even its name, successfully creating 'a distinct agenda from that of the party south of the border', a combination of 'Scottish distinctiveness' and 'staunch unionism' (Henderson and Mitchell 2018: 120, 123).

Davidson later observed that a separate Scottish manifesto had been 'vital' to success, shorn of the 'dementia tax' and cuts to the winter fuel allowance (*Evening Standard*, 10 October 2017), although as Murray Stewart Leith explores in Chapter 3, such documents were generally more British than Scottish in emphasis. On polling day, the Scottish Conservative Party managed to win 13 MPs, a dozen more than it had managed in any UK general election since 2001. 'Indyref2 is dead', declared Davidson, 'that's what we have seen tonight' (MailOnline, 8 June 2017).

A few days later, the Scottish Conservative leader hailed her MPs as 'Scotland's champions', a 'team' who would 'aim to stand up for Scotland's interests – and to show that those interests are best served by being part of the UK' (*Scottish Mail on Sunday*, 11 June 2017). There was even talk of the group acting as 'a party within a party', willing 'to defy Theresa May' in favour of Ruth Davidson (BuzzFeed, 10 June 2017). This, as Paris Gourtsoyannis explores in Chapter 4, was overblown, and in retrospect represented the hubristic highpoint of the Conservative revival in Scotland.

Unionist into Conservative Votes

The 2017 election, concluded Henderson and Mitchell, represented an opportunity for the Scottish Conservatives to build support by 'translating unionist votes into Conservative votes'. At the same time, they warned, 'their base is fragile and might easily fall away at the next election' (Henderson and Mitchell 2018: 120). There were indeed problems in store for Ruth Davidson, although these were not apparent after an election in which her party's 13 MPs apparently held a sort of internal 'balance of power', Theresa May having lost the slim majority gained by her predecessor in 2015. Seeking to stabilise her position, the Prime Minister emphasised the 'Unionist' in her party's name as she agreed a confidence-and-supply arrangement with the Democratic Unionist Party (DUP).

This provided Davidson with one of several opportunities to emphasise her UK influence as well as the Scottish party's new 'progressive' persona. Tweeting a link to a speech she had delivered at Belfast Pride in 2016 was a tacit warning lest the DUP (opposed, unlike the Conservatives, to same-sex marriage) nudge the UK Government to the right on social issues. 'I am practising Christian,' Davidson had declared during that speech. 'I am a Protestant. I am a Unionist. I am Scottish and British. I am engaged to a Catholic Irishwoman from county Wexford who was educated by nuns. For me, equal marriage isn't about one religion or county or community' (Davidson 2016).

Still Davidson rode high, attending the UK 'political Cabinet' and ranking second only to Boris Johnson as the party membership's choice as the next Prime Minister (*Scotsman*, 29 September 2017). The prospect of a Johnson premiership still apparently concerned the Scottish Tory leadership, Scottish Secretary David Mundell poking fun at the Foreign Secretary's failure to win a 2006 race to become Rector of Edinburgh University. Davidson, meanwhile, denied being in the running. 'I don't sit in the House of Commons,' she pointed out, 'let's get back to why we are here – to talk about the real issues and not about the Tory psychodrama.' Having firmly established themselves as Scotland's second party, Scottish Conservative strategy now focused on using the three years 'to show that we can be the next government in Scotland' (*Scotsman*, 1 October 2017).

With that once-unlikely aim in mind, Davidson began to articulate a broader vision for Conservatism, perhaps also to counter critics who said she lacked policy depth. 'Ctrl + Alt + Del. Conservatives must reboot capitalism' appeared on the UnHerd website in July 2017, a contribution (most likely written by former journalist Eddie Barnes) to a developing debate about saving capitalism from itself. The article drew from the Scottish Enlightenment thinker Adam Smith who, as Davidson pointed out, had been a moral philosopher as well as an economist. 'He argued that far from being purely self-interested, we care about the well-being of others, for no reason beyond the simple pleasure we take from their evident happiness.' This plea to read *The Wealth of Nations* alongside *The Theory of Moral Sentiments* was not new, having been made by Margaret Thatcher in the 1970s and Alex Salmond in the 2000s, but Davidson used it to conclude 'that people are not pieces on a chess board, to be moved around by outside forces' (UnHerd, 22 July 2017).

At Westminster, meanwhile, one newly elected MP, Paul Masterson, suggested that he and his colleagues might exercise influence over the Budget or 'big policy areas' by saying 'no sorry this doesn't work for Scotland, you need to listen to us', it being important for 'people back in Scotland to see that because for so long the nationalists have claimed they alone spoke for Scotland' (*The Times*, 4 September 2017). A backlash against the Conservative–DUP deal on the basis that Scotland had not derived 'Barnett consequentials' from £1 billion in additional spending for Northern Ireland had, although based on a misunderstanding of Barnett, been damaging for the party, something it sought to redress via Chancellor Philip Hammond's 2017 Budget, which granted Police Scotland and Scottish Fire and Rescue long-demanded VAT relief.

There was much talk of the Scottish Conservative MP group 'standing up for Scotland' at Westminster, a slogan shamelessly stolen from the SNP, and indeed Ruth Davidson's Scottishness was also an aspect of her party's revival. 'Ruth is seen as Scottish,' said a senior official, 'we heard voters say "we don't agree with everything Tories are doing in England but we like Ruth"' – thus her care in regularly disassociating herself from the UK party. It was, however, the 'association of Ruth with the defence of the Union which provides the relevance to be a Scottish party again' (interview, 11 February 2019). As Alex Massie observed, 'Davidson is a Conservative but, like almost every Scottish politician, she is also a nationalist':

> Nationalism in Scotland has always existed on a spectrum. When John Buchan said every Scotsman should be a nationalist he didn't mean Scotland should be independent, merely that Scottish politicians owed an allegiance to an idea of Scotland and a distinct Scottish national interest. Davidson is cut from the same familiar cloth as Baron Tweedsmuir. (*Spectator*, 9 August 2017)

Yet still rumours circulated of plans for Davidson to swap Holyrood for Westminster, either as an MP or as a peer. Noting that by the 2021 Holyrood election she would have been leader for ten years, she told the *Spectator* that she had not 'ruled it out. If devolution is going to work, then actually there has to be the ability to move between chambers and parliaments' (*Spectator*, 13 December 2017).

'The baby box is on the way!'

Even in early 2018 there were signs the Scottish Conservative revival was fragile, with several polls putting its rating below that achieved in June 2017, prompting John Curtice to suggest the party's recovery had 'seemingly hit the buffers, for now at least' (*Daily Record*, 31 January 2018). Perhaps with this in mind, Ruth Davidson reportedly banned 'toxic Tories' such as Boris Johnson, Liam Fox and Michael Gove (the latter two of whom were Scottish) from her party's spring conference, a source explaining that she did not 'want folk from the party down south dominating the conference' (*Sunday Herald*, 4 February 2018).

Davidson hailed that conference as the 'first time in 30 years' a group of Scottish Conservatives could gather together and ask 'how do we form the next government of Scotland?' (*Edinburgh Evening News*, 26 February 2018). Inauspiciously, they did not get the chance due to extreme weather (BBC News online, 1 March 2018). Boxes of a well-produced but rather lightweight pamphlet called *Scottish Conservative Unionist* sat in boxes. It spoke of setting out 'a positive agenda on social policy' by making Scottish education, once again, 'the best in the world', 'tackling the underlying causes of social injustice' and creating 'a genuine meritocracy' (Scottish Conservative Party 2018: 1). A few months later, Davidson fleshed out her vision of modern

Conservatism in a speech at Glasgow University, calling for an increase in NHS funding paid for, if necessary, by resisting further tax breaks for higher earners.

There was also trouble in the south. The Scottish Conservative MP group was divided over Brexit – its views ranging from 'a clean break' (i.e. no deal) to the softest possible deal – while Davidson repeatedly shored up Theresa May, praising her 'amazing resilience' (*Telegraph*, 2 March 2018) as she battled to win parliamentary approval. Davidson also teamed up (as 'proud Scots') with Michael Gove to demand the United Kingdom leave the Common Fisheries Policy (CFP) (*Telegraph*, 11 March 2018). So, when it emerged that the Withdrawal Agreement would bind the UK to the CFP until December 2020, Davidson called it an 'undoubted disappointment'. The Moray MP Douglas Ross was blunter, saying it 'would be easier to get someone to drink a pint of cold sick than try to sell this as a success' (*Mirror*, 19 March 2018). Davidson – named that month as one of 2018's 100 most influential people by *TIME* – had overpromised and underdelivered.

Then, towards the end of April 2018, Davidson surprised the Scottish (and UK) political world by announcing she was pregnant, having undergone IVF treatment with her fiancée Jennifer Wilson, making her the first leader of a UK political party to become pregnant while in post. The Scottish First Minister tweeted her congratulations, adding that one of the Scottish Government's trademark baby boxes was 'on the way' (*Scotsman*, 26 April 2018). As Davidson later wrote in the *Guardian*, in the last few years her party had sought to 'tell our own story . . . and in so doing, remove some of the negative stereotypes that follow us' (*Guardian*, 18 May 2018). With an obvious spring in her step, she also suggested UK Conservatives could 'learn to be a bit more joyful . . . something that I think we have tried to learn in Scotland' (Sky News, 22 May 2018).

Apart from trying to spread joy, Davidson's mantra was that Nicola Sturgeon should 'get back to the day job' instead of pursuing another independence referendum. The SNP leader hit back by suggesting that the Scottish Conservative leader loved 'nothing more than talking about the constitution – she just doesn't want the case for independence to get a hearing' (PoliticsHome, 26 May 2018). Attacks on Davidson had not let up since the previous year's electoral advances, with the pro-independence commentator Andrew Tickell charging that the 'solitary constant in Davidson's career has been its inconstancy. Her political polymorphism seems to have no limit' (*The National*, 1 June 2018). Later, the First Minister would attack what she called the 'breath-taking hypocrisy' of the Scottish Conservatives for leading a Holyrood vote against primary school testing which had featured in its 2016 manifesto. Others targeted the hitherto obscure Scottish

Unionist Association Trust – the 'historic proceeds', as trustee Peter Duncan put it, 'of raffles and tombolas' – which was charged with channelling 'dark money' to Conservative parliamentary candidates (*Scotsman*, 29 July 2018), largely spurious claims the party struggled effectively to rebut.

A Survation poll suggested the SNP would regain seats lost to Conservatives at the 2017 general election although, paradoxically, the same poll put Davidson four points ahead of Nicola Sturgeon in terms of personal popularity. In September, the Scottish Conservative leader published *Yes She Can: Why Women Own the Future*, just as speculation she might see her own future at Westminster reached its height. One plan had Michael Gove overseeing the end of Brexit negotiations before Davidson succeeded him after fighting the 2021 Holyrood campaign (*Sun*, 26 May 2018). Martin Kettle also revealed a more plausible scenario had David Cameron won the EU referendum in 2016 and stood down, as planned, a few years later:

> One of his moves would have been to confer a peerage on the Scottish Tory leader, Ruth Davidson, and make her defence secretary, sitting in the House of Lords . . . At some point between then and Cameron's departure, the plan went, Davidson would "do a Douglas-Home" and move to the Commons – as Harold Macmillan's successor, the Earl of Home, had done in 1963. Davidson would remain in the government, renounce her peerage, and be fast-tracked into a safe Commons seat. There would be a byelection, and she would then be in the Commons, in a box seat to win the leadership – the best bet to stop Johnson, and all with Cameron's backing. (*Guardian*, 3 May 2019)

The 'doing a Douglas-Home' part of Cameron's plan persisted well into 2018 but then, in an at-times intensely personal interview for the *Sunday Times*, a heavily pregnant Davidson danced 'unselfconsciously' for a photographer before putting an end to such speculation:

> Look, I'm 39, I'm leading a political party. No, I do not want to go and be a junior minister in the Lords. I'm coming back to do my job and beat Nicola Sturgeon. And on a human level, the idea that I would have a child in Edinburgh and then immediately go down to London four days a week and leave it up here is offensive . . . You have to want it. And I don't want to be prime minister . . . I value my relationship and my mental health too much for it. I will not be a candidate.

Presciently, Davidson also confessed to concerns that on returning to work in May 2019 she would be 'absent . . . the more remote of the two figures' in her same-sex partnership (*Sunday Times*, 16 September 2018).

The Scottish Conservative leader insisted there was no 'contradiction whatsoever' between her stated aim of becoming First Minister in 2021 and her having ruled out ever becoming Prime Minister because of the likely impact on her mental health. There was widespread praise from political opponents and allies, Theresa May saying she thought it had been 'incredibly brave' for a senior politician to be 'so open and so honest about her own mental health and what she's been through' (*Sunday Express*, 23 September 2018). Davidson arrived at the subsequent UK Conservative Party conference hand in hand with her fiancée, pitching herself as the 'pro-Union conscience of the party' (*Telegraph*, 1 October 2018) in a keynote speech. As Richard Hayton argues in Chapter 8, even by that point Brexit had put increasing pressure on the Conservatives' long-standing 'territorial code'.

Davidson's final major political act before going on maternity leave was to hint – alongside Scottish Secretary David Mundell – at resignation. 'Having fought just four years ago to keep our country together,' they wrote in a joint letter to the Prime Minister, 'the integrity of our United Kingdom remains the single most important issue for us in these negotiations.' They added that they 'could not support' a deal which created 'a border of any kind in the Irish Sea' or went beyond any 'differentiation' beyond that which already existed. Although this was a curiously 'unitarist' reading of the relationship between Northern Ireland and Great Britain, predicated upon 'uniformity across the whole of the UK' and 'underpinned by Westminster parliamentary sovereignty' (Sheldon and Kenny 2019), it found Davidson and DUP leader Arlene Foster in agreement (PoliticsHome, 14 October 2018). As Jonathan Evershed posits in Chapter 10, the relationship between Scotland and Northern Ireland had long been 'ambivalent'.

When the Scottish Conservative leader gave birth to a baby boy later that month, Foster tweeted: 'New life is wonderful . . . Many congratulations.' Davidson broke her maternity leave silence just once, to praise Theresa May's 'cojones of steel' as the UK Conservative leader faced a no-confidence vote. Serving as acting leader was Jackson Carlaw, who had been defeated by Davidson in 2011. 'I think I can see Ruth Davidson as the [First Minister] of Scotland,' he said in a February 2019 interview. 'I believe that it's perfectly possible, if not in fact now likely' (*Holyrood*, 12 February 2019).

Donald Cameron, the Scottish Conservative Party's policy co-ordinator, said results from 10 local authority by-elections (averaging 32.6 per cent of the vote) demonstrated that Scotland was ready to make Davidson First Minister in 2021, but as the *Scotsman*'s Paris Gourtsoyannis cautioned, Cameron and the party had yet to come up with a message 'that goes beyond Unionism and opposition to indyref2'. 'Davidson is not a details person,' he added. 'She is a saleswoman, and she needs a big, bold pitch to sell when 2021 rolls around' (*Scotsman*, 2 October 2018). As former Prime Minister Tony Blair later observed, 'the vulnerability of Ruth Davidson's Conservatives is that they are tied to Theresa May' (*Holyrood*, 22 February 2019).

'It is a pity that flip-flopping is not an Olympic sport'

Davidson had intended to return from maternity leave in May 2019, just a few weeks after the UK was supposed to 'exit' the EU at the end of March. 'Ruth is a very lucky politician,' remarked one senior colleague, 'she couldn't have chosen a better seven months to be away from all this . . . she's not associated with it' (interview, 18 March 2019). It did not work out as planned. Instead, Davidson returned to the helm as what she had once called the UK Conservative Party's 'psychodrama' reached its final, dramatic scenes. Talk of a long extension was deemed 'catastrophic' for the Scottish Tory revival. 'A lot of our voters are leave,' a shadow cabinet minister explained, 'and they just want us to get out' (*The Times*, 23 March 2019).

The previous year had also been dominated by a dispute between the UK and Scottish governments regarding the EU Withdrawal Bill and subsequent legislation in Scotland. The Scottish Government objected on the basis that certain powers should flow from Brussels to Edinburgh, rather than from Brussels to London, following exit day, whereas the UK legislation envisaged dispersal to the three devolved legislatures largely on Westminster terms. Scottish Secretary David Mundell later admitted having failed to 'manage expectations', which led to SNP claims of a 'power grab' and a showdown between the Holyrood and Westminster governments in the UK Supreme Court (*Scotland on Sunday*, 28 July 2019).

As Davidson observed in her foreword to an essay collection entitled *Britain Beyond Brexit*, 'rather than focusing on the things that matter, all of us have been consumed by parliamentary process, arcane technicalities and constitutional one-upmanship'. She then attempted to chart a middle way for post-Brexit Britain:

> Frankly, it is up to us whether we face this future with boldness or timidity. Whether we build something better or retreat into some misremembered past. We must be brave enough to remember that the free flow of ideas, goods, services, people and capital is always the right path. In or out of the EU, our task remains the same: to be open, not closed, to the world around us. To always look outwards for opportunities, not inwards for cold comfort and blame. (Davidson 2019: xi–xiii)

Elsewhere, Davidson suggested a new generation of New Towns, keeping every young person in education or training until the age of 18, a 'hydrogen revolution' and a 'union delivery unit at the heart of government' to ensure UK legislation was 'devolution compatible'. 'As a post-Brexit UK seeks to re-establish its position in the world,' she warned, 'it cannot do so merely as a little England' (UnHerd, 14 May 2019).

But having been, as one senior party official put it, 'protected, insulated to some degree from Brexit by the Scottish constitutional factor' (interview, 11 February 2019), that 'buffer' became worn as the battles of 2014 slipped further into the past. During one particularly fierce exchange at First Minister's Questions, Nicola Sturgeon – whose party had spent the last three years depicting Ruth Davidson as a hard-line Thatcherite – attacked the Scottish Conservative leader in personal as well as political terms:

> Perhaps the difference between Ruth Davidson and me is that I have principles, and I stick to my principles. Ruth Davidson would not recognise a principle. She used passionately to oppose Brexit; now she supports Brexit. She used to demand that we stay in the single market; now she wants us to be taken out of the single market. Of course, Ruth Davidson also used to call Boris Johnson names that I cannot repeat in the chamber. Now, she is cosying up to Boris Johnson – the arch-Brexiteer. I cannot help but think that it is a pity that flip-flopping is not an Olympic sport, because if it was, Ruth Davidson would be a guaranteed gold-medal winner. (Official Report, 22 May 2019)[11]

Some of this was pre-election rhetoric, for European Parliament elections took place the following day. Davidson's relative personal popularity did not prevent her party polling just 12 per cent of the vote, better than in any other part of the United Kingdom but still six points down on 2014. The outcome apparently prompted her to tell close associates for the first time that 'she really did feel as if she wanted to go' as party leader (*Financial Times*, 29 August 2019).

Sturgeon's allusion to Boris Johnson was also prescient, for two days after her attack Theresa May resigned as Prime Minister, having failed on three occasions to win parliamentary approval for her Withdrawal Agreement. Johnson had long been anticipated as her successor, which immediately put Davidson in a difficult position given her long-standing hostility towards the former Foreign Secretary. There had been reports of something called 'Operation Arse', an attempt by Scottish Conservatives to prevent a Johnson premiership, fearful of its likely impact on both the party in Scotland and, more broadly, the Union (*Guardian*, 2 October 2018).

Within weeks of May's resignation, however, the journalist Kenny Farquharson said that the 'message from Ms Davidson's allies' was that Operation Arse was being 'dismantled'. 'I have worked with him when he was foreign secretary,' the Scottish Conservative leader told the *Scottish Daily Express*. 'I will work with whoever the prime minister is.' Farquharson called this an 'abject . . . humiliation' for Davidson, given the 'damage done to her celebrated image as a no-nonsense straight-talker who tells it like it is' (*The Times*, 5 June 2019).

In the UK Conservative leadership contest that followed, Davidson supported everyone but Johnson (successively, Javid, Gove and Hunt), although three Scottish MPs – Colin Clark, Douglas Ross and Ross Thomson – emerged as cheerleaders for Johnson. 'Boris's moderate and modern conservatism,' they argued, 'is matched by that of our leader in Scotland, Ruth Davidson' (*Telegraph*, 23 June 2019). This seemed to many a considerable stretch, while the SNP made hay by unearthing old newspaper articles in which Johnson had criticised aspects of Scottish politics. For this he apologized (see *Press and Journal*, 5 July 2019), but it was clear the Scottish Conservative Party found the whole experience traumatic, particularly after three relatively harmonious and successful years. 'Looking at this sh*t show,' one senior figure told the *Daily Record*, 'I'm not sure I could vote for us. I don't know how anyone else is expected to be able to' (*Daily Record*, 11 June 2019).

Unusually, the Union – or rather the prospect of a second independence referendum – featured in the leadership campaign, with every candidate required to state their opposition to varying degrees. When Andrea Leadsom demurred by saying she would 'never say never', a backlash from Scottish Conservative MPs produced a swift U-turn, Leadsom tweeting that there would 'be no second referendums on my watch' (BBC News online, 12 June 2019). Davidson also came under pressure regarding her own interpretation of when 'now' *would be* the time, given the ambivalent nature of Mrs May's response to the Scottish Government's S30 order request two years earlier. In April she suggested that now would *never* be the time ('I'll say no, and this Prime Minister and the next prime minister should say so too'), while by June this had shifted to a negotiation 'in the same way as happened last time', provided the SNP won 'a majority outright' in 2021 (BBC Scotland, 29 April 2019 and 12 June 2019).

It did not help that a YouGov survey of Conservative members found 63 per cent would back Brexit even if it meant Scotland leaving the United Kingdom (a figure that would rise in the months ahead), while a Panelbase poll suggested support for independence would increase to 53 per cent in the event of a Johnson premiership. Davidson told party members to 'take a long, hard look at themselves', arguing that the 2016 referendum result ought to be delivered, just 'not at the expense of breaking up the UK' (BBC News online, 18 June 2019). Later she played on Johnson's own words, telling him: 'It's the Union do or die' (*Telegraph*, 27 June 2019). As the commentator Andy Maciver put it: 'In England, it's Conservative first, Unionist second; in Scotland, it's Unionist first, Conservative second, and that is manifesting itself in a very difficult way for the Scottish Tory Party' (BBC Radio 4, 28 July 2019).

The New Unionism

Strikingly, although Ruth Davidson had been strongly associated with a defence of the Union since the 2014 referendum, she had arguably made little contribution to unionist thought in the same period. After the 2017 general election, this emanated from London rather than Edinburgh, with Westminster asserting what Jim Bulpitt called 'central autonomy' over the Scottish periphery. Luke Graham believed the 'paucity of Scottish Conservatives pre-2017' had rendered Westminster 'complicit' in a Scottish nationalist 'agenda', 'rushing to devolve more and more powers to Scotland and Wales without considering the full economic, social and cultural impact' (Graham 2019: 34).

He and others particularly resented the Scottish Government's perceived incursion into 'reserved' territory, that is, international affairs. This informed what might be called the 'New Unionism', a multi-point agenda articulated in the Commons and in the media by several of the 2017 intake. The Stirling MP Stephen Kerr posited perhaps the most comprehensive plan: a 'powerful . . . Department of the United Kingdom led by a First Secretary of State for the Union'; 'stronger' (perhaps even statutory) intergovernmental and inter-parliamentary relationships; direct engagement between UK Government departments and 'stakeholders' in Scotland, Wales and Northern Ireland (rather than via the Scotland or Wales Offices); primary legislation to enable 'direct UK government spending in devolved areas in partnership with devolved administrations'; an 'urgent review' of English Votes for English Laws, something Kerr considered 'a badly advised and unnecessary circumvention of the work of the United Kingdom parliament'; and, finally, 'detailed proposals to replace EU regional funding' with 'a UK-level fund' (*Scotsman*, 24 July 2019). Andrew Bowie, Theresa May's former PPS (parliamentary private secretary), said he and his colleagues had spent months 'fighting' with the UK Government to 'fund directly . . . projects in Scotland', resisting the Treasury's 'instincts . . . to give the money to the Scottish Government' (*Press and Journal*, 1 October 2019).

In his contribution to *Britain Beyond Brexit*, John Lamont (who was close to Davidson, having backed her while an MSP in 2011) set out a slightly different agenda for 'the Union', which included highlighting 'hyperbolic' economic claims from the SNP, conducting 'a permanent campaign for the Union' to counter the 'permanent' campaign for independence, and ensuring 'that more Union is spread around the UK' via 'infrastructure and power' (Lamont 2019: 27). In a May 2018 speech to the Policy Exchange think tank, Davidson had also spoken of spreading 'the benefits of the union fairly and equally around the nation' with cultural institutions like the British Museum setting up 'second homes outside the capital' (Davidson 2018b). Other aspects of the Lamont agenda overlapped with those of Kerr, such as Whitehall having 'to consider the maintenance and promotion of the Union as one of its central tasks, not [as] a bolt-on extra'. He and Kerr both approvingly quoted a Theresa May line about the tendency to 'devolve and forget', so that 'in reserved areas, the UK Government explicitly looks after the interests of the Union in its policy-making while, in devolved areas, it must look for ways to collaborate and work together to improve outcomes for everyone' (Lamont 2019: 28)

To this Luke Graham wanted to add a rejuvenated sense of 'what being a British citizen actually means', perhaps by 'listing the entitlements and responsibilities involved' and creating a 'National Citizens Service'. This he called 'Federalism with British Characteristics', formalizing the 'mechanisms by which local, devolved and central government departments, assemblies and politicians interact' (Graham 2019: 35–7). All of this hinted at a less laissez-faire approach to the boundary between devolved and reserved powers, something taken up by Foreign Secretary Jeremy Hunt (in his bid for the UK leadership) in ordering his department not to provide any official support for Nicola Sturgeon's trips abroad if she used them 'to campaign' for Scottish independence (*Guardian*, 25 June 2019).

Symbolism was also important in the New Unionism. 'There's branding on every single thing the Scottish Government does in Scotland,' observed Andrew Bowie, 'it has a Saltire on the side of it and says paid for and delivered by the Scottish Government. Where's our UK flag? Where's paid for and delivered by HM Government?' (*Press and Journal*, 1 October 2019). Boris Johnson agreed, wanting Union flags emblazoned on anything in Scotland attributable to the UK Government. 'I don't mind seeing a Saltire or two,' he added, 'but I want to see the Union flag' (*Telegraph*, 30 September 2019), symbolic of what he called the 'awesome foursome'. Towards the end of his term as Scottish Secretary, meanwhile, David Mundell announced that a new UK Government 'hub' in Edinburgh would be called 'Queen Elizabeth

House', complete with 'dedicated Cabinet room, the first of its kind outside of London'. He viewed this as a 'focal point' to boost awareness of the UK Government's work in Scotland. 'The UK government needs to make the case every day for what it does in Scotland,' he said after leaving the Cabinet, 'the way the Scottish Government makes the case every day for independence' (*Scotland on Sunday*, 28 July 2019).

Kenny and Sheldon identified 'a new ethos of unionist activism' which involved 'the central state making and showing the case for Union, seeking to do much more to wean people away from nationalist politics by demonstrating the tangible benefits it can supply', something that might result – during a Johnson premiership – 'in a major shake-up of relations between the centre and devolved government across the UK' (Kenny and Sheldon 2019b). This suggested a move away from what Alan Convery identifies in Chapter 9 as 'devo-pragmatism' towards 'ultra-unionism', but falling considerably short of the 'federal offer' once proposed by Johnson following the 2015 general election (BBC News online, 11 May 2015).

In one of her farewell speeches as Prime Minister, Theresa May drew on some of this thinking (while rejecting other aspects) in an effort to move beyond the 'our precious union' mantra of her three years as premier. The Union, she said in Stirling, had 'never been about uniformity', diversity being 'part of the deal'. She also framed devolution as the 'form of government best suited to our geography, our history and our future'. But the answer to undeniable pressures on the devolutionary status quo, suggested May, did not 'lie in schemes of sweeping constitutional change', but rather in making 'better and more creative use' of the existing constitutional settlement. 'If we do not make realising the full benefits of being a United Kingdom of four proud nations and one united people our priority now,' she warned, 'then in the future it may be too late' (May 2019).

Denouement

The inevitability of Boris Johnson as the next UK Conservative leader and, therefore, Prime Minister, revived talk of a Scottish Tory UDI (unilateral declaration of independence). The BBC's Andrew Marr had asked Davidson in May 2019 if a party breakaway was possible, in response to which she had emphasised 'autonomy for candidate selection, policy, financing and all of the other things that come under my purview'. She acknowledged talk of a 'German CDU–CSU model' but said it was something she did not 'support and [would not] support in the future' (BBC1, 5 May 2019).

Murdo Fraser, however, clearly spotted an opportunity to revive his 2011 agenda. 'There is a growing consensus among Ruth's allies that this is an idea whose time has come', a senior figure told the journalist Stephen Daisley:

> We're almost there anyway. We're already a separate party in all but name. I keep hearing people describe relations between Ruth and Boris as transactional or business-like. That's true but it underlines the fact that these are now two separate entities rather than the one party. So why not hang a new brass plaque and make it official? (*Scottish Daily Mail*, 22 July 2019)

Channel 4 News reported that 'at least eight Conservative MSPs' were 'strongly considering' a split from the UK party a few days before Boris Johnson was elected its leader (*Channel 4 News*, 25 July 2019).

Davidson instead issued a 'defiant challenge' to Johnson, reiterating her refusal to back a no-deal Brexit before his first visit to Scotland as Prime Minister. 'As leader of the party in Scotland, my position exists independently of government,' she wrote in her *Mail on Sunday* column. 'I don't have to sign a no-deal pledge to continue to serve' (*Scottish Mail on Sunday*, 28 July 2019). Davidson was also reportedly 'livid' at the sacking of her ally David Mundell as Secretary of State for Scotland, something she had advised against. Alister Jack succeeded him, although the appointment of an MP with an English constituency to the Scotland Office (the first since A. J. Balfour in 1886), Robin Walker, provoked such a backlash that Gordon MP Colin Clark, an early backer of Johnson, was later added to the team (*Sunday Times*, 28 July 2019).

An online poll conducted by Lord Ashcroft in the wake of Johnson's visit put independence in the lead for the first time in two and a half years. Several surveys showed a clear upward trend, leading John Curtice to say it could 'no longer be presumed that Scotland would vote "no" again in an independence ballot'. Davidson sent a dossier of Scottish coverage of the Ashcroft poll to Number 10, where a new 'Union unit', led by a former Scottish Conservative Party aide, had been established to support Johnson as 'Minister for the Union' (*Scotsman*, 7 October 2019). The Scottish Conservatives had a partial reprieve when, on 6 August, Shadow Chancellor John McDonnell said a future UK Labour government would not block a second independence referendum, but it had been a torrid few months for their leader.

Then, on 29 August 2019, Ruth Davidson announced her resignation, effective immediately. 'You all know – and I have never sought to hide – the conflict I have felt over Brexit,' she said in a statement, which avoided any criticism of the Prime Minister or his recent move to prorogue Parliament.

Davidson said she could not face the 'efforts, hours and travel' needed to fight any forthcoming elections, contests in which the Scottish Conservatives were now expected to fall back on their 2016–17 gains.

Davidson later admitted her departure had 'been a long time coming', that the 'fire that had kept me slugging it out for all these years . . . had somehow become dimmed' (*Scottish Mail on Sunday*, 1 September 2019). The media and political response were largely sympathetic, although Nicola Sturgeon, who joked that Davidson had 'reclaimed her own independence', said it posed a 'bigger question': if 'the leader of the Scottish Conservatives can't reconcile herself to the extreme hard Brexit driven leadership of Boris Johnson, then why should the rest of Scotland?' (*The National*, 29 August 2019). But as Gerry Hassan observed, 'Ruth Davidson mattered in Scottish and UK politics', something confirmed by 'the identification with her, or antagonism felt by those who opposed her' (OpenDemocracy, 30 August 2019).

In interviews, Davidson held open the prospect of a political comeback, perhaps at the head of another 'Better Together' campaign. 'I will do what I can to stop that happening,' she said, 'but if it is happening there is absolutely no way that I am going to sit it out' (*Herald*, 6 October 2019). A few weeks later, the *Evening Standard* revealed that Davidson would be paid £50,000 for 25 days' work for City PR firm Tulchan Communications, news that prompted a considerable backlash and calls for her to resign as the MSP for Edinburgh Central. She later turned down the appointment, but the controversy cast doubt on her suitability as a No campaign leader in any future independence referendum.[12] Capitalism, she told the *Standard*, needed 'resetting'. 'But I don't have a 10-year plan,' Davidson added. 'Whether there is a second act I don't really know, but I would suggest that lots of people do have second acts' (*Evening Standard*, 23 October 2019).

'A referendum on a referendum'

Interviewed after his departure from the Cabinet, David Mundell viewed the 2021 Holyrood election as 'a referendum on a referendum' (*Scotland on Sunday*, 28 July 2019). This was prior to Davidson's resignation, although the former Scottish Secretary's framing most likely applied regardless. Speaking in early 2019, a senior party official predicted 2021 would be a 'change' election, in which the more Nicola Sturgeon talked about another referendum, the 'better' it would be for the Scottish Conservatives. 'We're in a sort of clinch of mutual destruction,' he admitted, 'it suits both of us to talk it up' (interview, 11 February 2019).

As Mitchell observed following the party's 2016 advance, the Conservatives 'need a strong SNP and the prospect of independence in order to sustain its support' (Mitchell 2016), but at the same time so much work had gone into establishing Ruth Davidson as 'the credible pro-Union voice', as one senior party figure put it (interview, 18 March 2019), that it seemed unlikely her resignation would lack an impact. As Alex Massie observed, Davidson had been 'the beneficiary of a great realignment of Scottish politics in which the dividing lines ceased to be between left and right and were instead between nationalist and Unionist', and thus her resignation deprived 'her party and, more importantly, Unionism of its most compelling champion' (*Sunday Times*, 1 September 2019).

At the same time, paradoxically, Davidson had not contributed 'any coherent or significant ideas to the intellectual or substantive case for the union' (OpenDemocracy, 30 August 2019), failing to turn, as Gerry Hassan argues in Chapter 12, unionist into conservative votes. And while her 'greatest achievement' as leader was moving her party 'in a decisively pro-further devolution direction' (Convery 2016a: 41), when it came to policy, as Jim Johnston and James Mitchell concluded, the Scottish Conservatives 'rarely led from the right', rather the party grew complacent, producing 'an upward electoral trajectory . . . fuelled by . . . little hard thought' (Johnston and Mitchell 2019: 27).

Another analysis held that Davidson's main contribution to the Scottish Conservative Party was 'managing to challenge prejudices simply by being herself' (*Guardian*, 27 April 2018). As the journalist Dani Garavelli put it, the 'kick-boxing lesbian', as she was often described, 'didn't just talk about change – she embodied it' (*Prospect*, 23 August 2018). Let us now consider the near-decade of 'Ruth Davidson's Conservatives' in greater depth.

TWO

Tory Revival in Scotland?
Recent Evidence, Future Prospects

Mark Diffley

Introduction

When the 1997 general election left the Scottish Conservative Party without any seats and with one solitary MP between 2001 and 2017, the running joke in Scottish political circles was that there were more pandas in Edinburgh Zoo than Scottish Tories in the House of Commons. This changed significantly in 2017 when 13 Conservative MPs were returned from Scottish constituencies (see Table 2.1). Long written off as a toxic brand, this result underlined the re-emergence of the party as an electoral force. While this did not represent a return to the party's dominance between the 1930s and 1950s, it was their best result since 1983 and a reminder of the potential the party had north of the border.[1]

As much as it was a departure from recent general elections, the 2017 result did not come completely out of the blue. A year previously, in May 2016, the Scottish Conservatives had produced their best result at any of the five elections since the inaugural Scottish Parliament vote in 1999 (see Table 2.2). In both the constituency and regional elements of the Holyrood electoral system, the party received more votes, measured proportionately and numerically, and had more MSPs returned, than at any of the previous four contests.

So, after several generations of decline in Scotland, the results of the most recent UK and Holyrood elections point to something of a revival in the party's fortunes north of the border. The increased support came later than the improvement in the party's performance in England and in Wales, where support for the Conservatives in both those parts of the UK had been on the increase since the 2005 general election. The extent of support for the Conservatives in Scotland also continues to lag behind that in England,

Table 2.1 Performance of the Conservative Party at general elections in Scotland since 1979

	Number of votes	Percentage of votes	Number of seats won	Ranking
1979	916,000	31.4	22	2nd
1983	801,000	28.4	21	2nd
1987	713,000	24.0	10	2nd
1992	752,000	25.6	11	2nd
1997	493,000	17.5	0	3rd
2001	361,000	15.6	1	3rd
2005	369,000	15.8	1	4th
2010	413,000	16.7	1	4th
2015	434,000	14.9	1	3rd
2017	758,000	28.6	13	2nd

Table 2.2 Performance of the Conservative Party at Scottish Parliament elections since 1999

	Constituency votes %	Constituency seats	Regional votes %	Regional seats	Total seats	Ranking
1999	15.6	0	15.4	18	18	3rd
2003	16.6	3	15.5	15	18	3rd
2007	16.6	4	13.9	13	17	3rd
2011	13.9	3	12.4	12	15	3rd
2016	22.0	7	22.9	24	31	2nd

where 45 per cent voted Conservative in 2017, and in Wales, where the figure rose to 34 per cent in the same general election (HoCL 2019).

Having acknowledged that Conservative support in Scotland continues to be consistently lower than in England and Wales, the scale of the rise in support north of the border is significant, with vote share almost doubling, in general election terms, between 2015 and 2017. In Holyrood election terms, the constituency vote share rose by around 60 per cent between 2011 and 2016.

Two overriding questions and issues arise from this observation, which we will consider in this chapter. In the opening section, we will focus on the reasons for this sudden significant increase in Conservative support. Explanations would appear to lie in a combination of having an appealing, youthful and charismatic leader; the party becoming the clear standard bearer for pro-union, anti-independence opinion; the continued fallout of the EU referendum vote in 2016; and being beneficiaries of disillusionment with the current Scottish Government.

The second question, which we will subsequently explore, is to consider the party's longer-term prospects in Scotland – in other words, whether the current progress will be short lived or whether its recovery is set to continue.

Explaining the Scottish Tory Revival

The first point to note in considering the Tory resurgence in Scotland is the timing. In particular, it is worth observing that revival *in general election terms* occurred in the two-year period between the 2015 and 2017 votes, while polling evidence *on voting intention* for the Scottish Parliament would suggest that the increase in Conservative support occurred fairly soon before the election was held, rather than representing the culmination of a gradual increase (see Table 2.3). Therefore, this would appear to have been a rather sudden rather than a gradual revival, and one which did not happen in the immediate aftermath of the independence referendum of September 2014. Indeed, it was the Scottish National Party (SNP) who were the main electoral beneficiaries, despite being on the losing side of the independence referendum, successfully harnessing and motivating those who had voted 'Yes' in 2014 to achieve a landslide victory in Scotland and a (less emphatic) third consecutive Holyrood election win in 2016. That the SNP swept all before them, capturing almost all the disaffected Labour and Liberal Democrat voters who had deserted those parties having voted for them in 2010, meant there was little potential progress for the Scottish Conservatives to make, their vote share falling slightly by 1.8 percentage points, to 14.9 per cent.[2]

Table 2.3 Voting intention for the Scottish Parliament, October 2014 to May 2016 (constituency and regional votes). Note that of the 56 polls on Holyrood voting intention, regional voting intention was asked in 52 polls.

	Oct–Dec 2014 (7 poll average)	Jan–Mar 2015 (9 poll average)	Apr–June 2015 (5 poll average)	Jul–Sep 2015 (10 poll average)	Oct–Dec 2015 (4 poll average)	Jan–May 2016 (21 poll average)
	%	%	%	%	%	%
Constituency VI	13	13	14	14	15	18
Regional VI	13	13	14	13	15	17

Source: What Scotland Thinks, http://whatscotlandthinks.org/questions/how-would-you-use-your-constituency-vote-in-a-scottish-parliament-election

Of course, both the 2015 general election and the 2016 Scottish Parliament election took place before the UK-wide European Union (EU) referendum of June 2016, an event that led to a narrow majority across the UK voting to leave the EU, while voters in Scotland expressed a much more significant preference to remain. Of the two constitutional referendums that have taken place in Scotland since 2014, it is the second vote that appears to have offered the Scottish Conservatives an opportunity to recover to become the second-placed political force in Scotland, both at Westminster and Holyrood.

Opinion polls conducted in Scotland illustrate the point perfectly. Having won less than 15 per cent of the vote at the 2015 general election, and with polls between that election and the EU membership referendum showing no discernible sign of progress for the party, polls between September 2016 and the 2017 general election showed support for the Scottish Conservatives consistently in the mid- to high 20s, and as high as 33 per cent (see Table 2.4).

Table 2.4 Voting intention for Westminster, September 2016 to June 2017 (Conservative support)

Date poll published	Pollster	Support for Conservative Party %
September 2016	Panelbase	24
October 2016	BMG Research	20
January 2017	Panelbase	27
March 2017	Panelbase	28
April 2017	Panelbase	33
April 2017	Survation	28
April 2017	YouGov	28
May 2017	BMG Research	30
May 2017	YouGov	29
May 2017	Ipsos MORI	25
May 2017	Kantar	27
May 2017	Panelbase	30
May 2017	BMG Research	27
June 2017	Survation	27
June 2017	YouGov	26
June 2017	Survation	26
June 2017	Panelbase	30
2017 general election result		28.6

Source: What Scotland Thinks, http://whatscotlandthinks.org/questions/how-would-you-be-likely-to-vote-in-a-uk-general-election

So, while the Scottish Parliament election of 2016 provided the first concrete evidence of a Tory revival, it was the local government elections of 2017 – conducted during the general election campaign of that year – which gave the party confidence it was about to make a significant Westminster breakthrough and reverse some of the gains the SNP had made in 2015. To begin with, it cemented the party's claim to be the second party in Scotland, outpolling Labour as it had done at Holyrood a year earlier. That Labour had once been the dominant force in Scottish local government made the Tory gains even more significant. And while the collapse of the Labour vote became the main story of that election, the gains made by the Scottish Conservatives represented confirmation of their revival.

The party gained more than 25 per cent of first-preference votes in that election and gained an additional 164 local councillors, giving it 276 in total, more than double its previous council representation and 2012 vote share, representing by far its best local election result in the devolved era. However, the real significance of the result lay in the geographical location of these gains. Far from being confined to victories in rural Scotland or leafy suburbs, the party won seats in areas including Shettleston in Glasgow and the Paisley North West ward in Renfrewshire, which included Ferguslie Park, two of the nation's most deprived areas. It was a taste of things to come at the general election which followed.

In the period since the EU referendum of June 2016, the Scottish Conservatives appear to have been successful in broadening their appeal even more widely. In particular, they were now increasingly similar to the party south of the border in appealing to voters who identified as on the 'right' of the political spectrum (measured in response to questions about attitudes to inequality and government's responses to it).[3] A previous study of the Scottish Conservative Party noted that it was significantly less popular among those who identified as being on the right of the political divide than the party was in other parts of Great Britain (Torrance 2012). Although one might expect this group to be most likely to vote for the Conservatives, at the 2010 general election little more than a third (37 per cent) of Scots who identified as being on the right did so, compared with 57 per cent of the same group in England. Very little changed in the next five years, with 38 per cent of the same group voting for the party north of the border in 2015. However, it was largely – though not exclusively – this group of voters who powered the Conservative revival in Scotland at the 2017 election, with nearly six in ten of them (58 per cent) backing the party.

Of course, since 2014 politics in Scotland has been dominated by the constitutional debates thrown up by that year's independence referendum in 2014 and the EU referendum that followed two years later. Although, as noted above, support for the Scottish Conservatives did not show signs of substantial growth in the immediate aftermath of the independence referendum and in Westminster voting intention polling until after the EU referendum, it is clear that both of these events were instrumental in reviving the party's fortunes north of the border.

Comparing Scottish Social Attitudes data from 2015 to 2017 illustrates the progress the Scottish Conservatives made among the cohort of voters who wanted Scotland to stay in the United Kingdom. At the 2015 general election, just one in five of pro-UK voters backed the Scottish Conservatives, fewer than both Scottish Labour (38 per cent) and the SNP (27 per cent). By 2017, this proportion had doubled, with 37 per cent voting Conservative, 36 per cent voting Labour and just 15 per cent backing the SNP (NatCen 2017) (see Table 2.5). Opinion polls undertaken in Scotland since the 2017 general election reflected this stronger alignment between Conservative support and support for Scotland remaining part of the UK, suggesting that this was a longer-term trend. Indeed, if anything, the relationship was now even stronger, and the Scottish Conservatives were increasingly the party of choice for 'unionist' voters.[4]

Given the single-minded passion with which the Scottish Conservative leader Ruth Davidson advocated for Scotland to stay in the UK, and her opposition to a second independence referendum, it is unsurprising that pro-UK voters increasingly coalesced around the Conservatives. Polling suggested much of this progress for the Scottish Conservatives came at the expense of the Scottish Labour Party.[5] Again, this is perhaps unsurprising, given Labour's lack of clarity on the issue of a second independence referendum, which was seen as a possible bargaining position in the event of a minority Labour government reliant upon SNP support (*Independent*, 20 September 2018).

Table 2.5 General election vote among Scots who supported Scotland staying in the United Kingdom, 2015 and 2017

	Those who support Scotland staying in the UK, 2015 %	Those who support Scotland staying in the UK, 2017 %	Change 2015–17
Scottish Conservative	19	37	+18
Scottish Labour	38	36	−2
Scottish National Party	27	15	−12
Scottish Liberal Democrat	13	10	−3

Notwithstanding the progress made by the Scottish Conservatives among pro-UK voters, it was now clear the significant divides in public opinion thrown up by Brexit were instrumental in cementing the party's advances. The electoral fallout from the EU referendum was strongly felt across all parts of the United Kingdom, not least in Scotland where it had a significant impact on the nature of opinion around the independence question, and on support for different political parties north of the border.

As data from the Scottish Social Attitudes survey illustrated, support for the two main parties in Scotland, the SNP and the Conservatives, became much more closely aligned to the respective parties' supporters' stances on the European question. Scots who defined themselves as 'Eurosceptic' (either supporting the UK leaving the EU or supporting fewer powers for the EU) were now significantly less supportive of both Scottish independence and of the SNP, and significantly more supportive of Scotland staying in the UK and of the Scottish Conservatives (NatCen 2017). In other words, the Scottish Tories became adept at attracting Eurosceptic voters to a much greater degree than in pre-2016 elections, to the extent that the relationship was much more in line with the Conservatives in England.

Furthermore, there is evidence that, despite the enthusiasm with which the Scottish Conservative leadership backed a Remain vote at the 2016 referendum, it was those who backed a Leave vote who were more likely to move towards supporting the Conservatives (What Scotland Thinks, 1 October 2017). Indeed, around one in five of those who had voted 'Yes' in 2014 and 'Leave' in 2016 supported the Scottish Conservatives in 2017, abandoning the SNP in response to that party's unequivocal support for a Remain vote; this explained why 8 per cent of those who voted SNP in 2015 backed the Scottish Conservatives in 2017. Although, as outlined above, the evidence suggests the fallout from the referendums on Scottish independence and on EU membership have been the crucial factors in explaining the revival in Scottish Tory fortunes, there are other factors which might also have contributed.

Chief among these was the performance and appeal of the then Scottish Conservative leader, Ruth Davidson. As noted earlier, her unyielding position on Scotland's place in the UK became crucial in appealing to the most biddable cohort of voters. For the first three or four years after winning the leadership in late 2011, her 'net' approval rating was negative (meaning more voters were dissatisfied with her performance than satisfied), but by the 2017 general election she enjoyed positive net ratings and a higher score than the First Minister (Ipsos MORI 2017). A further measure of Davidson's performance, whether voters see her doing 'well' or 'badly', showed similar movement, with particularly positive ratings around the time of the 2017 election and immediately afterwards.

Table 2.6 Political parties' showing on social policy, 2015 and 2017

	Health/NHS			Education			Crime/antisocial behaviour			Environment		
	2015	2017	+/–	2015	2017	+/–	2015	2017	+/–	2015	2017	+/–
	%	%		%	%		%	%		%	%	
SNP	48	34	–14	49	34	–15	40	33	–7	28	14	–14
Scottish Labour	18	33	+15	16	25	+9	14	17	+3	9	11	+2
Scottish Conservatives	9	15	+6	10	18	+8	15	23	+8	6	10	+4

While Davidson's personal ratings moved in a positive direction during this period, the party and its leader were criticised by some for lacking detailed policy positions (see *New Statesman*, 1 October 2016), although Davidson did explain her broader socio-political philosophy in general terms (see, for example, UnHerd, 22 July 2017). Despite this criticism, there was polling evidence that the Scottish Tories had made some modest progress with voters on key devolved issues controlled by the Scottish Government. For example, an Ipsos MORI poll conducted on the eve of the 2017 general election showed an improvement in Conservative ratings on these policy areas compared with 2015. Given their social policy focus – on which parties of the left tend to score better than parties of the right – these ratings illustrate progress being made, albeit modestly, beyond the big constitutional issues (see Table 2.6).

Brexit Challenges

This revival in Scottish Conservative fortune, hard fought over a number of years, showed signs of stalling in the first half of 2019, as evidenced by both polling data and election results. It would appear that, albeit to a lesser extent than Conservatives south of the border, the party's support was squeezed by the emergence of the Brexit Party and its clarity of message over the ongoing negotiations to leave the EU. This meant that while the SNP continued to dominate among those who had voted to remain in the EU, the 38 per cent of Scots who had voted to leave the EU were divided between supporting the Scottish Conservatives and supporting the Brexit Party.

Polling on voting intention for a UK election throughout 2019 illustrated the changing fortunes of the Scottish Conservatives, with the party's potential vote share declining in roughly the same proportion as support for the Brexit Party grew (see Table 2.7). This trend was also observable at the European

Table 2.7 Voting intention for a UK general election among voters in Scotland, 2019

	Mar	Mar	Apr	Apr	Apr	May	June	Sept
SNP	40	37	41	38	43	38	38	43
Scottish Labour	23	22	24	21	17	19	17	15
Scottish Conservatives	24	27	22	22	20	18	18	20
Scottish Liberal Democrats	8	7	8	6	7	10	13	12
Brexit Party	–	–	–	5	4	9	9	6

Table 2.8 Changing vote share at European Parliament elections, 2014–19

	2014 result %	2019 result %	Change (+/−)
SNP	29	38	+9
Scottish Labour	26	9	−17
Scottish Conservatives	17	12	−5
Scottish Liberal Democrats	11	14	+3
Brexit Party	–	15	+15
UKIP	11	2	−9

Parliamentary elections of May 2019. This saw the most significant reversal of Scottish Tory support at any contest since the general election of 2015. Although the party retained the one seat it held in Scotland, the fall in its support from the previous 2014 European election was significant; indeed, the combined fall in support for the Scottish Conservatives and UKIP (UK Independence Party) mirrored the support received by the Brexit Party, which picked up one of Scotland's six European Parliament seats in the process (see Table 2.8).

Conclusion: Long-term Realignment or Short-term Revival?

Predicting political events and public attitudes has become increasingly difficult, and the fate of the Scottish Conservatives would appear to be significantly bound up with a number of related issues, many of which are beyond their control. While the 2017 general election witnessed a revival in the party's fortunes beyond that which they might have expected only a few months previously, analysis conducted immediately after the campaign pointed to the challenges the party faced in building on its 28.6 per cent vote share.

First, a YouGov poll suggested around a third of those who backed the Scottish Tories did so tactically, most likely for reasons outlined earlier around Brexit and the possibility of a second independence referendum. Tactical voting was the single most popular reason, ahead of the 22 per cent who voted Conservative because of Brexit and the 12 per cent who did so primarily because they supported the party's policies and proposals. Crucially, the figure for tactical voting for the Conservatives across Great Britain was just 4 per cent, indicating that tactical support for the Tories in Scotland was around nine times that in the rest of the country (YouGov 2017).

And what of the potential ceiling for Scottish Tory support? A poll conducted by Ipsos MORI immediately before the 2017 election offers some indication. For each party, it asked voters if they were their 'preferred choice', 'would *consider* voting for them', or whether they would 'never consider voting for them'. The results for the Scottish Conservatives suggested they were the preferred party for around one in five Scots (19 per cent) with a further 16 per cent saying they would consider voting for them, suggesting a potential support in the mid 30s, around 7 points higher than the party received in June 2017. The fact 60 per cent said they would *never* consider voting for the Scottish Conservatives suggests, however, the party will find it difficult to get much higher than the mid-30s, at least as things currently stand. And when we look more closely at that additional potential support, it is clear it is most likely to come from Liberal Democrat and Labour voters, among whose supporters, 41 per cent and 18 per cent respectively, said they would consider voting Conservative, compared with just 9 per cent of SNP supporters.

It should be noted, however, that growth in support to the mid-30s could produce significant change for the party, meaning the Scottish Conservatives would become contenders for devolved government in 2021; two of the five Holyrood elections held since 1999 have been won by parties with a constituency vote share of 35 per cent or less, even if these governments were conducted on a coalition or minority basis. If the current trajectory in support for the Scottish Conservatives continued in late 2020 and early 2021, then this would become a realistic proposition.

Polling since the 2017 general election highlights these challenges and suggests some caution in predicting significant further growth in support for the Scottish Tories. Indeed, as the analysis above highlights, there has been a significant fall in support for the Conservatives following the rise of the Brexit Party, reflecting the long impasse in agreeing a basis upon which the UK was to leave the European Union. In April 2019, potential support for the Scottish Conservatives at a Westminster election fell to below 20 per cent for the first time since 2017, while parties supporting a harder Brexit made gains at their expense, with 22 per cent of 2017 Scottish Conservative voters backing the new Brexit Party (Panelbase 2019). Similarly, voting intention polling for the Scottish Parliament indicated a decline in support for the Scottish Conservatives, with the same poll in April 2019 indicating that 13 per cent of those who had voted Conservative in 2016 said they would cast their constituency vote for the Brexit Party.

While all these factors are significant ones for the party, the hardest challenge the party faced was the loss of Ruth Davidson as leader in August 2019. This chapter has charted the electoral progress the party made under her stewardship, most notably at the 2016 Scottish Parliament election and the local and general elections of 2017. Although, as we have seen, support for the party had begun to falter in the wake of the emergence of the Brexit Party, it seems clear the loss of Ruth Davidson may prove a longer-term headache.

So, have we reached peak Scottish Tory? In truth, we simply do not know the answer to that question and the reality is that much of what will determine the answer lies outwith the control of the party. The electoral fortunes of the Scottish Conservatives rest as much with decisions made by the UK Conservative Party as they do with the party's political opponents closer to home. The timing of a second independence referendum is also likely to have an impact on the party's electoral fortunes; its stance against another vote in the foreseeable future is broadly in line with public opinion, but the Brexit outcome might change that. What *is* in the party's control is the prospectus it puts before Scottish voters at the next Holyrood election in 2021.

THREE

'We' in Scotland or 'She' in Scotland? Scottish Conservative Manifesto Discourse during the Davidson Era

Murray Stewart Leith

Introduction

This chapter considers the rhetoric of the Scottish Conservative Party through the lens of party manifestos issued for Scottish, UK and European elections between 2010 and 2017. Beginning with a short consideration of why Scottish Conservatism slipped from its historical high point after the Second World War, it goes on to illustrate the importance of both ideology and identity – and the interplay between the two – on party fortunes.

The chapter then considers the importance of leadership before emphasising manifestos to consider both rhetorical changes and continuities within parties. The analysis goes on to illustrate the rhetorical emphases within Scottish Conservative and Unionist Party manifestos during the last decade. It will be argued that while the Scottish Conservatives were clearly differentiating their discussion in Scotland, they remained firmly wedded to wider UK Conservative Party rhetoric during British elections, which arguably left it at the mercy of wider events.

Ideology and Identity as Drivers of Contemporary and Historical Change

This chapter examines rhetoric in order to consider whether it was a factor in the changing fortunes of Scottish Conservatism during the Ruth Davidson era. Whether the recent, much more positive, change in electoral outcomes for the Scottish Conservative Party was down to changes within (and emphasis of) the party's rhetoric, or simply the leadership style of Davidson, is a valid question. Yet, before considering the recent rhetorical emphasis of her party, we must stand back and consider, briefly and in a limited fashion, the driving changes that led to the decline of Tory fortunes in the first place. The rationale for doing so can be seen in the historical patterns and currents which continue to have an influence today.

Even a very limited analysis of twentieth-century Scottish political history points to the strength and presence of Scottish Conservatism throughout society and politics. Yet at the end of that century, when Scottish politics burst onto the scene with a discrete political stage all of its own, we witnessed the electoral nadir of the party within Scotland. While many point to devolution which, of course, Conservatives firmly opposed (something that clearly contributed to their poor electoral results), wider patterns can be discerned long before the 1990s. It is the argument of this chapter that these patterns were still in play under the Davidson leadership, the evidence for which can be found in her party's manifesto discourse.

A point made by several scholars with respect to the party's electoral decline in Scotland was the 1965 decision to change its name from the Scottish Unionist Party to the 'Scottish Conservative and Unionist Party', and for the previously autonomous Scottish party to amalgamate with the UK Conservative and Unionist Party (Seawright 1999; Kidd 2008; Torrance 2017). This was not just a simple change of nomenclature; it also resulted in significant organisational and behavioural changes. In fact, it has been argued that these changes resulted in the Scottish Conservatives becoming a territorial element of the wider Conservative Party, rather than a distinctly Scottish party in its own right (Deschouwer 2003). While this territorial-arm relationship remains as such today, at the same time the Scottish Conservatives are a territorial party with a 'high degree of autonomy' (Convery 2016a). However, it does not always exercise that autonomy fully, as this analysis of manifesto discourse will illustrate.

There is an alternative account of the Scottish Conservative Party's decline during the twentieth century. Kendrick and McCrone (1989) highlight the interplay between economic and ideological factors, with the move to a Thatcherite approach creating conflict between the rising rhetoric of Britishness and Scotland having needs as a particular economic and policy case. Thus, it was not only the ideologically driven change in Conservatism that had a negative impact, but the emphasis on identity, and specifically the 'national' identity of Britishness. Seawright (1999) also touched upon this, highlighting the conflict created between the Thatcherite ideology of the right and the Scottish electorate either becoming, or perhaps just remaining, more left wing than voters in the rest of the UK.

In discussing these and other works, Convery focuses strongly on both the identity and the organisational change aspects of such arguments, stating that this 'entrenchment of an ideological shift under Thatcher combined with earlier organisational changes to create the impression that a once distinctly Scottish party had started to become "alien" and "English"' (Convery 2016a: 40). He also clearly identifies a link between the organisational changes of the 1960s and the ideological changes of the 1970s/1980s, when he points to the arguments made by Murdo Fraser in the 2011 leadership campaign. Fraser argued that the Scottish Conservatives needed to disband and reconstitute themselves as a new right-wing Scottish party under a different brand and name, thereby seeking to detoxify the party within Scotland. However, as Convery points out, Fraser's campaign 'drew explicitly on the pre-1965 organisation of the party to argue that a separate Scottish party [would merely return] the Scottish Conservatives to their natural state' (Convery 2016a).

A move back to a clearly independent and organisationally distinct Scottish ('non-Conservative') party would be, it was argued, in line with history and perhaps even contemporary wishes. Indeed, in retrospect, the Scottish Conservative Party's organisational, structural and name changes of the 1960s were moves against the emerging currents of electoral transformation, as this was the very period when a sense of national identity had begun to stir itself as a clear socio-political element within Scotland. The SNP's movement from fringe to mainstream took place during this period, with the initial election of a large number of local councillors in the late 1960s (not to mention the famous Hamilton 1967 by-election), followed by the tumultuous Westminster elections of 1974. The Scottish Conservatives, meanwhile, were wedding themselves more firmly to the UK party. When in 2011 Murdo Fraser urged a move (back) to a party organisation and name that was distinctly Scottish, he was reviving an approach that had clearly worked before, albeit in a different time if not place. Could such a turn have led to an even greater revival of a right-wing, rebranded party in Scotland after 2011?

It must be stressed that since the advent of devolution, and especially during the last decade of Scottish politics, the importance of both ideology and national identity cannot be underplayed as a driving force within the socio-political realm. Electoral events since 2007 have witnessed the increasing rise of the SNP as *the* party of government in Scotland, as the Nationalists also grew to become the largest Scottish force at Westminster in 2015. Furthermore, the 2014 referendum on (potential) independence for Scotland, and the subsequent 2016 UK-wide referendum on British membership of the European Union, ensured that issues around national identity remained firmly at the centre of wider public and media debates.

Previous works (see, for example, Leith and Soule 2011) have demonstrated the strength and importance of national identity and ideology as a factor within wider Scottish politics. It must be remembered that all political parties operating in the Scottish context are engaged in a constant, habitually underlying (and just as often obvious) debate not just around politics, but around national identity, something even more pronounced in the contemporary period. While it seems clear from previous research that a conflict between ideology and identity drove Scottish Conservative fortunes in an ever-downward direction for several decades, we must consider whether they have been behind recent upturns under Ruth Davidson's leadership.

Party Leadership and Party Voice in Manifestos

The leadership election of 2011 presented Conservatives in Scotland with the first clear strategic and personality choice of the devolution era. Previous leadership changes had seen no contests, with Annabel Goldie elected unopposed in 2005. The one-member-one-vote system that saw Ruth Davidson elected leader in 2011 was both new and innovative, a recommendation from the 2010 Sanderson Commission, established following the party's poor showing at the 2010 UK general election.

However, it has been argued that these shifts did not result in any major policy changes (Convery 2016a). Convery argues that while Davidson clearly represented a generational change, overall she represented the 'no change' candidate. While subsequently the Scottish Conservative Party clearly moved in a more pro-devolution direction, Convery points out that this was not necessarily the path in 2011, rather being the strategy posited by Murdo Fraser, the defeated candidate. However, as Smith (2011) has argued, political reality left Conservatives in Scotland with little choice but to firmly engage with devolution in a way they had not done since 1999.

Being in opposition, and also one of several parties in a multi-party system, often leads to a focused emphasis on the leader of a party and the personalisation of the party around that leader. This has certainly been an operational tendency of the Scottish Conservatives in recent times. During the 2016 election, Ruth Davidson was 'cleverly focused', perhaps due to her being popular as an individual as well as avoiding the ongoing 'branding problem' facing Scottish Conservatism (Anderson 2016). Indeed, it is fair to say Davidson was initially more popular than her party, with even later successes attributed to her 'strong leadership' (*Guardian*, 9 June 2017). However, while popular as an individual, a party voice is wider than just one person. Party fortunes may be strongly influenced by leadership, but manifestos represent 'the recognisable statement of policy, which has the backing of the leadership as the authoritative definition of party policy for that election' (Budge et al. 1987: 18), and as such deserve attention for the focus and direction of the party beyond the 'leadership limelight'.

Of course, it is fair to say that 'only a small proportion of the electorate ever read [a] manifesto' (Brack 2000: 1), but their contents are widely disseminated through the media, with constant analysis and discussion around election times. Furthermore, the ability of a government to rely on its 'electoral mandate', especially through the Salisbury Convention, and to push for manifesto commitments in the face of entrenched opposition at Westminster remains a key aspect of UK governance. Manifestos, therefore, remain the 'best-known documents' of political parties (Cooke 2000), as well as serving as a 'hymn-sheet' for each party's candidates (Kavanagh 2000).

Manifestos also serve as another illustration of the importance of national identity within Scotland. From the 1970s onwards, all major political parties, including the Scottish Conservatives, issued separate manifestos for Scotland (and Wales), adding a distinctly Scottish voice to UK-wide elections. Previous analysis of these documents has clearly illustrated differences between the 'Scottish' and 'British' versions (Leith 2006; Leith and Soule 2011). While the production of Scottish and Welsh manifestos surely indicates the remaining document is for England only, they are rarely, if ever, identified as such. Thus, the manifestos considered here remain firmly Scotland-orientated documents even when the election is a UK-wide contest.

The 'Ruth Davidson' Conservative Party Manifesto Rhetoric in UK General Elections

We now consider the five manifesto documents issued for the 2010, 2015 and 2017 UK general elections and the 2011 and 2016 Scottish parliamentary elections (European election manifestos are discussed later). Given the two distinct differences of the elections, and the nature of electoral events, these are analysed separately, beginning with the UK electoral documents of 2010 and 2015, and then the Scottish documents of 2011 and 2016. Both these sets of elections straddled the independence referendum of 2014. The 2017 general election manifesto was issued after the 2016 vote on membership of the European Union and is therefore also considered separately.

Entitled an *Invitation to Join the Government of Britain*, the pre-Davidson 2010 manifesto front page did not provide the party name as the 'Scottish Conservative and Unionist Party', unlike the other four documents considered here, but instead referred to 'The Conservative Manifesto for Scotland 2010'. Otherwise, the front cover was mostly blank, apart from the small Conservative Party (UK) logo of a stylised tree. Also, leaving aside the leader forewords, the first by David Cameron and the second by Annabel Goldie and David Mundell, the very first word of the document was 'Britain'.

This was distinct from the first Davidson-era UK general election manifesto (2015), which carried the title *Strong Leadership: A Brighter, More Secure Future*, featuring pictures of David Cameron and Ruth Davidson, side by side, under the small heading of 'The Scottish Conservative and Unionist Party Manifesto 2015'. The words 'Scottish Conservative and Unionist' with the stylised 'X' logo, reminiscent of the St Andrew's cross or saltire, featured towards the bottom of the cover page. However, the text of the main document featured 'Britain' in the first two sentences, with the word 'Scotland' not appearing until page 12, which also mentioned England as well as cities such as Glasgow and Aberdeen. Under Ruth Davidson, the party may have moved Scotland more to the fore, but her party manifesto in 2015 remained a determinedly Britain-focused document.

Indeed, the signifiers used in these documents were firmly centred on the idea of Britain or the UK. There were few, if any, indications that the 'we' regularly deployed meant the people of Scotland, let alone Scotland as a nation. The country mentioned is Britain, and the 'we' usually a loose discourse that could have meant the Conservative Party (or UK Government in 2015) or 'the people'. While it could be argued that the geographical term was 'Great Britain' or (usually and simply) 'Britain', and the political (sovereign) term the 'United Kingdom' or 'the UK', such academic differentiations were not present, the Scottish Conservative Party in both 2010 and 2015 appearing to conceive of the whole country as being 'Britain' and its people 'British', with these terms used frequently throughout both documents. This was also the case for visual images. There were no real representations of Scottishness in these two documents; the images employed could, with one or two minimal exceptions, be UK-wide (indeed, they were simply amended renditions from the 'English' document). Unless one knew Glasgow or Scotland well, the bridge pictured on page 12 could have been anywhere. Also, while the Forth Road Bridge on page 14 was iconic to many, it meant little outside of the travel section in which it was featured.

Likewise, the term 'nation' was used somewhat loosely and without direct reference on many occasions. It was rarely linked to Scotland in both documents and terms such as 'we as a nation should not be piling up and passing on unaffordable levels of debt to the next generation' (Scottish Conservative Party 2015) clearly spoke to a UK-level perspective. This was, of course, challenging to anyone who considered their national identity to be Scottish. It has previously been argued that the people of Scotland can clearly differentiate between their national identity (Scottish) and state identity (British) (see Leith and Soule 2011), but the Scottish Conservatives played fast and loose with these terms in their UK election manifestos. The 'national' finances were the UK's, as was the 'national' legacy of international sporting events (both Commonwealth and Olympic).

Interestingly, the word 'Scottish' and 'Scot' were used, but sometimes linked to wider discussion on devolved policy (and direct reference to Scottish Parliament elections are often made on the same pages, or closer within the text). It would seem that, at times, the party was employing a very Scottish-centric view. This could be taken to mean the party emphasising its Scottish distinctiveness or basis. However, it frequently, almost within the same paragraph if not page, switched to a British perspective without any clear delineating lines. The section on travel – a fully devolved policy for rail and roads – employed a distinctly Scottish rhetorical focus, but the next section, on broadband, was firmly 'UK' and 'Britain'. Likewise, Big Ben/Westminster and the Old Bailey appeared as images, reinforcing a manifestly British connection in the 2015 document.

The independence referendum, as an event, seemed to drive the Scottish Conservatives to promote a more British-centric view after 2014 than before it, as while the 2015 manifesto regularly employed the term 'Scotland', it was often in a territorial sense, or referring to sub-groups of the population (young people *in* Scotland, or 'Scottish youth'). In other words, the term 'Scottish' appears regularly, mainly because it is a part of the party's title or self-referencing 'Scottish Conservatives'. It was also used to refer to Scottish towns and cities and the Scottish Parliament at Holyrood. The term was thus territorially or institutionally employed, rather than as an identifier of a people or a national identity. While the saltire did make an appearance, it was pictured alongside the Union flag.

Interestingly, any sense of European identity was also absent. The term 'Europe' or 'European Union'/'EU' was noticeable by its absence, and, if used, was often deployed in a mildly pejorative way. Specific policies, such as migration, were the most common context in which the EU was discussed, again negatively. Overall, the sense of identity, the sense of belonging, and the 'we' regularly employed by the Scottish Conservative and Unionist Party in 2010 and 2015 manifestos was a political one and a 'British' one.

It was 'we have done so much' when referring to Wales, Scotland, Northern Ireland and England all together, and it was 'we' when a popular or effective policy outcome was being highlighted. Likewise, the reference to place was UK or British in focus; only twice did it specifically seem to indicate Scotland, and as often it could have been taken to mean the wider UK. This could be interpreted as an indication of a multilayered identity, or it could be a deliberate attempt not to openly differentiate. Whatever the motivation, the end result was a firmly British document issued by a Scottish political party, but for a

British general election. Importantly, this did not change when the Scottish party leadership moved from Annabel Goldie to Ruth Davidson.

Conservative Party Manifesto Rhetoric in Scottish Parliament Elections

The 2011 Scottish Conservative Party manifesto was entitled *Common Sense for Scotland*, with the subtitle 'Scottish Conservatives' and the stylised tree logo; it was less than half the size of the UK document issued a year earlier. It did not have a picture on the cover of any individual (just a road sign with an arrow pointing in the direction of 'Common Sense'). The foreword did not have an image of the then leader Annabel Goldie. The 2016 document, *A Strong Opposition – A Stronger Scotland*, meanwhile, was half as long again (still shorter than its Westminster election equivalents), but did carry a picture of Ruth Davidson.

One fascinating aspect of this latter document was noted by Anderson:

> Strangely for a political party, the Scottish Conservatives began their electoral campaign conceding defeat to the SNP. Instead, they sought to put forward a case for a strong Conservative opposition with Ruth Davidson at the helm holding the SNP to account and focusing on bread-and-butter issues rather than constitutional matters. (Anderson 2016: 560)

This very point was clearly outlined in the foreword to the manifesto, illustrating that in 2016 such documents still served as the flagship vessel of a political campaign, carrying its core message front and centre. The document also reflected the realities of the Scottish political system at that time. The SNP were clearly going to win the election (it stated as much on page 6), but the Conservatives were aiming for second place as the principal opposition in the Scottish Parliament, a position they could only have dreamed about 10 years before.

Obviously, given the nature of the elections, the focus was firmly Scottish, with the first page of the 2011 text mentioning Scotland in the first sentence, and 'Scottish' in the second, although the UK was also mentioned in the same paragraph. The third paragraph began: 'With the help of the Conservatives at Westminster . . .' but did refer to Scotland as 'a more prosperous nation'. There was no ambiguity about what the nation was in this document. The same was true in 2016, although there was a twist. The terms 'Scotland' and the 'Scottish Conservatives' were present, but so was the leader's name: 'Ruth Davidson' was mentioned twice together with 'her strong Scottish Conservative team' or, in other words, 'Ruth Davidson's Conservatives'.

The United Kingdom also featured in the 2016 manifesto's second sentence. In fact, it was quite a personalised document on many fronts: Kezia Dugdale (then leader of the Scottish Labour Party) was mentioned by name, while the First Minister was also discussed but, interestingly, *not* mentioned by name, although it would have been safe to assume that anyone reading would have known that to be Nicola Sturgeon. Clearly, the target was not the SNP but Scottish Labour, the once-dominant party the Scottish Conservatives hoped to supplant.

The size of the 2011 manifesto could be ascribed to either the limited aspirations, or the limited opportunities, the Scottish Conservatives possessed at that point. Differences in policy, meanwhile, between this document and earlier manifestos could only be considered 'limited and incremental' (Convery 2016a), with its ideological emphasis firmly in line with the wider UK Conservative Party and distinctly out of sync with the other Scottish political parties. For example, the manifesto argued for a review of the structure of the Scottish NHS (but no longer advocated an internal market as per England) as well as a graduate contribution to university fees (a long-standing position). The imagery of the document was also very limited; there were no internal images other than the picture of the party leader in the foreword – again, firmly out of step with manifestos in other elections.

This 'Scottish' document bore textual similarity to UK election manifestos in that, overall, the sense of identity, the sense of belonging, and the 'we' regularly deployed by the Scottish Conservative and Unionist Party in 2011 was a political one first and a Scottish one second, and that second by some distance. The document also kept a firm sense of audience in that it was appealing to Scottish Conservatives, not Scots per se as the sense of 'we' clearly related to a political party. Ultimately, it was a Scottish Conservative Party document with a very conservative sense of reach and aim. The rhetoric appealed firmly to an audience the party seemed to have accepted it would reach, and not much beyond that. This would change during the Davidson era.

In the case of the 2016 Holyrood manifesto, the aims had changed, the style had moved and the leadership was clear. It began with the words: 'This is not a normal foreword, nor is this a normal manifesto' (Scottish Conservative Party 2016). As highlighted by Anderson (2016) and discussed above, the party was aiming to be the formal opposition and therefore conceded it would not win outright. However, to challenge Anderson's argument somewhat, the Scottish Conservatives, within the document, clearly adopted an ideological/constitutional position by framing itself firmly against a second referendum on independence. The first full section of the document was thus entitled: 'No to a Second Referendum'.

Also, the personalisation (not just of Ruth Davidson, but of the party itself) continued later in the 2016 manifesto with five candidates highlighted via short biographies and images, two men and three women all stressing their 'new' or 'different' ways of coming to politics, and how they were proud either to be part of 'Ruth Davidson's team' or facing down a 'second referendum' on Scottish independence.

Again, as in 2011, the document was firmly rooted in a sense of Scotland and Scottishness. Terms like 'Scotland', 'Scottish', 'Scots' and references to sub-groups, such as 'taxpayers in Scotland' or 'young Scots', were abundant throughout the text. The sense of nation was clear and clearly Scottish, although the UK was also present. Where the UK did make an appearance, it was usually allied to the term 'government' and focused on continuing the policy developments of that body, should they be devolved, or working in partnership with the Westminster Government to meet certain objectives.

The idea of further devolution was also an aspect of the 2016 document which set it apart from previous publications. Rarely mentioned in UK Conservative documents, and not mentioned at all in the 2011 Scottish manifesto, the idea of further devolution could be seen as having been (as discussed above) thrust upon the Scottish Conservatives by events (namely the closeness of the 2014 independence referendum), but it was, nevertheless, firmly adopted. The manifesto rhetoric of the Scottish Conservatives thus adapted, employing the idea of further devolution with gusto in key policy areas, while simultaneously rejecting both independence and another referendum on the matter.

The imagery of the 2016 manifesto was also different (although that was not difficult in that the 2011 manifesto carried no imagery at all). Edinburgh Castle and the Scott Monument made an appearance, as did individual candidates and Ruth Davidson (in several images). Davidson, the Castle and 'Say No to a Second referendum' placard-waving supporters featured in one image, many wearing jackets with 'Scottish Conservatives' pasted on the back. Hills, sheep, police cars, skylines, elderly people and other 'stock images' also made an appearance. But the number of Ruth Davidson full-page images was most striking of all. This was indeed a personalised manifesto unlike any other, with the Davidson brand firm, clear and unequivocal.

Overall, the sense of identity, the sense of belonging, and the 'we' regularly deployed by 2016 had changed dramatically from the 2011 manifesto. While Scotland remained and was even firmer, the 'we' had moved beyond the Scottish Conservatives of old; it was a new 'we', a bolder 'we' that embraced new policies, new candidates, a new leader and, by implication, a new vision of Scotland and *for* Scotland. Both might be Scotland-focused documents, but it was the 2016 manifesto that represented a concrete call to Scotland and evoked a much wider political 'we'. It was also a 'we' clearly headed by 'she'; the 'conservative' Conservatism of the earlier period had been replaced by Davidson-branded Scottish Conservatism, a new leader for a 'new' party.

The 2017 Scottish Conservative and Unionist Party Manifesto

Entitled *Forward, Together: Our Plan for a Stronger Scotland, a Stronger Britain and a Prosperous Future*, this 80-page document dwarfed the Scottish Parliament documents and matched the size of previous UK general election manifestos. Bearing the title and the full name of the party on its front cover with no imagery, a signed statement by Theresa May was flanked by a picture of her and Ruth Davidson. Brexit was mentioned in the second sentence of this short statement, and five times in a total of 130 words. This was followed by a formal foreword by May and another by Davidson. The latter appears to be, in keeping with previously British ('English?') documents, an addition to the wider 'British' manifesto.

Again, much of the document seemed identical to the UK version, with 'Scotland' only appearing in isolated sections. As an example, there were 10 mentions within Ruth Davidson's foreword, but it was then 15 more pages before Scotland was again mentioned. On page 16, Scotland makes several appearances, some in relation to the tax-making properties of the Scottish Parliament (which is, again interestingly, not mentioned specifically). What was stated was that 'taxpayers in Scotland should not be asked to pay more income tax than their friends, family or colleagues in other parts of the UK'. This pattern was then repeated, with large sections of the manifesto not mentioning Scotland at all, before resurfacing every seven or eight pages as a reference or term, often specifically geographic, or in reference to devolved policy areas.

The nuances of the 2017 general election must be considered. The 'snap' election was 'called' by Theresa May on 18 April 2017, with more than two thirds of MPs endorsing that call the following day, leaving less than two months until polling day. While this might have had an impact upon preparations and readiness for the election and the creation of a distinct Scottish manifesto, it remained the case that the document issued in Scotland was very much a British one, with additions and amendments as required. In addition to its limited mentions of Scotland, which were often linked to specific Acts of Parliament or devolved policies, there were even fewer uses of the word 'Scottish'. Technically, it appeared on every page as the title of the Scottish party, but beyond that it made few – if any – appearances in the text.

What becomes clear in considering the text of the 2017 manifesto are the divergences between the UK-facing and Scottish-facing documents. They were technically written for the same population – the Scottish-based electorate (EU/Commonwealth citizens aside). However, they also maintained differences that would almost seem to indicate the targeting of different audiences. Once again, as in 2010 and 2015, the 2017 manifesto used signifiers and terms centred around the idea of Britain and/or the UK. Within the first 15 pages that do not mention 'Scotland', the term 'nation' is used often, but clearly in relation to 'Britain'. Phrases like 'If we are going to make sure Britain emerges from Brexit as a strong and united nation' illustrate this. But the clearest example is the one that stated 'Britain is a great nation' and that 'we will, as a nation, go forward, together' (Scottish Conservative Party 2017a: 12).

However, this was also a perfect example of where there was a clear change in the sense of 'we' that was often deployed in other sections of the manifesto. In areas that related to specific policy or government actions, the 'we' was clearly a Conservative Party one, indeed a UK Conservative Party one. However, at other points, and especially when discussing Brexit, the 'we' becomes much more encompassing, although again from a strongly British perspective. The 'we' is 'we the people', the *people* of the United Kingdom, the *people* of Britain. The nation therein was not Scotland, although that was mentioned and discussed in places, but a larger geographical nation, *the State*.

Again, there was a challenge there for anyone who held their national identity to be firmly and exclusively Scottish, but not necessarily to those who held a multilayered sense of identity. Again, we can see that shifting frame of reference, or shifting sense of a centric viewpoint, and it could have been a subtle and distinct employment, or a by-product of an attempt to avoid challenging and clashing concepts. At times, and as in 2010 and 2015, the 2017 Scottish Conservative Party manifesto deployed a clearly Scottish-centric viewpoint and, at others (often in the same section of the document), a more clearly British vantage point.

One section of the 2017 document that requires highlighting in this respect is the section entitled 'Leaving the European Union'. Covering just over two pages, this explored an issue that clearly divided Scottish and English electorates. However, while the text mentioned Northern Ireland, Gibraltar, and London, Edinburgh, Cardiff, Belfast and, of course, the EU, it only mentioned Scotland once, when it stated: 'We will work closely with the devolved administrations to deliver an approach that works for the whole of the United Kingdom and reflects the needs and individual circumstances of Scotland, Wales and Northern Ireland' (Scottish Conservative Party 2017a: 37). Again, the 'we' is British, if not firmly Conservative.

In 2017, the sense of identity and belonging employed by the Scottish Conservative and Unionist Party remained both party political and British. It was 'we have the biggest defence budget in Europe' when referring to Wales, Scotland, Northern Ireland and England all together, and it was 'we' when 'we will build on the proud Conservative record'. When it made reference to a territorial or national sense of belonging, such references were UK or British in focus; only occasionally did Scotland make an appearance and, when it did, it was very much as part of the wider UK.

The Scottish Conservative Party European Election Manifesto 2014

There was only one European election manifesto issued while Ruth Davidson was Scottish Conservative leader, that of 2014. In 2019, no Conservative manifestos were issued. Of course, whether the United Kingdom would actually take part in that election had remained in question until quite close to polling day. Clearly, given their focus on Brexit, writing a manifesto remained a difficulty the party did not want to face. This was probably even more of an issue for the Scottish party, with a leader who had supported remaining part of the EU, confronting an electorate that had voted by a decisive margin for the same outcome.

A short document of only 28 pages, the 2014 European manifesto evoked both personalisation and a firm sense of identity. The front cover featured David Cameron and Ruth Davidson together, while the second page listed party achievements, mentioning 'Britain'/'British'/'UK' more than a dozen times but only 'Scotland'/'Scottish' twice, one of them being a reference to the party's name. And while Davidson's foreword appeared before that of Cameron, she mentioned the UK twice in the first four paragraphs, Scotland only making its first appearance in the fifth. This was not surprising as her message was entitled 'Scotland and Britain United'. Cameron's foreword, clearly written for a wider audience, did not mention Scotland at all. The focus of Davidson's message was also interesting. While written for an EU election, it mostly argued the benefits of Scotland remaining part of the UK. The manifesto, of course, was issued a few months before the independence referendum, a chronology which explains the document's twofold focus.

As with the documents issued for Westminster elections, the EU manifesto was firmly centred on the idea of Britain/the United Kingdom. There were, of course, mentions of 'Scotland'/'Scottish' in relation to specific policy areas or actions of the Scottish Conservative Party. For example, the section on agriculture referred to 'Scotland's rural economy' and, when discussing the need to limit migration, Scotland's largest city was used as a reference point for the number of incoming migrants 'twice the size of Glasgow'.

However, again as per Westminster documents, this remained a firmly British document. The Union flag appeared in several images, while major (Scottish and UK) Conservative Party figures featured prominently, not only Ruth Davidson and David Cameron but also (future Prime Minister) Theresa May and (former UK party leader) William Hague. The Scottish Conservative European manifesto's 'we' is a British one; the country is the UK, the people British, and the party too.

Conclusion

Our short historical overview at the beginning of this chapter considered how the shift in ideology – which led to more of an emphasis on identity and belonging – within Conservatism might have contributed to the decline in Scottish Conservative fortunes. By focusing firmly on the manifestos produced by the Scottish Conservative Party for elections over the past decade, we can see there have been significant shifts in the language used within Scottish electoral contests, although this has been inconsistent.

Our analysis of manifesto foci and rhetoric in 2010, 2015 and 2017 did not, however, indicate significant changes in the way Scottish Conservatives presented themselves at British or UK elections. It has been argued that the autonomy of the Scottish Conservative Party is not something it had always sought to emphasise, and it appears this has been the case in the Scottish versions of UK-wide manifestos.

The presence of a distinct Scottish voice in such documents has remained muted at best, and completely absent in certain respects. However, this may be a deliberate choice, or simply an attempt to speak to what the party conceives of as its core support. In either case, and in recent elections, it would seem to have been a positive happenstance. There can be little doubt that after the EU referendum of 2016, the Conservative Party presented a distinctly 'British' voice for Scottish voters. Curtice has argued that this may have spoken 'to the hearts of those who were most opposed to independence' (Curtice 2018a: 42). This was clearly the message in the 2014 EU document, and the 2017 Westminster manifesto too.

There was a clear shift in rhetorical emphasis, presentation, imagery and linguistic application between 2011 and 2016 when it came to Holyrood manifestos. The significant change was not only in tone, but also their sense of identity, belonging and nation, most evident in 2016, a clear factor that must be considered as having had an impact upon the electoral fortunes of the party. But this must also be considered alongside the presence of a new, more high-profile leader – not only a new leader, but a new message, new imagery and a new vision, albeit all allied to a familiar and UK-wide ideology.

What was different in the 2016 manifesto was that Scottish Conservatism stood out with a rhetorical flourish absent from preceding manifestos. Its sense of belonging and national identity was aligned to a clear ideological and constitutional message. Likewise, the leadership, and the party itself, had been personalised. Ruth Davidson as a leader was clearly seen as an asset and fully deployed as such. In this sense, 'Ruth Davidson's Conservatives' were presented as new, different and positive. Whether Davidson was the sole explanation for the Scottish Conservative revival is arguable, but when the party put her at the fore – especially in 2016 and 2017 – it undeniably achieved better results.

Without further consideration, research and analysis, it would be difficult to draw conclusions as to the nature of this 'Davidson factor'. Certainly, there appear to have been two distinct approaches employed when the election was *for* Scotland, or simply *included* Scotland. It could be that the impact of Ruth Davidson differed depending on this context. Yet, it is also clear that a personalised approach around the Scottish party leader appeared to pay dividends. A distinct rhetorical approach has been a feature of Scottish Conservatism during the last decade; the question is, will that endure beyond the Davidson era?

FOUR

'Standing up for Scotland' at Westminster?

Paris Gourtsoyannis

Introduction

It is an everyday hazard around the Houses of Parliament: dodging groups of people who have just arrived from all corners of the UK and the world, who clog the pavements and paths as they gaze up at the gothic splendour of Westminster and pause for selfies. In glorious June sunshine five days after the 2017 general election, some of them witnessed 12 newly elected Scottish Conservative MPs being unveiled to the media in the Victoria Tower Gardens adjacent to Parliament. The scene was chaotic, with apprehensive looks on a few faces as the new arrivals were swarmed by television cameras and photographers, and sized up by dozens of journalists.

The photo call was a clear statement: a new force had arrived. Ruth Davidson's Scottish troops were here to restore order to a Parliament and a Conservative Party thrown into turmoil by Brexit and a disastrous election campaign. It all began so well. Like conquering armies throughout history, word of their power travelled before them. Media reports announced that Davidson had secured unprecedented influence for a political figure outwith the Westminster system.

The Times reported that Davidson had 'sent a clear warning to Theresa May not to force a hard Brexit on the UK' (*The Times*, 10 June 2017), while the *Guardian* suggested that 'Scotland's new group of Conservative MPs will be expected to vote as a bloc to protect the nation's interests at Westminster' (*Guardian*, 11 June 2017). Even the editor of the London *Evening Standard* said of Davidson: 'The interesting thing about her is she is now flexing her muscles, and the most interesting thing she is flexing her muscles on is Brexit' (*Scotsman*, 12 June 2017) – an intriguing observation from the former Chancellor, George Osborne.

In the days after the election, Davidson herself promised the MPs would 'forcefully' make the case for Scotland at Westminster, and said she wanted to 'look again at issues like Brexit which we know we are now going to have to get cross-party support for' (BBC News online, 10 June 2017). She called for an 'open Brexit', which her spokespeople insisted was not a call for the UK to remain in the EU Single Market, but her comments clearly suggested a change of course to match altered political circumstances.

The moment felt full of potential in the midst of yet another twist in the UK's recent political and constitutional history. But the grand unveiling nearly did not happen: the MPs were late because government whips had discouraged them from breaking away from training and induction to take part. And despite being the woman of the moment, the Scottish Tory leader was not present – Davidson had held a separate event to unveil the new MPs in Stirling two days earlier. In London, David Mundell, the Secretary of State for Scotland, spoke on behalf of the group.

Two years on from that day, the details help explain why that Scottish Tory influence was only used cautiously, rather than with the force that was promised. And they also help explain why Davidson – a more reluctant leader of her Westminster contingent than was understood at the time – ended up quitting the field entirely, bringing to an end the daring but unlikely project to install her as Scotland's first Conservative First Minister of the devolved era.

Outnumbering Pandas

It is easy to see why the 2017 Scottish Conservative group was an object of fascination. The main reason was novelty – the number of Conservative MPs from Scotland was the largest in 35 years. There had not been more than a single MP from north of the border in two decades, and for four of those years there were none at all. Lately, the Scottish Conservative Party had become the butt of jokes about there being more pandas at Edinburgh Zoo than Conservatives in the House of Commons. But as Edinburgh Zoo was to learn, Scottish Tories multiplied faster.

The spotlight was also on the Scots because they had broken the narrative. Having called a snap vote after months of soaring poll leads that promised a crushing victory over Labour, Theresa May had ended up presiding over a disastrous election which paralysed Parliament and made it impossible for the UK to leave the EU on schedule. The Prime Minister clung to power thanks to a confidence-and-supply agreement with the Democratic Unionist Party (DUP) that gave her a slim Commons majority; however, without the 12 gains in Scotland the Conservatives might not have remained in government at all. Scottish Tories were acutely aware of this fact. 'Theresa May wouldn't have been Prime Minister if it wasn't for us,' one Scottish Tory MP says. 'We knew it, and Downing Street knew it.'

The Scottish Conservatives were also an object of fascination because their leader was fascinating: Davidson could not have looked more different from May in the aftermath of the 2017 election. Her party had come second in two elections in as many years, and by historic standards those were two huge victories. As a gay, kickboxing former Territorial Army soldier from Buckhaven, Davidson's story broke the mould for a senior Tory, and her personality shone compared to May, who had been ridiculed for saying in an election interview that the naughtiest thing she had ever done was run through a field of wheat.

So, the 2017 result fuelled hopes at Westminster that Davidson might one day take a Commons seat and rescue the UK party from itself, rumours that flickered for over a year until she finally stamped them out in a soul-bearing interview (*Sunday Times*, 16 September 2018). With that prospect completely shattered by her 2019 resignation, it is relevant to ask if the Scottish Tory group were ever really 'Ruth's MPs', and whose interests they represented if not hers. They had the potential to change the course of the UK's volatile constitutional debate, both on Scottish independence and Brexit – but how much did it actually gain them?

Using interviews with party sources at all levels in Edinburgh and London, including members of Theresa May's Downing Street team, this chapter examines the record and the prospects for the Scottish Tory class of 2017: can they survive, or will they return to the panda enclosure as a critically endangered political species?

A Scottish DUP?

Two potential blueprints presented themselves to the Scottish Conservatives when it came to leveraging their position in a hung Parliament. The first was that of the DUP, which had extracted £1 billion in return for its support; the other was that of the European Research Group, the Eurosceptic party within a party that helped deliver an unprecedented 230-vote Commons defeat for May's Brexit deal from which her premiership never recovered. There might have been a third (Scottish) force in Parliament, further complicating already challenging parliamentary arithmetic. Indeed, how this ought to organise itself was a matter of serious debate and disagreement among Scottish Conservative MPs.

Most, however, were wary of differentiating themselves too much from their colleagues, although not everyone agreed. 'We were very conscious that we didn't want to become a Scottish DUP,' one MP says, while another admits: 'I hoped we would become a Scottish DUP,' adding that a 'phalanx' or a 'wedge' of Scottish Tory MPs could have extracted its own DUP-like price from ministers. The government did not wait for them to decide. The then Chief Whip Gavin Williamson moved swiftly to block the Scottish Tories from becoming another party within a party, setting the tone for an at times uneasy relationship. He took a divide-and-conquer approach: despite requests for adjacent offices, the 12 backbench MPs were physically separated and spread around the Palace of Westminster and its modern annexes. 'I thought it was silly,' a senior Scottish Tory figure says, but a Downing Street source admits there was 'concern' as to how the group would behave.

In spite of government wariness, the MPs did take steps to organise themselves as a distinct group, initially sharing a small pool of up to four staff: researchers, a press officer and a chief of staff. John Lamont, the MP for Berwickshire, Roxburgh and Selkirk, was named convener, with his Moray colleague, Douglas Ross, as deputy convenor. Lamont and Ross had both been MSPs when they were elected to Westminster, and Lamont was the only one of the 12 new MPs with significant parliamentary experience, having served at Holyrood since 2007. He was also one of Davidson's closest allies, having run her leadership campaign in 2011 and serving as her chief whip in the Scottish Parliament. Lamont and Ross were themselves a tight unit, sharing a flat in London during sitting weeks at Westminster and representing the nucleus of a small MPs' running club.

The purpose of their leadership roles was organisational, arranging meetings and briefings, both among the MPs and with external parties including ministers and government departments. But Lamont was viewed with particular suspicion by the government whips' office. 'They saw him as being loyal to Davidson, and there was a belief that he was passing information back to Edinburgh,' an MP colleague says. Publicly, the Scottish Conservative Party maintained that the group never took its own whip, but the extent to which they would take a united and distinct position on key issues such as Brexit was, according to one MP, a source of 'confusion and tension'. Another says the group was issued with a 'chamber rota', instructing MPs which debates to attend. 'That might have worked at Holyrood, where business managers basically decide who speaks and everything is tightly scheduled, but it was ridiculous at Westminster,' the MP says.

Joint staffing arrangements broke down as the first Scottish MPs were promoted to be parliamentary private secretaries (PPSs), which changed the demands on their offices. Issuing joint press releases from Westminster, meanwhile, lasted just a few months as, according to one MP, 'some of the group felt things were going out in their name that they didn't agree with'. Inevitably, in the same way that it strained collective Cabinet responsibility, party loyalty and the Union, it was Brexit which ended any attempt to form a Scottish bloc.

The issue came to a head over the EU Withdrawal Bill, the first and most significant piece of Brexit legislation. In Scotland, this attempt to transfer EU law into British statute sparked an unprecedented constitutional row. The architects of devolution had never considered that the UK might leave the EU, and key devolved responsibilities – over areas like agriculture, fisheries and the environment, as well as state aid and geographical indicators for food and drink produce – would be handed from Brussels back to the member state, the UK. Where those powers rested had not mattered while Scotland and the rest of the UK were part of the wider European Single Market. But after Brexit, any divergence within the UK market would leave London unable to run an independent trade policy, one of the central aims of Brexiteers.

The only option for the UK Government was to assert its authority over key responsibilities while offering to create 'joint frameworks' which would give the devolved administrations some say over their management. The standoff put at risk another, relatively new, feature of the unwritten British constitution, the Sewel Convention, which required the consent of devolved parliaments or assemblies before Westminster could legislate on a devolved matter. Unsurprisingly, that consent was refused by the SNP government in Edinburgh, and initially by the Labour government in Cardiff too, both of whom accused the UK Government of a 'power grab'.

The row divided the Scottish Conservative group, with some casting doubt on their support for the Bill. East Renfrewshire MP Paul Masterton, who was among a group of Tories branded 'mutineers' in a now-infamous *Telegraph* front page, said the clause relating to devolution was 'not fit for purpose and it must be changed'. He added: 'I will not support a bill which undermines devolution and does not respect the integrity of the Union' (HC Debs 4 Dec 2017 Vol 632 c733). There were also tensions behind the scenes as talks between Edinburgh and London dragged on. 'It became clear that what we were being told about what the whips' office was saying, and what was actually going on, didn't match up,' one MP says.

The matter came to a head after David Mundell gave a commitment in the Commons that the legislation would be amended 'at report' (HC Debs 6 Dec 2017 Vol 632 c1021), the final legislative stage before the Bill moved to the House of Lords. At Cabinet the previous day, he had been given an assurance by Damian Green, the Cabinet Office Minister and May's deputy, that the dispute would be resolved in time to make amendments in the Commons. But Green was sacked later that month over allegations he had acted inappropriately towards a female journalist. 'It turned out that he had expected to go, and his department hadn't really done anything for weeks,' a government source says. 'All in all, we lost two months.'

There was no deal with the Scottish Government by the time the Bill left the Commons on 17 January 2018. Amendments would have to be made in the unelected upper chamber, an embarrassing position that some in the Scottish Conservative group had anticipated, but one that left the party's MPs feeling angry and betrayed. Stirling MP Stephen Kerr accused ministers of having 'let this chamber down', adding: 'It sticks in my craw . . . It's not really good enough, and as a member of the House of Commons I hang my head to think that we have somehow dropped the ball' (HC Debs 16 Jan 2018 Vol 634 c821).

Another MP says that it was 'a wakeup call to some in the group about how much trust we could put in the whips' office, and how much we should believe it when the government said something would definitely happen'. John Lamont also became the focus of blame. Previously, he had held talks with the whips, but after the Withdrawal Bill debacle, Chief Whip Julian Smith was invited to a group meeting. Sources present describe an awkward and tense atmosphere as Smith said he had been told they were content with the Bill and the government's actions. Alister Jack, the Dumfries and Galloway MP who joined the whips' office the following year (he became Scottish Secretary in July 2019), turned to Lamont and said: 'This contradicts what we were led to believe.'

Despite the moderate language, it was a serious accusation, and the beginning of the end for the Scottish Tories as a distinct bloc within the Commons. A group of 'malcontents' approached Scottish Secretary David Mundell to say they wanted to remove Lamont, but the attempted coup failed after the Borders MP 'did a John Major' and challenged colleagues to back him or sack him. The plotters could not command a majority. Nonetheless, it was clear Lamont did not enjoy total support. As a result, since 2018, rather than gathering in the Commons, Scottish Tory MPs have held their group meetings at the Scotland Office, which now performed a co-ordinating role. There was no longer a permanent group convener. The consensus in the group is that the arrangements were doomed to fail, but one senior Scottish Tory at Westminster says Mundell could have intervened. 'David should have put his arm around them, and guided them. But he was so used to being on his own. He didn't know what to do.'

And throughout all of this, where was Ruth Davidson? The Scottish party leader was aware of the internal tensions – at least one MP spoke with her directly about their unhappiness at the level of control being exerted on the group. But contrary to all the speculation when they were elected, Davidson does not seem to have played an active role in her MPs' work, or even attempted to. 'She's never sought to direct or instruct,' one said (prior to her resignation), 'she's always respected boundaries.' Indeed, despite the Scottish Tories having the greatest leverage in the Commons of any group from north of the border, Davidson's relationship with her MPs may have been the most detached. It was a cross-party complaint among Scots at Westminster that they felt neglected by their respective party leaderships in Edinburgh, but every Holyrood leader with parliamentarians in the Commons, including Nicola Sturgeon, made multiple visits to meet their MPs after 2017.

Davidson regularly visited Downing Street to take part in political Cabinet and obviously met her parliamentarians at party events but, remarkably, in the constant Brexit turmoil since the 2017 general election, her MPs say Davidson never held a scheduled meeting with the group. Sources in Edinburgh and London are unable to provide evidence of her having attended one. Regular face-to-face contact between Westminster and Holyrood was instead carried out by her deputy, Jackson Carlaw, and Davidson's head of communications, Eddie Barnes. It was in keeping with her leadership style – Davidson did not normally attend Scottish Parliament group meetings either – but it was a source of puzzlement among MPs. 'Perhaps she was intimidated by Westminster and the fact that we can do our own thing,' one suggests. Another says: 'I'm a huge supporter of Ruth's, but I think she should have gotten more involved.'

Strong and Stable?

It is not hard to see why the Scottish Conservatives were viewed with suspicion by government whips from the moment they arrived in 2017: May owed them everything, while they owed her very little in return. The Scottish gains were the only good news story on election night for two reasons: Ruth Davidson and Nicola Sturgeon. In 2014, independence supporters had watched their opponents snatch defeat from the jaws of victory by creating the 'Project Fear' bogeyman that reared its head again during the EU referendum, and by pushing ahead with 'English Votes for English Laws' in its immediate aftermath. It helped create a narrative that declarations of love for Scotland and the Union were only for the campaign trail, and that the SNP were the party who truly 'stood up for Scotland'.

In the year that followed the independence referendum, around 100,000 people joined the SNP, setting up an historic landslide at the 2015 general election. But a year on, it was Sturgeon who was ignoring the warning from recent history and misinterpreting the result of a referendum. On the morning of the 2016 result, she said Brexit made a second Scottish independence referendum 'highly likely' (BBC News online, 24 June 2016) and announced plans to make preparations for a second referendum.

Weariness at three years of constitutional upheaval boosted the Scottish Conservatives even as May's national campaign effort faltered. The Prime Minister's first visit to Scotland of the election confirmed the awkward, paranoid style of her campaign. Journalists were summoned to a town hall in rural Aberdeenshire for a 'rally', booked in secret as a 'children's party' and attended only by invited Tory activists. Theresa May took questions from preselected media outlets and repeated her 'strong and stable' line nine times, helping to justify her 'Maybot' nickname (BuzzFeed News, 29 April 2017).

A brief door-knock in Banchory followed with a local candidate who, on paper, had little hope against an SNP majority of 7,033. As news channels carried their progress down a row of houses in live broadcast, at first no one came to the door. The metaphor was abject and accurate. The apparently unlucky candidate was Andrew Bowie, but on election night he built his own majority of nearly 8,000, a few hundred more than the number of votes lost by the Liberal Democrats, who had held the seat for 18 years prior to 2015. Across Scotland, tactical voting lifted all three unionist parties. Constitutional fatigue had rescued the Scottish Tories from the same fate as colleagues in the rest of the UK.

Devolution had also insulated them from the worst disaster of the campaign, unveiled by May at the party's manifesto launch in a redeveloped Victorian mill in Halifax, an indication of where the Tories expected to pick up seats in 2017. A plan to factor the value of people's homes into a means test for elderly care, with no cap on costs over £100,000, was branded a 'dementia tax', disowned by furious MPs and abandoned by the Prime Minister within four days (*Guardian*, 23 May 2017). The manifesto had been written by May's policy chief, the MP Ben Gummer, and Nick Timothy, Downing Street's co-chief of staff alongside the former Scottish journalist Fiona Hill.

Just how tight a grip that small group of people had, and how hard the Scottish party had to fight to escape it, was revealed on the margins of the manifesto launch. Despite being hemmed in together by protesters who surrounded the mill, Cabinet ministers had been told not to speak to journalists. But with the Prime Minister due back in Scotland the following day to launch her Scottish manifesto alongside Davidson, another potentially damaging story had to be squashed before the next morning's front pages: a plan to means-test winter fuel payment, which would not apply in Scotland. Along with reporters from ITV Border and the *Herald*, I was summoned to a briefing with Mundell in the alley leading out of the mill, near the bins.

The attempt at secrecy failed as the Prime Minister's motorcade swept out of the back entrance just as Mundell was being interviewed on camera. He quickly received a text from Fiona Hill demanding to know why he had been speaking to the media. But if he had not, the Scottish manifesto launch could have turned into another disaster. This set the tone for a constant need on the part of Scottish Conservative MPs to mitigate the unintended consequences of their English colleagues' words and actions.

Ruth's MPs?

After 2017, Scottish Conservative MPs were under no illusions as to the external factors behind their victories. 'There's nothing about me as a human being that means I won my seat,' one MP says. 'We made gains in Scotland because of Ruth's personal brand and because we were effective at convincing people that we were the only alternative to the nationalists.' New Scottish MPs took the clear message from their constituents: while the result was no endorsement for May, they were being sent to Westminster to fight the SNP and protect the Union, not to oppose the UK Government from within. It seems unlikely, when considering the new MPs as individuals, that they would ever have reached a consensus on that in the first place. Even in a group of just eleven men and one woman, there were significant differences in political experience and motivation.

Some really were 'Ruth's MPs'; the suddenness of the 2017 general election meant several candidates had effectively been hand-picked by Davidson herself or party chairman Lord (Mark) McInnes. Some had to be talked into turning their lives upside down at short notice for what looked likely to be scant reward: the last Scottish polls before the election was called had given the SNP a 19-point lead. John Lamont was one of three new MPs who had been serving at Holyrood when elected. Candidates like the 67-year-old retired firefighter Bill Grant in Ayr, Carrick and Cumnock had served on his local council for a decade and stood for Westminster before. At the other end of the spectrum, at 27 years old Kirstene Hair became one of the youngest members in the Commons; she had not been born the last time her Angus constituency was represented at Westminster by a Conservative. Some MPs, particularly the younger ones, arrived with hopes of a career in government, while others were willing to get on the wrong side of the whips.

While only one member of the group played a significant role in the campaign to leave the EU, there was a broader range of opinion on Brexit than was first apparent. Aberdeen South's Ross Thomson was a leading figure in the Leave campaign in Scotland, while Luke Graham was finance director for the official Remain campaign, Stronger In. Among the rest – who occupied a spectrum between those two points – support for Davidson's vision of Brexit could not be taken for granted. Alister Jack, for example, had voted to leave the EU (*i* newspaper, 26 July 2019).

Ross Thomson's constituency shared its boundaries with Moray Council, which recorded the narrowest EU referendum result in Scotland, a margin of just 122 votes for Remain. Analysis of that result by Chris Hanretty of the University of East Anglia suggested that David Duguid's Banff and Buchan constituency – which included major fishing ports at Peterhead and Fraserburgh, bearing a decades-old grudge against Brussels – voted 'Leave' (Hanretty 2017). An 'open Brexit', therefore, would have limited appeal for many of their own voters.

Scottish Conservatives have always had a strained relationship with devolution, opposing the creation of the Scottish Parliament before grudgingly coming to accept it. Ruth Davidson won the party leadership with a promise to draw a 'line in the sand' (*Scotsman*, 9 September 2011) on further devolution, before rubbing it out when the threat of independence loomed (BBC News online, 26 March 2013). So, despite the Scottish Tories' long exile from London, for several members of the 2017 group Holyrood held little or no interest – Westminster was at the centre of their political aspirations. For a few, David Cameron's reforming project had drawn them into Conservative politics rather than Ruth Davidson's charisma. 'I would never consider standing for the Scottish Parliament,' one MP admits.

Personality and personal relationships also mattered, and while all the MPs would credit Davidson for their victory, some had distant or even strained relationships with their Scottish leader. A dispute over selection for the West Aberdeenshire and Kincardine constituency – the top Scottish Tory target in 2017 – was understood to have caused tensions when Andrew Bowie was personally asked by Davidson to stand just months before the election was called. As some Scottish Conservative MPs won promotion while others did not, these differences only became more prominent.

The first Members became PPSs within eight months. It was, according to one MP, an obvious campaign of preferment in order to secure obedience. 'The whips were very clever in picking off those who were vulnerable, to win their loyalty,' they said. 'You can see by who it was that got promoted.' A Downing Street source admits there was an effort to bring Scots into government to show the administration cared about the Union. Others point out that the three Scottish Tory MPs who opposed May's Brexit deal – initially Lamont, Ross and Thomson in the first 'meaningful vote', then only Thomson in the following two – were, with Bill Grant, the only Scottish Tories who were not offered positions in May's government. The dividing lines might not have been as clear as those in the 1980s and 1990s, when the Thatcherite Michael Forsyth represented one end of the spectrum and Malcolm Rifkind the other, but they were nevertheless there.

Standing up for Scotland – and against the SNP

While political interests and ambitions varied, there was always total unity among the Scottish Tories as to their main objective: opposing the SNP and defending the Union. Ironically, pursuing that goal sometimes put the group in direct conflict with its own side. Between 1997 and 2017, the Conservative Party at Westminster had come to regard Scotland as foreign territory, and the Unionist near wipe-out in 2015 merely reinforced that idea. Scottish Tories say they arrived at Westminster to find that even their own MPs and ministers, as well as civil servants, had absorbed the message that only the SNP 'spoke for Scotland'.

In the Commons chamber, re-education was swift and thorough. In a June 2018 debate, Northern Ireland Secretary Karen Bradley made the mistake of taking an intervention in a Commons debate from the SNP's Joanna Cherry by saying she would 'hear the voice of Scotland' (HC Debs 5 Jun 2018 Vol 642 c220). 'Karen got an earful,' an MP says, and indeed she swiftly withdrew the comment. With a dozen extra bodies, the Scottish Tories could now fully take part in the parliamentary pantomime, offering a morale boost to ministers and MPs who had grown used to being shouted down by 56 SNP voices. From June 2017, they had competition. 'Colleagues told us they used to hate having to do Scottish Questions, and avoided it,' another MP says. 'Now they bring popcorn.'

But louder voices in the Commons could not conceal what Scottish Tories saw as a deeper, structural problem. They were quick to pick up on a lack of consideration for Scotland in day-to-day governing and policy-making. All Conservative MPs were part of a group on the mobile messaging platform WhatsApp which fed them updates of every government spending announcement. Scottish MPs made a point of responding to each message with the same question: 'How does this affect Scotland?' Often, government departments did not have the answer. 'I think they were shocked by the extent to which government and the Westminster system wasn't set up to consider Scottish needs and Scottish politics,' a Scottish Tory source in Edinburgh says:

> It's like we've been through this 20-year revolution, where devolution has changed hugely but the Union hasn't caught up. You can't have a stable Union when Westminster is so unfocused when it comes to Scotland. Ministers, Spads [special advisers] and civil servants, they all know this stuff. It isn't that they don't care, they just forget, which is slightly different.

Scottish Conservatives describe having to do battle with civil servants who had come to see the division of responsibilities under devolution as inviolable. 'Officials lack imagination and hate change, and they believe that if something is devolved, it's got nothing to do with them,' one MP says. That resistance to change is strongest within the Treasury, according to Scottish Tory MPs, who described Philip Hammond as 'the least political Chancellor ever'. 'If George Osborne was still Chancellor, we'd be investing in Scotland all over the place,' the MP adds. The frustration of Scottish Conservatives was familiar to journalists in what was known as the 'Scottish Lobby'. At all levels, from departmental press officers to the Prime Minister's official spokesman, getting answers to questions about Scotland was near impossible. It was not so much that they did not have the answer, they just seemed surprised to be asked the questions at all.

Another MP reflects that 'we've been effective at stopping things from happening, when an idea comes through government that is obviously not going to work, and we shut it down'. In some cases, that meant intervening to stop their own government handing the SNP a political victory. In January 2019, for example, it was suggested that Nicola Sturgeon could be given a seat at the table in future trade negotiations between the UK Government and the EU, and eventually with other countries too (*Herald*, 5 December 2018). A senior Scottish Tory MP briefed against the plan, warning that the group was 'very wary' and insisting that the Scottish Government 'would be taking part purely to sell Scotland and nothing more – if they're there at all' (*Scotsman*, 23 January 2019).

Protocol and precedent dictates that when the First Minister travels abroad, the Foreign Office provides logistical support. But when Scottish Tories learned that Sturgeon's February 2019 trip to North America had received Foreign Office assistance, they were furious. Her itinerary included an appearance at the United Nations and an interview with US media in which she suggested that 'in the not too distant future . . . Scotland will be an independent country' (PBS, 2 August 2018). David Mundell 'hit the roof' and complained to Foreign Secretary Jeremy Hunt, who ordered that, in future, only trips where Sturgeon did not try to 'drum up support for independence' would be supported. Not all politically damaging decisions could be stopped, however, and Mundell in particular found himself caught between Scottish interests and government policy.

The Scottish Secretary had been left isolated by his party's confidence-and-supply deal with the DUP, particularly after saying he would not support 'funding which deliberately sought to subvert the Barnett rules' and was 'not going to agree to anything that could be construed as back-door funding to Northern Ireland' (*Sunday Post*, 25 June 2017). No money was forthcoming for Scotland through the Barnett formula, not least because he had misunderstood how it worked, and Mundell had to walk back from his previous comments (BBC News online, 27 June 2017). Barnett consequentials were also the subject of a row over the UK Government's Stronger Towns Fund, an investment drive announced in a bid to win over Labour MPs representing Brexit-voting constituencies in the north of England. Neither Downing Street, the Treasury nor the Ministry of Housing, Communities and Local Government could say how the fund would operate in Scotland. It eventually emerged that Scottish councils and organisations would bid directly to Whitehall for funding, prompting the SNP and Labour to accuse ministers of 'rolling back devolution'. The president of the Convention of Scottish Local Authorities added that the UK Government was 'not playing by the rules' (*Scotsman*, 15 March 2019).

At its heart, the problem was one of proximity to power. Under Labour, both Number 10 and Number 11 had Scottish tenants; during the 2010–15 coalition government, meanwhile, the presence of Danny Alexander – the Highland Liberal Democrat MP who served as Chief Secretary to the Treasury – in the decision-making 'quad' with the Prime Minister meant Scotland's voice was at the heart of government. There was also widely shared praise for the role played by Lord (Andrew) Dunlop, who alongside Ramsay Jones was Cameron's special adviser for Scotland at Number 10. Jones maintained close links with the Scottish media while Dunlop monitored decisions made across government. A source within May's Downing Street operation defends its record, saying Dunlop was working during an independence referendum campaign that focused minds on Scotland. But the key was Dunlop's close relationship with Mundell, ensuring that, together, Downing Street and the Scotland Office could make sure political decisions landed well north of the border. Dunlop was also effective at negotiating with the Treasury to establish the first 'city deal' for Scotland, boosting UK Government investment in Glasgow. 'He always squared the money away first,' one senior government source says, contrasting it with the 'mess' of the Stronger Towns Fund. 'He [Dunlop] didn't seek any praise or limelight . . . he was happy to do it all behind the scenes.'

Dunlop was rewarded for his work with a peerage in 2015, and made a junior minister at the Scotland Office. After the 2017 general election, however, he left the government. 'I spent the first few months after Andrew left wondering why everything was much more difficult,' a government source says. 'That's when I fully appreciated the job that he'd done.' There had been a plan to install Ian Duncan, the Scottish Tory MEP and a close ally of Davidson, at the Scotland Office but he was narrowly defeated by the SNP's Pete Wishart in Perth & North Perthshire. Duncan, however, was made a peer and given Dunlop's old portfolio. But he also had responsibilities in Northern Ireland, where his time was increasingly monopolised by negotiations to restore the

Northern Ireland Assembly. As a member of the House of Lords, Duncan was also physically removed from the Scottish group of MPs.

There was a Scot at the Prime Minister's side when May entered Downing Street: Fiona Hill had been born and raised in Inverclyde before working as a journalist for several Scottish outlets. But she was controlling rather than collaborative, and insiders say her more recent links with Scottish politics and opinion were limited. Besides, along with Nick Timothy she was ousted as a consequence of the terrible election campaign in 2017. 'You have to have someone who has immediate access to the Prime Minister at all times, who can give instructions to other Spads and even ministers,' a senior government source says. 'Whatever her deficiencies, Fiona Hill had that immediate access and authority. Since she left, we haven't had that.' The crucial Scottish axis between Dover House and 10 Downing Street lost its strength.

Hunting as a Pack

Despite frustrations, rows and disagreements over tactics, where the Scottish Conservatives did work together to maximise their influence, they had a significant impact. The group hunted as a pack to extract 'retail' wins from various government departments, a strategy that often involved pictures posted on social media of 12-on-1 meetings with Cabinet ministers. Defence Secretary Gavin Williamson – who was Chief Whip when the Scottish Tories first arrived at Westminster – was among the first to get this treatment, agreeing to relief for military officers based in Scotland who were paying a higher income tax rate set by the Scottish Government (BBC News online, 19 July 2018).

The group also made its budget submissions jointly and were particularly successful ahead of the 2018 Budget, securing continued tax reliefs for the oil and gas and whisky industries despite the Chancellor being under pressure to find £20 billion of new investment for the NHS. In Philip Hammond's Budget speech he credited 'the concerted lobbying of my Scottish Conservative colleagues' for the decision to extend the freeze on spirit duty, adding that the MPs could now 'all afford to raise a wee dram to Ruth Davidson on the arrival of baby Finn'. Of the eight city region deals agreed in Scotland, those covering Edinburgh and South East Scotland, Stirling and Clackmannanshire, the Tay Cities, Ayrshire and the Borderlands were all signed off after the 2017 election.

And while Brexit put strains on group unity, Scottish Tories could claim to have had a major role in shaping developments. Until 2019, the Prime Minister insisted that 'no deal is better than a bad deal', a position that

Davidson, Mundell and many of the Scottish Tory MPs found it difficult to agree with, both on its own terms and because of the risk they believed it posed to the Union. Parliamentary opposition intervened and whatever resolve May had to push ahead with a no-deal Brexit disappeared, but Scottish Tory lobbying played its part, too. 'There are many factors that combined to stop a no deal,' a Downing Street source says. 'But the Scottish dimension was one of them.'

Scottish Tories added their voices to those of the DUP in blocking May from considering the possibility of a Northern Ireland-only 'backstop' for the Irish border, with Davidson and Mundell signing a letter to the Prime Minister warning that such a deal 'would undermine the integrity of our UK internal market and this United Kingdom' and would therefore not have their support, leading to reports they had both threatened to resign (*Scotsman*, 15 October 2018). Scottish Conservative MPs were also influential in another respect, opposing the idea of extending the post-Brexit transition period (floated in order to allow more time for trade negotiations) on the basis that it would have risked adding years to the UK's involvement with the Common Fisheries Policy, something deeply unpopular with many Scottish Tory voters (*i* newspaper, 14 November 2018).

A major step forward for Scottish influence in Number 10 came with two key promotions to the government payroll: in December 2018 Andrew Bowie became May's PPS – a mere 18 months after their leafleting round during the 2017 election – while Luke Graham, the MP for Ochil and South Perthshire, took on the same role at the Cabinet Office. At high-level meetings taking place at Downing Street, the government's most senior ministers and officials now had someone to whom they could turn when questions about Scotland come up.

Bowie in particular became a conduit for requests and reminders of Scottish issues, big and small; sometimes, even the most trivial of these proved of political value. Standing in for the Prime Minister at Prime Minister's Questions (PMQs), for example, the Cabinet Office Minister David Lidington delivered a warm and lengthy tribute following the death of Billy McNeill, the Celtic captain who had led the Lisbon Lions and become the first British footballer to lift the European Cup in 1968 (HC Debs 24 Apr 2019 Vol 658 c736). It was a story that led every Scottish newspaper and bulletin but an opportunity that might otherwise have been overlooked in Downing Street. 'That's when I knew we had the ear of Number 10,' an MP says.

Greater influence in Downing Street had far-reaching consequences, too, with a toughening in the government's line on a second independence referendum. The Prime Minister's stock response when challenged by the SNP had been 'now is not the time', a formulation based on deference to the

Cameron-era 'respect agenda'. From early 2019, that became a more direct 'no', to the extent that when the Tory leadership candidate Andrea Leadsom suggested she would 'never say never' to granting the powers to hold another independence vote, it was immediately seen as a gaffe. Scottish Tory MPs reacted with disbelief, and made their feelings clear in public and in private (*Scotsman*, 12 June 2019). Leadsom U-turned the next day.

Beyond the immediate question of an independence referendum, the Scottish Tories also sought a more long-term constitutional impact. The main front in their battle with the Treasury was the replacement for EU Structural Funds which were to invest £16 billion in the UK over the seven years to 2020. Crucially, Scottish Tories said a new UK Shared Prosperity Fund should be administered centrally from Whitehall, rather than via the devolved administrations. Projects supported by funds from Brussels had often been branded with the flags of the EU and Scotland, a source of frustration given the funds ultimately derived from the UK's contribution to the EU budget. While outwardly superficial, the desire to 'put a Union flag' on investment went to the heart of the Scottish Tory mission to remind voters they still had a government at Westminster looking out for their communities (*Scotland on Sunday*, 30 September 2018). As signalled by the row over the Stronger Towns Fund, it also represented a major departure from the way the UK Government had interacted with devolution in the past.

Not content with breaking down barriers in Whitehall, Scottish Tories also wanted to reshape it entirely. Their experience of the Scotland Office – the lack of coordination with Downing Street, the breakdown in trust over Brexit and frequent rows with the Scottish Government – led the Scottish Tories to view Dover House with disdain. Despite the prospect of a new Prime Minister offering the chance of swift promotion to the Cabinet, few Scottish Tory MPs showed much enthusiasm for the post of Secretary of State for Scotland. Tory members of the Scottish Affairs Committee backed a report on intergovernmental relations that was hostile to the department, and called for a review that could see it replaced (Scottish Affairs Committee 2019). Led by the Stirling MP Stephen Kerr, the group argued that the UK Government needed a new locus of power representing all the devolved nations as well as the Union as a whole. MPs had differing visions as to what shape this should take: Kerr won cross-party support for his vision of a 'Secretary of State for the Union'; Ruth Davidson backed the creation of a 'Union Unit' at Downing Street to co-ordinate policy; while others suggested the Prime Minister (or their deputy) should become 'Minister for the Union', thinking derived from the Canadian model.

Scottish Conservative MPs believed their constitutional agenda represented a completion of the unfinished business of devolution, a review after

20 years that corrected what they saw as fundamental errors in its original design and in the approach of successive Westminster administrations in having 'thrown powers at Edinburgh', as one MP put it. Taken together, it could represent the 'line in the sand' once drawn by Davidson, only this time chiselled to make it more permanent.

'Operation Arse'

Theresa May's resignation confronted Scottish Tories in Edinburgh and London with a stark reality: in 2017, Ruth Davidson was thought to control the Prime Minister's fate, now the man she least wanted to become Prime Minister controlled that of the Scottish Conservative Party. And while the reasons for her own resignation might have been deeply personal, Davidson's departure represented a political failure that overshadowed any legacy the Scottish Tory MPs might have secured at Westminster. By the middle of 2019, we might have reached the halfway point of the Scottish Tory redemption tale; instead, it began to look as if the story had already ended.

Despite a shared love of an eye-catching photo opportunity, Davidson's dislike of Boris Johnson was common knowledge to the point of being Scottish political folklore. He represented everything Davidson wanted to change about the Tory image, not just in being an Old Etonian, Bullingdon Club Oxford graduate – Johnson shared that background with David Cameron, after all – but because of a fundamental clash of political values. Drawing on her Church of Scotland faith and her military service, Davidson's mantra was 'serve to lead'; even some of Johnson's friends and allies, by contrast, admit his career has been an exercise in service to his own ambition. Facing him in the final televised debate of the 2016 EU referendum campaign, Davidson went further on the attack than Cameron and other senior Conservatives were willing to go by repeatedly accusing Johnson's Leave campaign of 'lying' to voters (*Telegraph*, 22 June 2016). Some Scottish Tories also believed Johnson's commitment to the Union was inconsistent and opportunistic: he made no visits to Scotland to campaign during the 2014 independence campaign, a fact remembered by its veterans (*Herald*, 20 July 2019).

Long before May's fate was sealed, the Scottish party leadership regarded a Johnson premiership as an existential threat to Davidson's already slim hopes of breaking the glass ceiling in Scottish politics by taking power at Holyrood. Internal surveys (Conservative Home, 3 May 2019), later confirmed by polling once the leadership race was underway, found that Johnson had an approval rating of around -40 in Scotland, below that of Jeremy Corbyn (*Sunday Times*, 23 June 2019).

At the 2018 Conservative Party conference in Birmingham, Johnson confirmed his ambition to become Prime Minister, delivering a speech that directly challenged May over her Brexit policy. On the fringes of the same conference, a senior Scottish Conservative briefed me and journalists from the *Daily Record* and the *Herald* on covert efforts to stop Johnson. We were told that leading Scottish party figures were lobbying their colleagues not to support him, warning of the impact north of the border. The source guaranteed front-page coverage by claiming the plot was being called 'Operation Arse', 'so we'd all be clear who we were talking about' (*Daily Record*, 2 October 2018).

But, from the start, it was clear Operation Arse was a general's campaign, and enthusiasm for it never extended beyond Davidson's closest allies and into the trenches. So close was the relationship between Ross Thomson and the UK Tory leadership pretender that he was seen pressed up against Johnson, ushering him through a media scrum to his speech like a Hollywood bodyguard. The start of the leadership campaign confirmed the rout. Among Tory party members, Johnson was the runaway favourite. Davidson insisted she would 'work with whoever the Prime Minister is' (*Daily Express*, 22 May 2019), while Mundell, who had previously claimed Johnson was 'not an asset' to the Conservative Party (BBC News online, 2 October 2018) and could not see himself 'being able to serve' in a Johnson administration (*Sunday Politics Scotland*, 9 December 2018), now claimed he had never ruled out serving in a Boris Johnson-led Cabinet (*Representing Border*, ITV, 13 June 2019).

When the full field of candidates was confirmed, Scottish Tory MPs spread their support across five of them, including four who eventually backed Johnson. Davidson's opposition to the frontrunner counted for little – and her endorsement counted for even less. The Scottish Tory leader gave her strong backing to the Home Secretary, Sajid Javid, even flying down to London so she could introduce him. None of the Scottish Tory MPs joined her in endorsing Javid in the first round, however – not even his former PPS, Paul Masterton, who only backed him after his first, and then his second choice were eliminated. Javid's crime was failing to listen to Scottish Tory concerns about immigration restrictions in a white paper setting out the government's post-Brexit plans (*Scotsman*, 26 June 2019).

Davidson showed how much political capital she was willing to expend trying to stop Johnson with a snap endorsement of Michael Gove in the few hours between the penultimate and final ballot of Tory MPs, to decide the two candidates that would face a vote of the party membership. Gove had been the hope of most of the Scottish Tory MPs, who believed he was the candidate who 'got' the Union the most. But he lost by two votes – another case of Scottish Tory numbers being decisive.

They didn't unite behind a candidate, but the leadership contest also demonstrated that where they did work together, the Scottish Tories could influence the debate. The final five candidates backed a joint 'manifesto' calling for direct UK Government investment in devolved areas, reform of Whitehall structures to defend the Union and, most ambitiously, flexible immigration rules that took account of rural business needs in Scotland (*The Times*, 12 June 2019). So complete was the U-turn on immigration that Javid was forced to ask for a review of the Migration Advisory Committee advice behind his department's own white paper.

But there was no reconciliation between Johnson and Davidson, and within hours of his entry into Downing Street, the relationship was damaged beyond repair. Despite Mundell's previous hostility, expectations had grown during the leadership race that Johnson would keep him on as Scottish Secretary for at least a short period, given the lack of Despatch Box experience among the 2017 Scottish Tory intake. A personal appeal from Davidson had no effect, however, and Mundell was sacked and replaced by Jack. In the days that followed, the depth of his relationship with Davidson was revealed: she asked the man she described as her 'work husband' to officiate at her wedding (*The Times*, 27 July 2019). It was a personal loss and a very public political humiliation for the Scottish Tory leader.

Johnson compounded the slight by appointing an English MP to a junior ministerial role at Dover House for the first time in well over a century (BBC News online, 26 July 2019). But the most significant breach of faith was the confirmation, once in office, that Johnson intended to deliver on his 'do or die' commitment to leave the European Union on 31 October, whatever the cost. Davidson made her views clear: 'I don't think the government should pursue a no-deal Brexit and, if it comes to it, I won't support it' (*Mail on Sunday*, 28 July 2019).

The protest only served to underline how powerless she was to stop it. Meanwhile, it became increasingly clear that Downing Street's aggressive strategy to capture the pro-Brexit vote in England, orchestrated by Johnson's controversial senior adviser Dominic Cummings, would have to be built on the rubble of Scottish Tory MPs' re-election hopes. The snap election desperately sought by Johnson to finally correct the mistake of 2017 would certainly mean significant losses; in the final months before the 31 October deadline, some polling warned of a near-wipeout that would take the Scottish party back into panda territory (*The Times*, 4 September 2019).

The Scottish Tories would also have to go into that campaign without the figurehead who they credit with getting them elected in the first place. Davidson's resignation came the day after the government announced it would prorogue parliament for five weeks – a deeply controversial move that was eventually struck down by a historic judgment of the Supreme Court.

'You all know I have never sought to hide the conflict I have felt over Brexit,' Davidson admitted at a press conference announcing her departure. But the underlying reason was personal: 'I fear that having tried to be a good leader over the years, I have proved a poor daughter, sister, partner and friend,' she revealed. 'The party and my work has always come first, often at the expense of commitments to loved ones. The arrival of my son means I now make a different choice.'

Davidson's resignation came as a shock, but if it felt inevitable after the fact, that may be because it had been on the minds of senior Scottish Tories for weeks, if not months. One source close to the former leader says questions about her future began to be discussed as soon as she returned from maternity leave in May. 'We tried to convince her to take a bit of extra time off,' the source says. Another senior party figure described, two months before Davidson's resignation, their belief that having a family had changed her perspective on leadership. 'When you messaged her before, she always replied with a point on politics or policy,' the source said. 'Now it's baby photos.' Similar sentiments were shared by several Scottish Tory MPs before Davidson stood down. It feels important to note that everyone who expressed them was a man.

Conclusion

Preparations were already underway for a snap election when the Scottish Tory leader resigned, with at least one MP forced to pulp an early run of leaflets describing themselves as 'Ruth Davidson's candidate' (*Scotland on Sunday*, 8 September 2019). The Davidson 'project' was cut short – but as we have seen, it never fully reached as far as Westminster. In terms of how they've gone about their jobs, the Scottish Tories rejected being 'Ruth's MPs' – and none of them have yet broken faith publicly with Boris Johnson, even throughout the prorogation crisis and the effective expulsion of 21 senior MPs who rebelled over legislation seeking to block a no-deal Brexit.

An election campaign will be the ultimate test of their approach of being a group of individuals rather than a Scottish bloc. Will it confirm the Tories as part of the Scottish political landscape, or will 2017 have been the high-water mark? The MPs know they have to demonstrate that they have had an influence, in this parliament. 'For voters, it isn't going to be enough to say: we stopped these things from happening,' one member of the group says. 'I think that's going to have to change. We will have to demonstrate a record that we can stand on.' With plenty of promises made to Scottish Tories during the leadership campaign, a party source in Edinburgh adds: 'It'll be our job to remind the new Prime Minister: "You said this".'

For some, their approach has been a success. 'We're like the Avengers,' one MP says. 'We assemble when we're needed.' But other Scottish Tories wonder what might have been with a more aggressive strategy. 'It's been a total failure,' a senior figure in London says. 'The Scottish Tories ought to have more power now than at any time in 20 years or more, but instead we've gone backwards. We have less influence than we did under Cameron, when we had just one MP. The Scotland Office should be our base of power, and instead you've got Scottish MPs calling for it to be abolished. It's a shambles.'

For the past two years, the Scottish Conservatives have inverted the DUP strategy: rather than a highly visible performance of power, with photo opportunities in front of 10 Downing Street, they've gone through the back doors of Whitehall. Rather than £1 billion upfront, they've accepted a promise of future investment and reform. Whether the strategy pays off is a question that can only be answered at the ballot box. The answer looks set to come sooner than is comfortable.

FIVE

The Scottish Conservatives and Local Government

Lauren Toner, Chrysa Lamprinakou and Neil McGarvey

Introduction

Prior to 2017, a book chapter on the Scottish Conservative and Unionist Party's experience in local government was likely to be a very short one. Indeed, the Conservatives and local government has, until recently, been something of an oxymoron in Scotland. After the 1995 reorganisation, the Scottish Conservative Party was on the powerless fringes of town halls across Scotland, and, judged against local election results, the party was in seemingly terminal decline and Conservative councillors became a rare breed. However, following the 2017 local government elections, that is no longer an appropriate narrative.

As institutions, however, it could hardly be said that Scottish local authorities were thriving during the same period. The profile of local government has diminished due to a loss of powers (e.g. police, fire, water, sewerage and transport) and restricted financial autonomy (council tax capping and freeze). They now exist in the shadow of the Scottish Parliament and Government, the existence of which has undoubtedly created pressure for greater national conformity, a creeping centralism that somewhat contradicts localism (Evison 2019; McGarvey 2019).

The Scottish Parliament inherited a finance system 'characterised by a high degree of grant dependency, based on an inelastic property tax, under a strict capping regime to control expenditure' (McGarvey 2002), and that rather centralised system remains in place today. This, coupled with the long-standing 'tradition' of almost invisible local political leadership (the post-1997 English elected mayor agenda never registered in Scotland) has produced a diminished emphasis on local politics. Very few members of the Scottish public can name any council leader, and one suspects almost none could name a Conservative one. Overall, the political profile of local government in Scotland has been lowered in recent decades, and the profile of the Conservative Party within that has also been marginalised.

There is a long-standing academic orthodoxy that local elections are 'second order' (see Miller 1988). Party support at the local level is heavily influenced by politics nationally; the focus and coverage tends to be national, thus they are akin to a mid-term high-sample national opinion poll. Such 'second-order' elections typically attract smaller turnouts, and the electorate are more susceptible to switching their preference to minority party or independent candidates. Scottish electors, if they turn out to vote in local elections, tend to be more promiscuous, encouraged – since 2007 – by the existence of the single transferable vote (STV).

Capitalising on this, in 2017 the Conservatives won 276 of the 1,227 council seats available in Scotland, achieving their most impressive local election result in Scotland in almost four decades. Their continual campaign mantra of 'no to a second referendum' was highly effective, in that it deliberately emphasised their unionist credentials to successfully expand their support base. Aided too by the decline of the Scottish Labour vote and multi-member STV wards, the party secured representation in traditionally Tory-free areas such as the East End of Glasgow, Ravenscraig, Ferguslie Park and Cowdenbeath. North Lanarkshire, traditionally a Labour heartland, saw Conservative representation increase from zero to an unprecedented nine. It was, however, in existing Tory strongholds such as the Borders, Dumfries and Galloway, East Renfrewshire, Perthshire and Aberdeenshire, where the Scottish Conservatives performed most strongly.

This chapter reviews the Scottish Conservative and Unionist Party's experience in local government in the contemporary era, with a review of the post-1974 period, traditionally viewed as the inception of modern Scottish local government. It analyses the impact of the Conservative Party over the past 40 years, and then shifts the focus to how Scottish Conservative local manifestos and electioneering has changed, looking, in particular, at the 2017 contest.

The Marginalisation of Conservatism in Modern Local Government

Prior to the 1970s, local government in Scotland was a rather humdrum affair, and in many areas of Scotland party politicians were notable only for their absence. Then came the advent of 'modern' Scottish local government following the mid-1970s reorganisation that created the dual region–district structure. It was the Conservative UK Government of 1970–4 which implemented the Wheatley (1969) recommendations for of the creation of a new two-tier structure in Scotland. From the 1974 elections, therefore, party politicisation became the norm across the vast bulk of Scotland's densely populated new council areas, with manifestos, party selection and group discipline becoming the norm.

Since the 1980s, Scotland's cities, towns, regions and districts have tended to be dominated by Labour, SNP and – to a lesser degree – Liberal Democrat and independent representatives (this tradition survives in the Highlands and Islands as well as large tracts of rural Scotland). Since then, large swathes of Scotland have remained immune to the attractions of Conservative local councillors. Until 2017, Tory representation in Scottish local councils was in single (or singular) digits without any committee or executive authority, prompting Allan McConnell's (2004) summary of the party's experience as 'a slow death in Scottish local government'.

The party's disappearance from Scotland's municipalities largely mirrored their declining Scottish representation in the House of Commons throughout the 1980s and 1990s. Its worsening electoral performance saw the marginalisation of Conservative councillors and groupings across the vast bulk of Scotland's local authorities and, despite controlling the Scottish Office between 1979 and 1997, with so few councillors the party reaped little influence within the Convention of Scottish Local Authorities (COSLA). Being the only mainstream Scottish party to oppose constitutional change, the Conservatives became the 'other' of Scottish politics, both nationally and locally, and by 2003 controlled no Scottish councils. Not since the 1950s and 1960s had the party performed in Scotland at a level consistent with their English counterparts. The reasons for this are multiple and not the concern of this chapter (for detailed discussion, see Torrance 2012).

Decreasing Scottish Conservative representation was not even halted by the introduction of the single transferable vote (STV) in 2007. This electoral system is designed to reflect the representation of parties broadly in line with their proportionate share of the vote, yet as Table 5.1 outlines, by 2012 only 13.3 per cent of Scots voted Conservative in local elections. In Scotland's three- and four-member wards, a larger candidate vote share tended to be required in order to gain fully proportionate representation.

These figures confirm the Scottish Conservative Party has never been strong during the post-1974 'modern' Scottish local government era in terms of either vote share or councillor representation. Their most successful performance was witnessed in 1978 when a 30.3 per cent of the regional election vote share was achieved, which then translated into a 28 per cent

Table 5.1 The Conservative Party and Scottish local government in council elections, 1974–2017

Year	Tier	% Vote	% Seats	Con. / Total councillors
1974	District	26.8	21.7	241 / 1,110
1974	Region	28.6	25.9	112 / 432
1977	District	27.2	23.4	259 / 1,107
1978	Region	30.3	28.0	121 / 432
1980	District	24.1	19.6	232 / 1,182
1982	Region	25.1	27.0	119 / 441
1984	District	21.4	16.0	189 / 1,182
1986	Region	16.9	12.4	65 / 524
1988	District	19.4	13.7	162 / 1,182
1990	Region	19.2	9.9	52 / 524
1992	District	23.2	17.3	204 / 1,182
1994	Region	13.7	5.9	31 / 524
1995	Unitary	11.5	7.1	82 / 1,155
1999	Unitary	13.5	8.8	108 / 1,222
2003	Unitary	15.1	10.0	122 / 1,222
2007	Unitary	15.6*	11.7	143 / 1,222
2012	Unitary	13.3	9.4	115 / 1,222
2017	Unitary	25.3	22.5	276 / 1,227

*From 2007 vote share = first-preference votes

councillor share across Scotland's nine regional and three island councils. Since then, the story has been one of steady decline, sprinkled only with the occasional upward blip – that is, until the most recent elections in 2017, when the party almost doubled its vote share from 13.3 to 25.3 per cent, which paralleled the party's improved electoral performances at the 2016 Scottish Parliament and 2017 UK general elections.

It is notable that neither the single member plurality, nor single transferable vote electoral systems (used since 2007) were particularly kind to the party in terms of the translation of votes into seats. At all but three of the elections, the party has gained a smaller proportion of seats that its proportion of votes. This largely reflects the bias in each system in favour of 'winning' parties that achieve around 30 per cent or above of vote share, something the Conservatives last achieved in 1978. Still not managing to break that threshold in 2017, they gained more than a quarter of the vote and elected 22.5 per cent of Scotland's councillors.

Post-2017, despite their rising success and being part of coalitions with either independents or Scottish Liberal Democrats in Aberdeen City, Aberdeenshire, Angus, Argyll & Bute, East Dunbartonshire, Perth & Kinross and Scottish Borders (see COSLA 2019), the Scottish Conservative Party very much remains 'the other' where council leadership is concerned. This is due to the formal policies of both the Scottish Labour Party and the SNP not to enter into any local coalition arrangements with the Conservatives.

Conservatism in Modern Local Government

Prior to modern local government, Scottish Conservative and Unionist-orientated candidates often campaigned without a party label, opting to stand as independents, progressives, moderates or some other neutral label. In Glasgow, for example, a 'Progressive Association' of such councillors was formed in 1936 as an anti-Labour alliance. In 1951 it boasted a sizeable 58 councillors on Glasgow Corporation (Kemp 2011). In this era, the role of local councillor was considered a voluntary, unpaid civic duty, consistent with Conservative philosophy. The councillor professionalisation and salary agenda of recent years was largely driven by other parties. One suspects the evolution of attendance allowances, public funding and salaries may not sit comfortably with many local Scottish Conservatives who still remain of the view that being a councillor is not a full-time occupation (most evidence however, suggests the contrary, see APSE 2014; Thrasher et al. 2014; Kerley and McGarvey 2017).

The immediate post-war decades saw a strand of paternalistic conservatism and unionism feeding into 'One Nation' Conservatism. This form of municipal Toryism was likely to give emphasis to social cohesion and loyalty to established values, as well as fiscal prudence, local autonomy and decentralisation of power. An emphasis on localism and personal freedom combined with a scepticism of both local and central government interference, was consistent with traditional conservative philosophy. In the post-war era, such an approach stood in direct contrast to the British Labour Party's post-war 1945–51 centrist socialism, which tended to be of a top-down, state-centred variety.

As Gilmour observed, pre-Thatcher Conservatism was 'generally welcoming of the welfare state; full employment; the encouragement of ownership of property; the acceptance of trade unions; the mixed economy; support for private enterprise; and strong defence' (Gilmour 1978: 19). Thatcherism, of course, did not embrace that outlook. Her conservatism placed more emphasis on economic liberalism rather than the obligations of leadership, voluntarism and community service. The point to stress, as

McCrone et al. (1993: 138) note, is that traditional Scottish unionism (the party only reincorporated the Conservative nomenclature in 1965), placed emphasis on 'civic duty and social responsibility'. However, in the Thatcher years, the emphasis shifted to neoliberal individualism.

For McCrone et al., the party's philosophy moved away from its Scottish social and ideological base, and thus many previously Scottish Conservative voters placed their vote elsewhere. Added to this was a perception of the party as English. This reached its epoch with the introduction of the Community Charge in Scotland a year before it was introduced in England and Wales. Ironically, this wound was self-inflicted in that the Scottish Conservative conference had voted in favour of earlier introduction in order to avoid another rates revaluation (see Torrance 2009). The 'Poll Tax', as it was almost universally labelled, consolidated perceptions of the party as 'anti-Scottish' and fuelled the campaign for a devolved Scottish Parliament.

Following this came another centrally imposed reorganisation of local government structures in the 1990s (Midwinter and McGarvey 1997: 23). Labour leadership and control of large local councils such as the Strathclyde and Lothian Regions provided a potent platform base for opposition to Conservative-run Scottish Office policies. The Conservative solution was abolition via reorganisation. When it proposed reorganisation in 1991, the Conservative Party had control of none of the 12 Scottish island and regional councils and only three of Scotland's 53 district councils. Those three councils were among the smallest, covering only 2.4 per cent of Scotland's population (McCrone et al. 1993: 10).

The Conservative-controlled Scottish Office under the John Major-led UK Government replaced that structure with 32 unitary authorities in 1995–6. Influential Conservative interests lobbied against larger local authorities prior to that reorganisation (Midwinter 1995: 99), resulting in the creation of several smaller councils and the break-up of old counties such as Ayrshire, Lanarkshire, Renfrewshire, Lothian and Dunbartonshire. The boundaries of councils such as East Renfrewshire, East Dunbartonshire, South Ayrshire, Stirling and an abortive attempt to enlarge Berwickshire looked to have been gerrymandered with the partisan interests of the Conservative Party in mind. Ward-level adjustments were made in Dundee to enhance the prospect of Tory control in Angus (Black 1994). Such partisan party-political considerations were cited as unduly influencing the contours and boundaries of Scotland's new unitary local government map (see McVicar et al. 1994; Black 1994; Midwinter and McGarvey 1997).

Though the Scottish Office legislation did not adopt the very small units some in the party had lobbied for, the reorganisation did result in a Labour-controlled COSLA campaign of non-cooperation from 1994. The hostility of central–local relations in Scotland was not alleviated by the appointment of Michael Forsyth as Secretary of State for Scotland in 1995. He had been part of the Scottish Office team that initiated the reorganisation, having served as minister of state between 1990 and 1992, and was widely perceived to be on the Thatcherite wing of the party in Scotland.

These perceived anti-Scottish policies, imagery and narrative of the Thatcher era are ones that the Scottish Conservative Party has only recently begun to shake off. There is some debate whether it was economic, political or ideological rationale that inspired the Conservatives' restructuring of local government across Great Britain. Whatever the motivation, the period undoubtedly witnessed the beginnings of a transformation in the rationale and purpose of local government. The Conservative UK governments of that period became embroiled in local affairs on an unprecedented scale. While 'New Left' councils were predominantly an English phenomenon (for example, Greater London, Sheffield and Liverpool), the Labour-led Lothian Region was the closest Scottish example. As Scottish Secretary, Michael Forsyth adopted an adversarial approach in response to such councils, or, as Conservatives might have referred to them, 'municipal socialists'.

Traditional Conservative philosophy had a clearly demarcated idea of the appropriate role and competences of local, territorial and national governments in the UK, local government's appropriate role being the efficient administration of local services within a framework of financial rectitude (see Bulpitt 1983). In the Bulpittian analysis, this stable 'dual polity' of 'high' (UK central government) and 'low' (territorial/local government) politics broke down in the 1980s. Local councils began to develop policies that were inconsistent with, impinged upon or were in direct opposition to central government policy. Policies such as alternative economic strategies, declaring nuclear-free zones and campaigning against South Africa's apartheid regime were all anti-Thatcher in tenor. In response, central government increasingly began to interfere in what were traditionally the autonomous concerns of local politicians. Examples included capping or setting local tax rates, deciding appropriate models of service provision, regulating the local economy and the like. Policies such as the right to buy council housing, compulsory competitive tendering, enterprise zones and transport deregulation were at the forefront of the new Conservative local public services agenda.

For Conservatives, the value of local government in this dual polity tends to de-emphasise its political component in favour of a focus on the efficient and effective administration of local public services. Representative, democratically accountable and responsible government are long-standing British political traditions (see McGarvey 2019). And emphasis on these traditions lessens focus on other roles of local councils such as their status as units of local democracy, pluralism and participation. The Bulpitt argument suggests policies such as 'right to buy', compulsory competitive tending, school opt-outs and transport deregulation, though portrayed as ideological in orientation, were actually motivated by politics – a desire to ensure local authorities delivered services as efficiently as possible.

An alternative, and more conventional, analysis gives emphasis to Conservative ideological motivations. Right-wing think tanks such as the Adam Smith Institute and Institute of Economic Affairs were at their most influential during the Thatcher era. A new framework of legislation, dictation, regulation and rate-capping compelled Scottish local councils to pursue national Conservative-inspired policies which gave emphasis to competition, privatisation and lower taxation. These policies were underpinned by an ideology of distrust in the performance, efficiency and effectiveness of in-house council workforces and the broader public sector. In theory, more marketised arrangements meant that 'politics' was removed from service delivery and thus trade unions were weakened.

For many in the Scottish Conservative Party, despite its somewhat rapid electoral decline and the disappearance of Conservative-led local administrations, the 1980s are an era to be celebrated, for then the party won successive UK general elections and dominated the broader political agenda. To the party's opponents, however, it is the era in which the Scottish Conservatives were 'othered' as alien to the twin aspirations of enhanced Scottish autonomy and egalitarianism. Although COSLA continued to participate in the formal machinery of intergovernmental relations with the Conservative-run Scottish Office, relations became increasingly strained and Tory policies were often met with hostility, resistance and non-compliance (Midwinter 1995: 115–6).

The intergovernmental dynamics of 1979–97 were dominated by a creeping centralisation and gradual diminution of local authority power in fields such as local taxation, expenditure, education, housing, utilities and transport. In 1991 even the Association of Scottish Conservative Councillors acknowledged that among its members 'a large number of councillors have indicated that they feel local government's powers have been very much eroded under the present Conservative Government' (cited in McCrone et al. 1993: 12).

Overall, the task of describing the typical governing practice of a post-1974 modern Scottish Conservative local administration is almost impossible. In social scientific research parlance, we lack reliable, sustained case studies of Conservative local authorities and have too small an 'n' (number) at our disposal. Thus, the empirical base of any evidence is virtually anecdotal and it would be improper to generalise from such a small sample. Following the

1995 reorganisation, the party had, until 2017, struggled to gain a foothold even in areas such as Eastwood/East Renfrewshire, Stirling, East Lothian and South Ayrshire, areas in which it was once the predominant political force.

Modern Scottish Conservatism, the 2017 Local Government Manifesto

So how exactly did the Scottish Conservative's 2017 local election campaign buck the trend of recent decades and almost double the party's support? Brexit has undeniably brought new dimensions of politics to the fore throughout the UK, and in Scotland specifically, it has unequivocally bolstered the Scottish Question (that of Scotland's place in the UK) with partisan lines firmly entrenched (Curtice 2017b; Henderson and Mitchell 2018). A transformation of the Scottish political environment had been underway long before the EU referendum, and therefore to understand the Scottish Conservatives' success during this election, it is first necessary to recognise how voting trends have evolved in Scotland.

Stable party alignments based upon social class had long characterised voting behaviour throughout the UK (Pulzer 1975). Then, as notions of class became increasingly less relevant to many in British society due to deindustrialisation, changing employment trends and increased access to education, the working-class cleavage was diminished. Evidence of this effect on Scottish voting behaviour can be witnessed initially in the 1974 general election results when the SNP won more than 30 per cent of the vote by securing support across all social classes, thus diminishing the previous Labour–Conservative duopoly.

The resulting ideological convergence led to the decline of 'positional' issues, under which different sections of the electorate had distinct positions, and the rise of 'valence' issues (e.g. a growing economy, better-managed public services) where the vast bulk of the electorate were in agreement. Consequently, the Scottish electorate – in line with British voting trends – came to rely upon perceptions of competence and strong leadership that would, in turn, enable a party's delivery of positive outcomes such as economic stability and efficient public services (Green 2007).

Following the referendum result in 2014, however, Scotland's place in the Union continued to be at the centre of Scottish political debate and political allegiances were accordingly redrawn along constitutional lines (McAngus 2016). Thus, a perfect storm of valence and constitutional politics emerged for the historically electorally weak Scottish Conservative Party ahead of the 2017 local government election. Having gained ground among unionist supporters at the 2016 Holyrood election following the sharp decline of Scottish Labour, the Conservatives appeared to have adapted their local campaign strategy accordingly.

While the Scottish Conservatives had previously campaigned in council elections on the basis of local issues, the 2017 local election manifesto and campaign signalled a distinct shift in party messaging. Historically, a key feature of Scottish Conservative and Unionist ideology was the recognition of the scope for local policy differentiation and prioritisation of Scotland's differences within the Union. However, little of this was evident in 2017. Instead, there was the overarching, dominant and consistent message of preventing a second independence referendum. Thus, this became the primary platform (and by extension the mandate) upon which the Scottish Conservatives were elected to local government. Although Scotland was no stranger to constitutional politics, this was the first time the Scottish Conservatives had utilised such influence over the electorate in the fight for control of local councils, institutions which lacked much constitutional authority.

Despite dominating the conversation at the time, for example, constitutional politics had been absent from the Scottish Conservatives' 1999 local government election campaign. With the passing of the Scotland Act 1998, legislative devolution for Scotland became a reality, a reform the Scottish Conservatives had historically opposed. Yet, once established, their attitude towards the Scottish Parliament was one of co-operation, exemplified by their involvement in cross-party processes which saw the extension of devolved powers via the Calman and Smith Commissions. But this transfer of power from Westminster to Holyrood had little effect on how the party conducted politics at a local level.

The 1999 Scottish Tory campaign (conducted concurrently with that for the Scottish Parliament) displayed all of the hallmarks of a typical council election contest, with candidates highlighting their opponents' perceived failures in administration and offering their alternative policy ideas to improve local communities. Contemporary election leaflets saw candidates promising action on issues such as council spending, youth programmes, dog fouling, investment in libraries, social services and education, repairing roads and saving town centres from closure. The primary commitment by Scottish Conservative candidates in 1999 was perhaps portrayed most effectively by the campaign in Renfrewshire, which stated that 'we are not entering into any confrontational politics, we simply promise that when elected to Renfrewshire Council on 6th May – Conservatives will . . .' (Scottish Conservative Party 1999b). The leaflet then proceeded to promise changes only in local policies. It may be somewhat surprising that the beginning of the devolution process did not influence the party's local politics, given the campaign's antithetical nature compared with the political climate of 20 years later.

Four years of a Labour–Liberal Democrat coalition Scottish Executive also failed to prompt any cross-over to the local level. The 2003 Scottish Conservative council election campaign very much mirrored that of 1999 with its sole focus on local policies. This was perhaps best exemplified by a Conservative candidate in Glasgow, Alan Rodger, who issued handwritten letters to voters explaining his awareness of the local residents' concerns, such as council tax rates (Rodger 2003). In stark contrast, however, the streamlined manifesto (Scottish Conservative Party 2017b) of the 2017 local election campaign highlighted (in the first three lines of its foreword) both the importance of electing strong local representatives to tackle local issues and the need to oppose a second independence referendum.

Contrary to previous local election campaign material which criticised the records of outgoing local governments, the same foreword utilised language more pertinent to the prospect of another independence referendum than to local government. Statements such as 'rather than pushing for separation, Scottish Conservative councillors will . . .' and, 'rather than trying to manufacture a case for independence, Scottish Conservative councillors will . . .' With almost every local policy pledge in the statement prefaced by declarations of the like, the tone of the campaign was overtly defined.

In 2017, the Scottish Conservatives placed constitutional politics front and centre, occasionally omitting local issues from their campaign material altogether – for example, leaflets distributed in Midlothian which promised to 'send a message to Nicola Sturgeon' (Winchester 2017). Individual campaign material advertising specific Scottish Conservative candidates also followed this trend, most of which began with vehement opposition to a second referendum before listing any local concerns or policy pledges.

The slogan 'No to a second independence referendum' that heavily featured on Scottish Conservative local campaign material, compared with their area-specific policy slogans of the past such as 'No further congestion in Troon town centre' (McIntosh 1999) from the 1999 local election campaign, or 'No to 600 houses' (McNally 2003) from a 2003 leaflet for the Dundonald & Loans ward, suggests that the ideological shift underway in the Scottish Conservative and Unionist Party has undoubtedly penetrated their approach to local government.

Conservative Local Candidates in 2017: A Profile

Looking at Conservative election candidates in the 2017 local elections, we can seek to gain a deeper understanding of those who championed the 2017 manifesto by analysing candidate demographics and their political views. Using data from the University of Strathclyde's 2007, 2012 and 2017

Scottish Local Candidate Surveys, we can conduct a comparison with the Scottish Conservative candidates of previous local elections. How do Conservative local election candidates in 2017 differ from those standing in previous elections? Have there been any major changes in the background and political positioning of candidates?

A distinct shift in campaign style and policy concern in 2017 from previous years is clear from a review of campaign material, yet it remains to be determined whether this is also a symptom of new influence within the party or whether the party has simply capitalised on, and adapted to, changing trends in Scottish voting behaviour. Statistical analysis suggests that when compared to all other candidates, being a Conservative candidate in 2017 increased the likelihood of emphasising the Scottish Question as an important campaign issue over local concerns. These results remained consistent when running the same analysis for parties favouring the Union (Labour, Liberal Democrat) only. Given the dichotomous nature of the independence debate, the same analysis was undertaken comparing SNP candidates to all others. Interestingly, our results suggest that belonging to the SNP significantly reduced the probability of a candidate emphasising the Scottish Question instead of local issues. By comparison, no such effects were observed concerning the Conservative candidates' likelihood of campaigning on Brexit or the constitution more generally, which suggests Conservative candidates' constitutional concerns were confined to internal UK matters.

When we look at the demographics of Conservative candidates, however, some contradictions concerning the origins of British unionism are apparent, especially when comparing 2017 local candidates with those in 2012 and 2007. With the help of data from the Scottish Social Attitudes Survey, we can also compare these candidates with voters. Given the increasing significance of identity politics pertaining to the Scottish Question in 2017, it is pertinent to address candidates' national identity and examine possible change over time. Over many years, the 'Moreno question' on the extent to which respondents see themselves as Scottish and/or British has been used as a measurement of national identity. Looking at how Conservative candidates, voters and the general public have responded to this question over the years (see Table 5.2), there are signs of continuity but also of subtle changes.

The responses of the Scottish public to this question have been fairly stable, with minimum variation from year to year. Conservative voters have identified as more 'British' than the general public throughout, but again we find relatively few changes. Turning to Conservative candidates, we do see a certain shift between 2012 and 2017. The proportion of candidates who saw themselves as 'More British than Scottish' increased from 22 to 31 per cent, while those who regarded themselves as 'More Scottish

Table 5.2 National identity of Scottish Conservative candidates and voters compared with the Scottish population (2007, 2012 and 2017)

Which of the following best describes the way you think about yourself?	2007			2012			2017		
	Conservative candidates	Conservative voters	General public	Conservative candidates	Conservative voters	General public	Conservative candidates	Conservative voters	General public
Scottish not British	3	10	24	1	6	23	1	11	23
More Scottish than British	18	20	30	8	22	30	4	19	30
Equally Scottish and British	46	43	28	64	46	30	42	44	30
More British than Scottish	16	15	4	10	7	6	16	12	6
British not Scottish	12	9	5	12	16	6	15	5	6

Sources: University of Strathclyde Local Election Candidate Surveys; Conservative voters and general public: Scottish Social Attitudes Survey (SSA).

Note: Numbers do not round to 100 because a sixth option, 'none of these', is not included in the table.

than British', or 'Scottish not British', declined from 9 to 5 per cent. This is perhaps a fairly small shift, but it is in line with a greater degree of polarisation in terms of national identity in Scotland.

Turning to other demographic variables, there have been relatively minor changes over the years. The share of female candidates, for example, declined from 27 per cent in 2012 to 24 per cent in 2017, while the average age of Scottish Conservative candidates increased slightly from 54 to 57. Despite religion no longer being closely aligned with political allegiance in Scotland (see McCrone 2001), almost 47 per cent of local Conservative candidates in 2017 indicated that they identified with some form of the Protestant faith. The respective percentages for 2012 and 2007 were 60 and 67 per cent. Thus, there has been a notable decline in the number of Protestant Conservative candidates over the years. Only around 38 per cent of the Scottish population identified with some form of Protestantism in the 2011 census (Church of Scotland and other Christian statistics combined; see Scottish Government 2011). This provides scope for further research on the role of religion in Scottish party politics more widely. Overall, the survey analysis suggests that while not as relevant in overall voting as it once was, religion and national identity continue to play an important role in support for modern Scottish Conservatism.

Conservatisms? Local, Scottish, British and European

As already indicated, the success of the Conservative Party at the 2016 Scottish Parliament election validated their new campaign approach centred on opposition to a second independence referendum. This same streamlined message saw the party secure councillors in traditional working-class areas which for decades had lacked any Conservative representation. The same tactic and message was subsequently deployed during the 2017 general election and 2019 European Parliament elections. Yet in spite of the many manifesto pledges reflecting those of a typical campaign covering policy areas such as the economy and public finances, much political commentary attributed this Conservative revival to the sub-national (Scottish) party having kept the main focus of the campaign on a rejection of Scottish independence with less focus on policy.

While adopting a British unionist outlook has undoubtedly bolstered the Scottish Conservative Party's electoral success, this was not mirrored in the Conservative Party's approach to local government elections in England. In fact, despite English councillors being elected via a single-member plurality system, the English Conservative campaign style was more akin to that of Scottish candidates elected via the single transferable vote. The Scottish system provides scope for candidates to emphasise personal attributes in that multi-member wards encourage active engagement with the electorate, as voters can indicate multiple preferences and thus candidates may rely on a personal vote in order to compete with party colleagues standing in the same ward (Curtice 2007).

In contrast to the centralised manifesto delivered by the Scottish Conservatives, their English colleagues offered no such uniform promises, instead tailoring individualised campaigns to ward-specific needs. The absence of a national manifesto may have been due, in part, to the fact that only 34 councils were up for re-election, or that the party was already focusing its efforts on the snap general election announced during the local campaign period. Whatever the reason, local policy remained the focus of the Conservatives' English local government campaign.

This was apparent with their candidates for the Isle of Sheppey pledging to address traffic issues and cleanliness on the street (Booth and Pugh 2017); those in Lyndhurst and Fordingbridge promising to keep local libraries open (Heron 2017); and those in Winchester emphasising school placements (Grajewski 2017). Despite the aftermath of the Brexit vote eliciting a shift in voting behaviour (see Curtice 2017c, 2018b) similar to the changing allegiances of Scottish voters after the 2014 independence referendum, constitutional politics was notably absent from English Conservative local election campaign material. If British unionism were a feature of Conservative local politics across the board, policies relating to the UK constitution and the existing devolution settlements might have been expected to have formed a prominent part of this campaign, but they did not.

The fact that constitutional politics were not highlighted in the English local Conservative campaign at a time when the Brexit deadline had only just been extended further suggests that a campaign centred on British unionism was unique to the Scottish wing of the Conservative Party. This conclusion is compounded by the similar circumstances of the 2017 Scottish and 2019 English local elections, during which both branches of the Conservative Party fought campaigns in political environments dominated by constitutional politics, yet the localised policies of the latter left no room for unionist rhetoric. So, Scottish local election campaigning in 2017 was uniquely different in character and scope from both previous Scottish Conservative local electioneering and the practice of the party in other parts of Great Britain.

Conclusion

We ought to be wary of the suggestion that the Conservatives are 'back' when it comes to Scottish local government. Many in 1999 suggested that the first Scottish Parliament elections and the return, as a consequence, of Scottish

Conservative parliamentary representation were a prelude to a renaissance that never came. The party's first devolved manifesto even opened with the phrase 'this is a new party' (Scottish Conservative Party 1999a). That 'new' party, however, remained stuck at between 13 and 17 per cent of the vote in local elections until 2017. Offloading old political baggage therefore took some time.

The Scottish Conservative and Unionist Party's recent electoral success, meanwhile, was driven by constitutional rather than local factors. There is little evidence that the 2017 election success was a locally driven, bottom-up process involving a renewal of the party in town halls across Scotland. It was rather, and somewhat ironically, down to the 2014 Scottish independence campaign and its fallout. The party at a Scottish national level successfully harnessed the energy of an anti-independence/SNP platform to deliver a clear and succinct message to 'No' voters in Scotland: back the Conservatives and we will stop a second independence referendum.

The Scottish Conservative Party's minority status in Scottish local government since the 1970s created something of a challenge in narrating a Conservative approach to local governance in Scotland, so limited were contemporary examples of it in practice. The Conservatives' decline in town halls followed much the same trajectory as the party's broader decline at UK general elections after 1955. From being a vibrant mass-membership Scottish political party with thriving local constituency associations across the country, the party became, in many local areas, a moribund, decaying and almost defunct political organisation. The local election results in 2017, coupled with the new normal of 'no overall majority' in Scottish council chambers, offers some political space, therefore, for the party to expand its local support base.

Locally, the Scottish Conservatives were, until 2017, heading towards the status of a marginal minority party in virtually all of Scotland's local councils. The 2017 local election results could signal a turning point, although the party's challenge remains how to convert a defensive unionist message into a broader Scottish policy platform and vision. Recasting local electioneering as a debate concerning the Scottish constitution is a short-term electoral tactic that worked in 2017 but is unlikely to be a longer-term electoral strategy. Reflecting on unionism as a political philosophy may be a worthwhile exercise for the party, for at its height Scottish Unionism was very much rooted in the idea that Scotland should retain its own identity and scope for autonomy *within* the Union. But whether such a philosophy is in tune with contemporary Scottish Conservatism, or can find space in the post-Davidson Scottish party and post-Brexit Johnson-led UK party, is debateable.

Acknowledgement

The authors would like to thank Dr Wolfgang Rudig, University of Strathclyde, for his assistance and permission to use data from the Scottish Local Election Candidate Surveys funded by the British Academy, the Nuffield Foundation and the Carnegie Trust for the Universities of Scotland.

SIX

'A lesbian with family values': Gender and Sexuality in Ruth Davidson's Leadership of the Contemporary Scottish Conservative Party

Jennifer Thomson

Introduction

Ruth Davidson is unique – a married lesbian[1] and mother of one; a practising member of the Church of Scotland and past Sunday School teacher; a former member of the Territorial Army; a woman who is outspoken about past struggles with depression and mental health; a survivor of two serious accidents which both required months of painful recovery; and the owner of a 'ballsy wit' (*Vogue*, March 2018) that seems to charm every press interviewer she encounters. She also happens to have been the youngest and the first openly gay political party leader in the UK – and of the Scottish Conservatives, no less, a party which, in her lifetime, had fluctuated wildly in its position on gay rights.

This chapter focuses on Davidson's position as a gay female political leader, looking at how gender and sexuality have figured in her media coverage, self-presentation and her own political positions from her election as leader of the Scottish Conservatives in 2011 to her resignation in 2019. It moves chronologically from her election as leader to the present day, focusing on key moments – primarily the passage of same-sex marriage in Scotland; the Conservative–DUP confidence-and-supply alliance following the 2017 general election; and the publication of Davidson's 2018 book, *Yes She Can*. It opens with a discussion of the Conservative Party's contemporary policies regarding women's representation and sexuality. In doing so, this chapter argues that Davidson can be seen as part of a broader trajectory within contemporary British conservatism concerning attitudes towards women in the party and policies on sexuality (especially same-sex marriage).

The Conservative Party and Women's Representation

Traditional attitudes to encouraging women's representation within the Conservative Party differ starkly from those adopted by their main electoral rival, Labour. Under Tony Blair's leadership during the 1990s, the Labour Party instituted a programme of all-women shortlists (AWS), which led to a huge increase in the number of women MPs. At the 1997 general election, 120 female MPs – the largest-ever cohort – was returned to the House of Commons. The vast majority of these (101) were Labour Members, constituting 24 per cent of the Parliamentary Labour Party (Childs 2001).

By contrast, the Conservative Party lagged behind. In 2005, the Conservatives only returned 19 female MPs compared with Labour's 98 (Childs and Webb 2012: 1). This paucity of Conservative women MPs was acknowledged in David Cameron's leadership, which began in the wake of the 2005 elections, a key feature of his attempts to move his party in a more socially liberal direction. That year also saw the establishment of the Conservative Party organisation Women2Win, co-founded by future prime minister Theresa May, which existed to encourage women to seek Conservative candidacies. These new approaches saw the Conservatives elect 49 women in 2010, their largest-ever number of female MPs (Childs and Webb 2012: 1). However, these methods were notably less prescriptive than Labour's use of AWS, focusing on encouraging women to stand rather than changing the structures through which candidates were chosen and elected. They reflected a broader approach to autonomy and local candidate selection more in line with Conservative political ideology and organisation.

Attitudes to women's representation in the Scottish Conservative Party appeared reflective of those at Westminster, even if the Scottish context was somewhat different in terms of women's representation. Scottish politics has, since 2014, been remarkably feminised. At one point, all three leaders of the main political parties were women and two were openly gay. The Conservative Party, both UK-wide with Prime Minister Theresa May, and with former Scottish Conservative leader Annabel Goldie, who headed the party between 2005 and 2011, followed by current leader Ruth Davidson, has also seen key elite female representation.

Indeed, the Scottish Parliament, since its inception in 1999, has generally seen higher levels of women's representation compared with the UK Parliament, although Westminster is catching up. In 2019, Holyrood had 34.9 per cent female representation compared with Westminster's 32 per cent (*Holyrood*, 13 May 2016). Yet these figures mask huge differences across party political lines, as Table 6.1 demonstrates.

Table 6.1 Percentage of female MSPs in the 5th Scottish Parliament (2016–21) by political party

Scottish National Party	44
Scottish Labour	48
Scottish Conservative and Unionist Party	23
Scottish Green Party	17
Scottish Liberal Democrats	20

Source: Scottish Parliament Fact Sheet: Female MSPs, Session 5, http://www.parliament.scot/ResearchBriefingsAndFactsheets/Cumulative_List_of_Female_MSPs_S5.pdf.

The differences across parties reflect very different approaches to women's representation. Scottish Labour continued to use all-women shortlists in the 2016 Holyrood election, as it has done since the Scottish Parliament's inception, returning almost 50 per cent female MSPs. Labour's position on women's representation has, until recently, had little impact on other political parties' (Kenny and Mackay 2014). At the 2016 election, the SNP used all-women shortlists in constituencies with retiring MSPs for the first time (*Holyrood*, 13 May 2016). This saw their numbers jump dramatically, having elected fewer than a third female MSPs (27.5%) in 2011.

The Scottish Conservatives' low level of female MSPs was particularly notable given 2016 was a breakthrough election for them, more than doubling their number of seats and becoming the second-largest party in Holyrood. It also reflected, as detailed above, a more laissez-faire attitude to women's representation, one centred around encouraging women to stand rather than dictating structural change as Labour and, more recently, the SNP (to clear results in 2016) had done via AWS. In this context, while the Scottish Conservatives are comparatively weak on female representation, the fact the party has now been led by women for the majority of the period following devolution appears an aberration rather than part of a broader representation strategy. As discussed below, Davidson's personal approach was in line with her party's approach to women's representation, in politics and elsewhere, and the prospect of the party adopting more prescriptive attitudes under her leadership appeared slim.

The Conservative Party and Sexuality

The Conservative Party's position on gay rights was also liberalised in the period following its electoral defeat in 1997. Under the leadership of William Hague, Iain Duncan Smith and Michael Howard in the late

1990s and early 2000s, the party adopted a socially conservative outlook. Respectively, Hague and Duncan Smith imposed three-line whips on votes to repeal Section 28 and to allow same-sex and unmarried couples equal adoption rights (Hayton 2010: 494–5; Monahan 2018: 140–4). Yet these decisions, particularly around the adoption issue, sparked tensions and arguments within the party about the direction of its social policies: 35 Conservative MPs (including future leader David Cameron) absented themselves from the adoption vote, and eight voted with the then Labour government to change the law (Hayton 2010: 495; Monahan 2018: 141).

The issue of sexuality, and in particular policy towards same-sex relationships, was therefore another key part of Cameron's modernisation of his party. While Cameron stressed his position as a 'family man', he did so in a way that was not anchored in heterosexual marriage. In a 2008 speech, he spoke about marriage as a 'positive social norm' but also stressed that any future tax cuts for married couples under a Conservative government would also extend to same-sex civil partners (Hayton 2010: 497; Monahan 2018: 142). This moved further after the 2010 election, with Cameron (now Prime Minister) voicing clear support for same-sex marriage legislation. In his 2011 speech to the Conservative Party conference, Cameron presented this as fundamental to his Conservative identity:

> And to anyone who has reservations, I say: Yes, it's about equality, but it's also about something else: commitment. Conservatives believe in the ties that bind us; that society is stronger when we make vows to each other and support each other. So I don't support gay marriage despite being a Conservative. I support gay marriage *because* I'm a Conservative. (*Telegraph*, 5 October 2011)

Monahan depicts this positioning as part of an ongoing 'Tory-normativity' of attitudes to gay rights within the Conservative Party, a conscious decision to rebrand 'a group previously seen as outside of acceptable Conservative behaviour has been identified as "one of us" all along' (Monahan 2018: 134). Although, as Monahan shows, this rebranding has deep roots in the Conservative Party from the 1960s onwards, this has not necessarily been fully taken on board by party activists and supporters.[2] Yet same-sex marriage passed through the Commons in 2013, with the Scottish Parliament following suit in 2014. Davidson's speech to Holyrood at the time, discussed below, echoed the sentiments of then Prime Minister Cameron in his 2011 conferences speech.

Contemporary 'compassionate' Conservatism was thus anchored in more modern approaches to women's representation and gay rights. The modern Conservative Party sees the lack of women's presence within the party as a problem and is willing to take incremental steps to address it; and it regards gay rights as an extension of the social liberalism the party now largely espouses, even if these positions are not necessarily accepted across the board.

Early Years and Same-Sex Marriage in Scotland

It was against this increasingly socially liberal position and the modernisation of the party that Ruth Davidson joined the Scottish Conservatives. In 2008, she left a career in the media and joined the party, working at Holyrood before becoming an MSP (via the Glasgow regional list) in 2011. Following Annabel Goldie's decision to step down shortly after that election, Davidson was elected party leader, the youngest person ever to lead a UK political party (her 33rd birthday was just a few days away) and the first openly gay individual to do so. But while she won a Stonewall award in 2012, her sexuality and private life were far less part of her public persona than in later years. In a 2012 interview with the *Scotsman*, for example, her sexuality was discussed, particularly in relation to her faith (Davidson was a practising member of the Church of Scotland and a former Sunday School teacher), but questions about her then partner, the interviewer was warned, were 'a no-go area' (*Scotsman*, 24 January 2012). With the Conservatives still a minor political force in Scotland, Davidson possessed a relatively low media profile.

Following passage of the same-sex marriage bill through Westminster in 2013, similar legislation progressed through the Scottish Parliament in 2014. In the debate, Davidson related her personal circumstances to the passing of the Bill, declaring that she had 'no doubt that this could be the most personal speech that I will ever make in the chamber'. Davidson began her argument by stressing the importance of marriage and the stability that marriage and family life had brought to her own childhood:

I believe in marriage. I believe that marriage is a good thing. I saw the evidence of that every day growing up in a house that was full of love. My family had the stresses and strains that are common to all, but there was never any doubt, question or fear in my mind that our togetherness was in any way insecure. The bedrock of that stability and security was my parents' marriage. That stability helped me and my sister to flourish and have confidence that we could be whoever we wanted to be. After more than 40 years of marriage, my parents still love each other. I look at what they have and I want that too, and I want it to be recognised in the same way. That recognition matters. (Official Report, 20 November 2013)

Much like Cameron's 2011 party conference speech, Davidson's personal invocation acted as a reminder that marriage was a quintessentially conservative tradition, thus continuing the aforementioned 'Tory-normativity' (Monahan 2018). By evoking it in terms of family, stability and the important role it played in childrearing, like Cameron before her, Davidson staked her support for equal marriage not 'in spite' of her conservatism, but because of it. As such, same-sex marriage became a continuum of the modern Conservative Party.

Later in the same speech, Davidson spoke of the importance that same-sex marriage legislation would have for young people and future generations in Scotland:

> We have an opportunity today to tell our nation's children that, no matter where they live and no matter who they love, there is nothing that they cannot do. We will wipe away the last legal barrier that says that they are something less than their peers. We can help them to walk taller into the playground tomorrow and to face their accuser down knowing that the Parliament of their country has stood up for them and said that they are every bit as good as every one of their classmates. They will know that their Parliament has said that they deserve the same rights as everyone else.

Elsewhere (especially in her 2018 book, *Yes She Can*, discussed below) Davidson has spoken passionately about the public responsibility she feels she holds as an openly gay figure, particularly in relation to younger people. She concluded her speech by declaring: 'I believe in marriage. I believe that it is a good thing and something to be celebrated, and I want everyone in Scotland to know that marriage is important to them' (Official Report, 20 November 2013).

Beyond the passing of same-sex marriage legislation, the 2015 general election, the Scottish Conservatives' success at the 2016 Holyrood election and the 2016 EU referendum increased Davidson's profile, both in Scotland and throughout the rest of the UK. Davidson, meanwhile, spoke in increasingly personal terms about her sexuality. In a BBC radio interview during 2015, she spoke about the difficulties of reconciling her Christian faith with being gay:

> It's something I struggled with, I didn't want to be gay. I'm not sure how many people do. It's been amazing the difference, even in my lifetime, how things have changed. I struggled with it for a number of years actually before I would admit it to myself, never mind to anybody else. But there comes a point at which you make a decision and that decision is either that you're going to live a lie for the rest of your life, or you're going to trust yourself, and that's what I had to do. (BBC News online, 5 November 2015)

In a party political broadcast the same year, Davidson's partner appeared alongside Ruth's mother and father (*Telegraph*, 18 February 2015). Moving into her first UK general election as leader of the Scottish Conservatives, Davidson therefore seemed increasingly comfortable addressing her sexuality and embedding it within her growing media profile.

The 2015 and 2017 General Elections

The 2015 general election was widely perceived to be an incredibly close race between Labour and the Conservatives, to the extent that both David Cameron and Ed Miliband ran tightly orchestrated campaigns, fearful that the smallest slip might damage their electoral prospects. Such was this fear that Cameron's aides would not even allow a puppy within reach of the Prime Minister during a trip to Cheltenham (*Daily Mail*, 12 April 2015). Davidson, sheltered from this given her devolved role, was instead photographed 'at the bingo, driving a tank, playing a set of bagpipes, holding a falcon and an eagle, and staring lovingly into the eyes of a trout – although not all at the same time' (BuzzFeed News, 29 April 2015). Such press coverage displayed a developing interest in her as an individual and a generally warm relationship with the media.

A growing media presence for Davidson was also coupled with a continued willingness to speak out on LGBT (lesbian, gay, bisexual and transgender) issues. In a lecture to Amnesty's Pride event in Belfast in 2016, Davidson repeated part of her speech made to the Scottish Parliament during the passage of the same-sex marriage bill, evoking her parents' long marriage and the family stability this had provided her with. She went on to argue that Northern Ireland was being held back through its continued denial of same-sex marriage laws:

> [F]or a foot-loose employer who can contribute to a local economy, why would you base yourself where some of your employees can't be married? If you're a global business, deploying people around the world, why would you send them to a place if some of them aren't equal? It's also about where you find the smart, young, mobile, educated workforce. How many people have got on a boat or a plane to go to college or uni or start work away from here because it's easier to be your whole self somewhere else? How many of Northern Ireland's daughters and her sons have chosen to build a life in friendlier climes? (Davidson 2016)

Again, Davidson's linkage of the issues of marriage, employment and business opportunities and growth embedded LGBT equality within a broader conservative spectrum. Marriage was again framed as part of Conservative Party ideology and policy.

This speech was to prove especially important given the result of the snap UK election held the following year. The 2017 general election did not return the Conservative majority which was anticipated; instead, the party at Westminster had to enter a confidence-and-supply arrangement with the Democratic Unionist Party (DUP) in order to secure a Commons majority. The DUP were the main unionist party in Northern Ireland and held a series of strongly socially conservative positions, particularly on abortion and same-sex marriage. Indeed, the DUP's invocation of a particular feature of the Northern Ireland Assembly, the 'petition of concern', meant it had managed to block same-sex marriage proposals several times (Thomson 2015).

Following the deal, Davidson spoke to May and sought assurances that LGBT rights would not be under threat in Great Britain as a result. Speaking to the BBC, she said that she was

> fairly straightforward with her [May] and I told her that there were a number of things that count to me more than the party. One of them is country, one of the others is LGBTI rights. I asked for a categoric assurance that if any deal or scoping deal was done with the DUP there would be absolutely no rescission of LGBTI rights in the rest of the UK, in Great Britain, and that we would use any influence that we had to advance LGBTI rights in Northern Ireland. It's an issue very close to my heart and one that I wanted categoric assurances from the prime minister on, and I received [them]. (Press Association, 10 June 2017)

Davidson also tweeted a link to her 2016 Amnesty Pride lecture, with the words: 'As a Protestant Unionist about to marry an Irish Catholic, here's the Amnesty Pride lecture I gave in Belfast' (indy100, 10 June 2017). Taking this public stance illustrated a bolder position regarding her sexuality and her private life, and their relation to her public and political role. Davidson was willing not only to publicly take on the Prime Minister in relation to LGBT rights, but also potentially to undercut her party leader's position at this pivotal moment for the Conservative Party.

Yes We (She?) Can

Following the 2017 general election, Davidson enjoyed her highest media profile yet. In April 2018 she was interviewed in *Vogue* and later the same year announced she was pregnant. In September 2018, meanwhile, she published a book, *Yes She Can: Why Women Own the Future.* The book managed to be both a biography of Davidson and a series of vignettes regarding the setbacks women experienced in their personal and professional lives, accompanied by short interviews with a range of successful women including Theresa May, the journalist Tina Brown, the philanthropist Melinda Gates and BBC journalist Laura Kuenssberg. In doing so, Davidson provided an insight into her personal life but also linked that to the broader liberal feminist struggle for equal pay and representation that she described in the book.

In the book, Davidson set out the clearest sense yet of her thinking on gender and women's role in public and political life. In a chapter entitled 'Role Models and Mentoring', Davidson discussed her difficulty, until she became Scottish Conservative leader, in understanding why people sought out role models. Following her election, she recounted, she began to receive emails from young gay people:

> A number said they were not out yet in their school or to their families – or they were out and were getting bullied. Some were incredibly personal, others were absolutely heartbreaking. But the message in all of them was that these young people were interested in politics but thought it was something they could never do because of their sexuality. It mattered to them to see someone gay take on a national leadership role. (Davidson 2018: 63)

Davidson went on to stress that she always took the time to reply to every single email, 'often in very personal terms about my own situation', and that this wave of people reaching out to her resulted in a feeling that she 'wouldn't let gay people down' (Davidson 2018: 64). In this way, Davidson linked discussion of her sexuality back to the speech she had made during the passage of same-sex marriage legislation at Holyrood: the importance of making things easier for the next generation and the responsibilities she carried as an elected gay politician, whether or not those contacting her were her constituents or voted for her party.

Yes She Can further linked interest in Davidson as a gay politician to broader issues around mentorship and people's perceptions about what was and was not achievable in their own lives. She interviewed one chief executive who was in favour of workplace quotas, and another who instead advocated training and mentoring. Davidson closed the chapter by saying (in characteristically direct language) that:

> The idea of *needing* a quota really grates on me. It offends my inner feminist – that spaces have to be set aside or special accommodation afforded to women

just because of their gender. I want to scream a massive 'fuck you' to a system that says we must ration and apportion seats at the decision-making table because, without such dispensation, women couldn't be able to take those seats on their own.

Yet Davidson goes on to acknowledge that

the outcome is more important than the journey. If quotas lead to all the other ways of opening doors – creating more role models, allowing for more mentoring, encouraging a critical mass of new entrants, supporting greater company networks – perhaps they can speed that journey up. I'm conflicted as to whether that is an admission of defeat, or simply a practical tool. (Davidson 2018: 71)

This depiction of quotas – as insulting to women in the assumption that they somehow need extra help, but perhaps also at times a necessary evil – largely fits with broader understandings of positive discrimination within the Conservative Party. Quotas are against the principles of meritocracy which underpin the party's understanding of candidate selection and democracy. Indeed, in even considering quotas as 'a practical tool', Davidson places herself on the more liberal wing of her party in her approach to thinking about women's representation. This did, however, lead her to a rather woolly conclusion: acceptant that quotas might do some good but steadfast in her belief that they were nevertheless offensive to women's merit and ability.

Beyond the issue of quotas, *Yes She Can* focused largely on themes that resonate with contemporary mainstream feminism: the wage gap, juggling motherhood with a career, and online abuse. Davidson talked about 'finding out my (male) co-presenter at the BBC earned 40 per cent more than I did for doing exactly the same job', and writes about her experience of having IVF as 'invasive, joyous, mortifying, fearful and hopeful'. She worried what combining motherhood with front-line politics would look like, presciently observing that she had 'no idea how changing family responsibilities will affect the way I do my job' (Davidson 2018: 35, 79, 89).

In further linking her own experiences to a broader cacophony of female voices, and to wider struggles to which the presumed reader could relate, Davidson inserted herself into a resurgence of mainstream liberal feminist thinking. Recent years had seen broad discussion around women's public and political roles, including debate on the gender pay gap, women on corporate boards, women's symbolic representation in public artworks and sexual harassment under the #MeToo movement. In

Yes She Can, Davidson skilfully linked her own story to a broader conversation around women's rights, such that we were presented not with a traditional political biography, but rather a personal twist on the contemporary feminist conversation. As such, it read as both biography and Davidson's political manifesto, an outline of what she hoped women in public life might achieve and what her own future political career might go on to promote.

Conclusion

Ruth Davidson resigned as Scottish Conservative leader in August 2019. Her announcement (made the day after Boris Johnson's controversial decision to prorogue Parliament) was ostensibly related to a desire to spend more time with her family, and the difficulties of balancing political life with a young child. While Davidson's gender and sexuality played a key role in her self-presentation as leader, ultimately they remained bastions of traditional, conservative British society and ideals. Defining her departure from politics through motherhood reiterated this.

The institutions that defined Davidson – the Church, her past roles at the BBC, her former membership of the Territorial Army, her marriage and her family – were still backbones of a type of conservatism/Conservative understanding of the nation that had long existed. Likewise, in her 'fuck you' approach to quotas for women in public life, and her pro-mentorship and encouragement position, Davidson aligned herself with a broader understanding of the approach to women's representation in the Conservative Party as a whole. Structural changes were best avoided, with incremental change and mentorship the best way to improve women's public and political representation.

To situate Davidson in this way is not to belittle her uniqueness as a politician; indeed, it is difficult to think of another politician who would consent to the various photo opportunities she undertook in the run-up to the 2015 general election, let alone pull them off. Neither is it to deny the substantial obstacles that existed (in terms of her gender, sexuality, pregnancy in office and past mental and physical health issues) to her having reached the heights of Scottish party political leadership. Yet it does remind us, with little surprise, that Davidson was a C/conservative. In her near decade as leader of the Scottish Conservatives, her public presentation and political positions remained situated within conservative understandings of family life and social and political change. Her gender and sexuality were, in this sense, not aberrations but rather continuations of a conservative political projection her party had promoted for some time.

Acknowledgement

This chapter is dedicated to the memory of my late grandmother, Christina 'Ina' Geddes, who, like Ruth Davidson, was a strong Scottish woman with deep roots in the Borders. It is also dedicated to the many other strong Scotswomen who loved, cared for and supported my grandmother throughout her life, not least of all my mother, Jane.

SEVEN

Riding the Unionist Wave: Ruth Davidson, the Media and the Re-emergence of the Scottish Conservatives

David Patrick

Introduction

Given that any perceived Tory revival in Scotland would in large part be influenced by media representations of that party, this chapter seeks to explore the nature of this relationship from 2011 to 2019. It presents findings from an overview of media coverage of the Scottish Conservatives in this period, drawing liberally from comment and opinion pieces, political sketches, blogs and magazine profiles, as well as news reports. With a particular focus on Ruth Davidson, the discussion shows that the 2014 independence referendum – and the parallel polarisation of Scottish politics – provided the Scottish Conservatives with a necessary platform upon which to build a new identity and relevance.

The (at times myopic) focus on unionism was an idea that found fertile soil in both Scottish and UK press titles, many of which were editorially pro-Union in 2014. Thus, the Tory revival, which arguably reached its peak in 2017, can be seen as partly down to the often-positive coverage of Davidson as a uniquely prominent champion of Scotland's remaining in the Union. Davidson's resignation, and continuing confusion over Brexit, may indicate that the Conservative resurgence has lost much of its momentum, though with the constitutional question remaining a central concern of Scottish politics, an explicit commitment to unionism evidently remains an effective campaigning strategy moving forward, not least in media terms.

Early Years and the Independence Referendum

Such was the extent of the Scottish Conservative Party's electoral misfortune after 1997 that it was regarded as of little importance in the initial years of Davidson's leadership, with voters across the political spectrum believing the party to be of marginal significance (*Scotsman*, 28 October 2013). Continuing to be little more than 'a mildly political neighbourhood watch group, doing the round of leafleting between tea dances and community litter pick-ups' (*Scottish Daily Mail*, 22 July 2019), the party struggled to convey a coherent political message which resonated with voters, a factor made more difficult due to policies of the UK Conservative Party (in coalition government since 2010).

The lack of any significant shift in the party's fortunes between 2011 and 2014 also drew criticism regarding Davidson's suitability for the leadership (see, for example, *Scotsman*, 23 May 2013) and capacity to halt and reverse long-standing decline. Though by no means regarded as a failure, her early performances at First Minister's Questions were also seen as uninspiring – competent, but 'without really landing too many punches on Alex Salmond during the weekly political joust at Holyrood' (*Scotsman*, 13 August 2012). Davidson was yet to establish herself as the media darling she would later become.

Therefore, the referendum campaign, which began early in Davidson's leadership (January 2012) but only gathered pace after March 2014, was to prove a turning point for both the Scottish Conservatives and Scottish political culture in general. Receiving prominent media coverage was the unionist 'Better Together' alliance, typified by press photographs or television coverage of Ruth Davidson alongside Scottish Labour leader Johann Lamont and Scottish Liberal Democrat leader Willie Rennie. Although this camaraderie would dissipate following the referendum result, the sight of former rivals sitting 'sitting side by side, smiling' (Pike 2015: 23) did much to project a united front on the constitutional question.

Given they were starting from a position of weakness, the referendum also provided the comfortably unionist Scottish Conservatives with something of an open goal, facilitating ample opportunity to gain (often positive) publicity, particularly for Davidson. As Garavelli put it, 'it wasn't until the indyref campaign – when she was one of the strongest voices speaking up for the Union – that she began to establish herself as a force in Scottish political life' (*Scotsman*, 7 May 2016). But although ever present in terms of photo opportunities, Davidson was rarely the focus of any major news stories, the media narrative concentrating predominantly on Alex Salmond, Alistair Darling, Gordon Brown and David Cameron.

The Scottish Tory leader, however, did take part in televised debates, including a 'town hall' format which saw Davidson appear alongside Kezia Dugdale and Douglas Alexander to argue the case for the Union against Nicola Sturgeon, Patrick Harvie and Elaine C. Smith; and in another, notable for its explicit engagement with first-time 16- and 17-year-old voters, at the SSE Hydro arena where she appeared with George Galloway. While the choice of Davidson as a headliner of this latter event has since been described as 'inexplicable' (Macwhirter 2014: 96), Davidson also pushed 'hard to be involved, realising that a political event on this scale would never be repeated' (Pike 2015: 134).

In addition to Davidson's increased public and political profile, the referendum was also crucial in crystallising the political position upon which the Scottish Tories would henceforth campaign. The party started to define itself increasingly in terms of a single issue, rejecting Scottish independence and any calls for a second referendum. This was not a particular gamble; 'No', after all, had won in 2014, while the 'Conservative Friends of the Union' group was said to have some 80,000 backers (*Holyrood*, 15 March 2014). Perhaps most importantly, continuing to articulate an anti-independence position was also in line with the editorial positions of most major Scottish newspapers.

Still, the Scottish Conservative Party would see few gains immediately after the referendum, its focus on the Union not yet paying electoral dividends. But the 2012–14 campaign had planted a seed. In the post-2015 period, Davidson and her party had the advantage of continuity and stability as Scottish Labour went through a particularly turbulent phase, which meant there was an opening for a 'unionist' champion. This position Davidson effectively filled (aided by often positive media coverage of her and her party), attracting former Labour voters in the process, a conversion potential highlighted in the press as early as 2015 (*Scottish Daily Mail*, 18 November 2015).

Gender and Sexuality

From the first weeks of her leadership, a focal point of media coverage concerning the Scottish Conservative leader was her sexuality. Prior to the referendum, for example, Ruth Davidson's split from a former partner received newspaper coverage (*Express*, 1 March 2013), with Cochrane (2014: 179) intimating in his diary that he might have gone easy on her in his opinion pieces due to these romantic troubles. As the UK's first openly gay party leader, Davidson was consistently frank about her sexuality, discussing the difficulties she faced in coming to terms with being a lesbian, including the impact it had on her mental health and the difficulty of reconciling her sexuality with her faith (*The Times*, 16 September 2018; BBC News online, 5 November 2015).

As a result of this, Davidson, whom Cochrane once described as 'a 30-something leader who not only makes no secret of her sexuality but

makes jokes about it in what often seems like a deliberate attempt to shock'
(*Telegraph*, 5 November 2012), was in many ways defined by her sexuality
in her early years as leader, particularly in the period before she became so
closely associated with opposition to another independence referendum.
Certainly, this aspect of her identity may well have contributed to her early
exposure beyond strictly political circles, with outlets in the gay press providing Davidson with a level of coverage invaluable in building her media
persona (*PinkNews*, 20 September 2011).

This is not to say, of course, that coverage within these particular outlets
was uniformly positive (Davidson was booed, for example, while speaking at the Stonewall Awards), but she was named politician of the year by
PinkNews in 2015 (*PinkNews*, 2 November 2012; *Herald*, 24 October 2015).
Later in her leadership, Davidson's sexuality continued to influence both
her politics and media attention, particularly her engagement to Jennifer
Wilson and the arrival of their first child. While the Scottish Tory leader
was initially protective of her partner's privacy, their relationship was later
discussed more openly, with a number of sketches and interviews finding
Davidson talking warmly about her partner, how they met and the positive
impact Wilson had had on her life outside politics (*Sun*, 26 October 2018;
Vogue, 26 April 2018).

An important aspect of this dynamic was the inclusion of the couple in an official 2015 Tory campaign broadcast, the first time Wilson
had appeared alongside Davidson in such an explicitly public medium
(*Telegraph*, 18 February 2015; *Sun*, 26 October 2018). Speaking of this
move, Deerin said 'it felt like a big moment, not just for the Scottish
Conservatives, but for wider British society' (*Scottish Daily Mail*, 9 April
2015), echoing a more general narrative that the party was becoming
more progressive. The day after the 2017 general election, the *Telegraph*
showed the couple leaving a polling station hand in hand on its front
page (*Telegraph*, 10 June 2017). This proved mutually beneficial: not only
was Davidson's status as the UK's first openly gay party leader newswor-
thy, but the resulting coverage also allowed her to frame the Scottish
Tories as tolerant, progressive and different from their UK counterparts.

Other aspects of Davidson's background and personality were also used
to support the idea she was something of a break from the party norm, a
'counter-intuitive Conservative', in the words of David Torrance (*i* newspaper, 25 January 2016). Davidson was thus presented as a more authentic
politician, in tune with the concerns and desires of ordinary voters: 'State-
educated, charismatic and emphatically unentitled, the socially progressive
centrist has since become the poster girl for detoxification of the Tory brand'
(*Vogue*, 26 April 2018). Key in this respect were persistent references to her

lower-middle-class upbringing, something regularly contrasted with the wealthy elites seen to represent the party in London. Davidson even went as far as claiming she had never encountered the class system before attending Edinburgh University (*Vogue*, 26 April 2018).

Davidson, 'drawing strength and popularity from her strong sense of humour, comprehensive education and Protestant middle-class background' (Simpkins 2018a), thus utilised another aspect of her personality to her electoral advantage, with the larger Conservative Party also keen to publicise and highlight her background (*Holyrood*, 15 March 2014). Cultivating the idea that Davidson was 'the antithesis of the hunting-shooting-fishing caricature of the Scots Tory' (*Scotsman*, 28 October 2013) therefore became a key aim of the Conservative publicity machine, with a view to harnessing Davidson's pro-unionist message and making her 'more palatable for Scottish voters who had massively turned away from the Conservatives for several decades' (Simpkins 2018b).

These aims were aided by Davidson's ease and openness with the media (*Telegraph*, 18 February 2015), which arguably helped mould a generally positive image within the Scottish press. With a variety of political campaigns taking place between 2012 and 2017, the Scottish Tory leader thus had several opportunities to hone her media-handling abilities, building on experience and skills she had learned in her previous career as a broadcaster. Discussions of her performance in this regard were often highly positive, painting the Tory leader as a political titan within the ever-changing Scottish political landscape. Chris Deerin would describe Davidson as 'always well prepared, often unpredictable, and a formidable debater who is not easily deflected' (*Scottish Daily Mail*, 9 April 2015), while a feature article would say of her performance at First Minister's Questions that she was 'so uncommonly comfortable in her own skin, with an effortless confidence and charm that goes a long way towards explaining why she's the Tory that Labour frontbenchers fear the most' (*Vogue*, 26 April 2018).

This is not to say, however, there was no criticism. Alan Cochrane records in his diary that he considered her 'good on the telly but crap everywhere else' (Cochrane 2014: 11), and it is clear that Davidson became a more effective campaigner as her party's position became centred around a defence of the Union. Perhaps one of her most high-profile and celebrated appearances came during the 2016 EU referendum process, where her debating technique, passion and persona helped bring her to the attention of an audience beyond Scotland and Holyrood. Her appearance at Wembley Arena has been described as 'career-making' (*Vogue*, 26 April 2018), while Kevin McKenna opined that it had 'brought her to U.K.-wide attention', emerging 'at just the right time for Scottish unionists' (*Observer*, 26 June 2016).

Indeed, such was Davidson's personal popularity that at times a potential career in Westminster – including even the possibility of leading the UK Conservative Party – was mooted, with a variety of commentators believing this to be a natural progression. This idea gained particular traction in the period leading up to the 2017 general election, and inevitably grew following Scottish Conservative gains in that contest. Though some questioned whether her 'distinct brand of Scottish unionist Conservatism' would be as popular in England (Simpkins 2018b), Davidson was among the early favourites to eventually succeed the Prime Minister and was 'widely considered one of the party's brightest stars' (*Daily Mail*, 13 December 2017), with some commentators suggesting she was among David Cameron's preferred candidates for the role during his own time in office (*Guardian*, 3 May 2019).

Media coverage often reflected this perceived change in status, with the general election campaign of 2017 seeing Davidson become 'the focus of the sort of gushing profiles that Nicola Sturgeon once enjoyed' (*Herald*, 19 June 2017) and cited as a possible 'kingmaker' in any future Tory leadership contest (*Scotsman*, 29 September 2017). Despite such high expectations regarding her future in politics, Davidson largely distanced herself from such notions, publicly stating on several occasions that being Prime Minister was not an ambition. Fearing the impact on her family life and mental health, the Scottish Tory leader instead emphasised her desire to become First Minister, arguing that she had a 'job to do in Scotland' (*Vogue*, 26 April 2018).

Some commentary would also question whether navigating the London media environment might prove too big a contrast with her experiences in Scotland, with a *Scotsman* piece hypothesising that 'being the subject of queries about her ability in the right-wing press might persuade the Lothians MSP that the slightly more collegiate inter-party atmosphere of Holyrood is still preferable, no matter her ambitions' (*Scotsman*, 13 December 2017). However quixotic such speculation, the fact the media entertained, debated and in some cases propagated the idea of Davidson as UK Tory leader said much about her standing within Scottish politics and its media.

There were dissenters, unsurprising given the Labour tenor of several leading newspapers such as the *Daily Record*. Though it did not make it into a lot of his regular columns, Alan Cochrane – despite working for the Conservative-supporting *Telegraph* – had a particularly poor opinion of Davidson's early leadership period, variously describing her as 'absolutely useless', 'a disaster' and 'a real dodo' (Cochrane 2014: 203, 56, 88). There were occasional gaffes, including when Davidson tweeted a provocative photograph of an American actress in her underwear, to which author Yvonne Ridley responded: 'I just can't believe the leader of a political party who wants to be taken seriously would be so demeaning to women' (*Daily Mail*, 1 July 2017).

Perhaps the most damaging and sustained criticism Davidson received was a result of her stance on the so-called 'rape clause' (an exception to the two-child cap on Child Tax Credit for conception during non-consensual sex), a position over which she was 'virulently attacked' (Simpkins 2018a). The impressive Tory returns in the 2017 election – which followed controversy over this policy – demonstrated that the issue was not enough to derail the momentum of the Tory revival in Scotland, but for some it tarnished some of Davidson's more feminist and progressive credentials: 'Ruth Davidson was supposed to represent a fresh break with crusty Tory tradition. She is in a gay relationship and has been assumed to be in favour of women's rights. That reputation all but evaporated over the past week' (*Sunday Herald*, 16 April 2017).

Overall, however, Davidson managed to steer clear of damaging allegations, personal scandals or high-profile media gaffes, and this also aided her ability to articulate a coherent – if narrow – message regarding her party's unionist commitment with a greater level of legitimacy than might have been the case with an individual not so well versed in handling the media.

(Scottish) Women in Politics

Before going on to discuss the manner in which the Scottish Tories harnessed and cultivated the unionist message in the years following the 2014 referendum, a key disclaimer must be made in order to more accurately contextualise Ruth Davidson's particular contributions to Scottish political life: that in relation to both UK and Scottish politics, women are notably under-represented in terms of their proportional numbers of MPs or MSPs. This pattern is repeated in the make-up of political journalism and the wider political commentariat, with these branches of the media being disproportionately male, a trend which is often most entrenched in the more right-wing newspapers that may be expected to give a Tory leader more favourable coverage.

Essentially, there is evidence to suggest female politicians are often evaluated and critiqued against different standards than their male counterparts, and that in several instances this institutionalised sexism can be a hindrance to political advancement. As Walsh notes, 'female political leaders continue to be judged according to different and often more taxing standards than their male counterparts by largely male or male-identified political commentators within the mainstream media' (Walsh 2015: 1032), with stylistic or sartorial choices, for example, receiving disproportionate coverage when reporting on female politicians.

Though both Nicola Sturgeon and Theresa May have been subjected to far greater scrutiny with regard to their dress and appearance than has been the case with Ruth Davidson (Pedersen 2018: 711–12), this dynamic is seen to affect the reporting of virtually all female politicians in the UK, resulting in 'the double standard whereby the appearance of male politicians attracts far less critical comment from the media, with the result that women with serious political ambitions have to subject themselves to more critical self-scrutiny than their male peers' (Walsh 2015: 1029). Thus, a number of female politicians find themselves framed more as celebrities (O'Neill et al. 2016: 295) than as serious politicians, with policy positions or other opinions often being secondary.

Regularly reproduced in language and frames of reference, it has been noted that 'much reporting implicitly resumed certain kinds of masculinity as the unmarked norm against which women were, if considered, marked as different' (Adcock 2010: 150), and it is a trend that obviously influences a variety of options and decisions available to women with political ambitions (North 2016: 357; O'Neill et al. 2016: 302; Pedersen 2018: 710). The wider implication of this is that female representation, remaining marginalised, thus discourages other women from seeking political office or engaging in public debate and the like; therefore, Davidson assuming the centre stage (in a national debate, directly opposing another prominent female politician) in Scottish politics had potentially greater implications for society than is generally appreciated.

By all conventional norms, Davidson might have been expected to receive far less coverage than she actually enjoyed. Put another way, neither her gender nor her sexuality damaged her prospects of securing positive coverage from the mainstream press, despite established trends of female marginalisation and trivialisation being institutionalised within both Scottish politics and media (Ross and Carter 2011). That Davidson could command consistent attention from various media outlets is testament to both her ability as a campaigner and, more tellingly, the comparative importance which came with propagating a unionist position.

The Unionist Revival

The constitutional question has come to define much of Scottish politics since 2014. As David Torrance noted,

> Paradoxically, the 2014 referendum proved the impetus for a Tory – or more accurately, a unionist – revival; the Scottish National Party's 2015 landslide proved a double-edged sword, a peak that provoked an anti-independence backlash of which Ruth Davidson and her colleagues took skilful advantage. (*Financial Times*, 9 June 2017)

This observation was echoed by Ben Borland: 'Ironically for the National-ists, and this must be a particularly bitter pill to swallow, it was the inde-pendence referendum of 2014 which did most to power the Tory revival' (*Scottish Daily Express*, 4 March 2017).

As already noted, with the Scottish print media largely holding an explicitly unionist editorial position in 2014, Davidson's developing cam-paign skills – coupled with the continuing relevance of the constitutional question – thus found a sympathetic audience, particularly in the middle-market and broadsheet newspapers with a more centre-right perspective. Reference to this friendly media environment is not to diminish David-son's contribution to the turnaround in Scottish Tory fortunes, but rather to further emphasise the effectiveness of unionism as a campaigning tool, particularly when wielded by an experienced leader.

Certainly, as Simpkins has argued of Davidson, 'Her embodiment of a distinctly Scottish brand of unionism has been able to mirror the views of a majority of the Scottish electorate, lending her the "authenticity" that is key to her popularity' (Simpkins 2018b). Arguably then, Davidson's most notable personal achievement was articulating this to Scots who remained unconvinced by independence, presenting her party in a way which could see unionist loyalty overcome historical aversion to the Tories. As Stephen Daisley opined, 'Her most important work . . . has been in helping to rein-vigorate Scottish Unionism as a confident political tradition. National-ism no longer preaches in an echo chamber, now the other viewpoint, the majority viewpoint, answers back' (*Scottish Daily Mail*, 22 July 2019).

Though effective, this myopic focus on the constitutional conundrum also drew criticism from some sections of the media, with Joyce McMillan high-lighting that the Scottish Tories seemed 'more reactive than proactive, more interested in saying "no" to independence than in saying "yes" to any viable set of policies' (*Scotsman*, 7 July 2017). The emergence of British national-ism – less commented upon by the media in Scotland – and Davidson's use of jingoistic language and imagery also drew limited comment, such as Garry Scott's observation regarding the hypocrisy of Davidson's campaign style: 'Her party and the wider Unionist movement were eager to suggest [in 2014] that nationalism encouraged ideas of Scottish superiority. This wasn't long before Ms Davidson appeared atop a British Army tank waving a Union Flag' (*Herald*, 27 January 2018).

Nevertheless, Davidson was to enjoy consistent characterisation as an emerging political heavyweight within both Scottish and British politics. Writing in the *Guardian*, Martin Kettle described her as 'just about the only Conservative with wide appeal in Scotland; and one of the most articulate defenders of the union in a thin field' (*Guardian*, 3 May 2019), while Chris

Deerin would describe her personal impact on her party as 'a remarkable achievement in a nation where "Tory" has largely been used as a term of abuse' (*Daily Mail*, 19 April 2017).

Other commentators, while accepting Davidson's achievements and progress as leader, also put such advances within a broader context, notably that she had been fortunate to have been in a position to react to constitutional developments. As Alan Cochrane noted, 'Whereas Maggie had the Falklands war as well as only Michael Foot and Neil Kinnock to contend with, Ruth has had Alex Salmond's and Nicola Sturgeon's obsession with independence . . . to boost her popularity' (*Telegraph*, 20 March 2018). Wright (2017) also drew attention to this dynamic, commenting that 'it is unlikely that the party could have reaped the full benefits of having a widely respected leader had there not also been shifts in Scottish public opinion that make the party's British Unionism . . . much less electorally toxic than used to be the case'.

Ruth Davidson's Media Style

A significant aspect of Davidson's personal political marketing was a willingness to engage in public relations stunts. 'She is a dab hand at photo opportunities,' wrote Daniel Boffey, 'aware that much of her job is to keep her party on the map' (*Observer*, 17 April 2016). Other media commentators drew attention to this image-conscious aspect of her campaigning style, with Pike describing how Davidson had 'appeared to be enjoying herself with a series of wacky photocalls' (Pike 2015: 248) during the 2015 election, and Jan Moir listing how the then Tory leader had 'ridden a bull, played bagpipes, served ice cream cones and – my favourite – straddled the gun of a tank flying the Union flag as it trundled through a glen' (*Daily Mail*, 27 May 2017).

Press photographs of Davidson tended to be positive – showing her open and smiling in public settings, or looking serious and authoritative during First Minister's Questions – and in the later years of her leadership, as highlighted earlier, her relationship with her partner was also utilised for publicity purposes. Pieces for soft news or magazine articles tended to be full of various shots, often aside glowing reviews of Davidson's personality and career achievements (*Vogue*, 26 April 2018). In an age of increasingly 'aestheticised' political presentation, partly as a result of 24-hour news and social media, it has been noted that the *image* of politicians has become far more important than their character, policies or values, this concern with style and appearance often seen as an established part of the political media (see Walsh 2015: 1026).

In a similar vein, Davidson was also adept at exploiting television appearances, both in terms of delivering the types of packaged soundbites which made up the main news bulletins (O'Neill et al. 2016: 303) and in less offi-cial or 'soft news' (North 2016: 356) settings. For example, her 2015 appear-ance on the news-based BBC panel show *Have I Got News for You* 'appeared to go down well with the audience, with a large positive response from the viewers posting online' (*Herald*, 24 October 2015), with Davidson's selec-tion for the 23 October broadcast being the first time a Scottish politician had appeared on the show since Charles Kennedy in 2009.

Davidson's ease in such a setting was already well developed by 2015, having been commented upon from the earliest days of her leadership, with Cochrane observing, 'Where she does score well is on television, where she looks self-assured and, above all, approachable. As a former broadcaster, this ability may not come as a huge surprise but it is one that the Scottish Tories should play for all it's worth' (*Telegraph*, 23 September 2012). Pre-dictions of a Tory revival at the 2015 general election, however, were more muted, and with good cause. Amid polls indicating that the party would come 'at best a poor third in Scotland' (*Financial Times*, 20 February 2015), Davidson tried to appear publicly confident of a comeback, stating that she would be 'bitterly disappointed if they did not make any gains' (*Scottish Daily Express*, 26 April 2015).

In the end, David Torrance's earlier belief that it was 'highly likely they will go into the election with one MP and come out of it with one or maybe two' (*Financial Times*, 20 February 2015) proved correct, with a post-referen-dum bump for the SNP seeing Nicola Sturgeon's party taking 56 out of 59 possible seats, leaving Labour, the Liberal Democrats and the Conservatives with a single constituency each. Davidson tried to put a positive spin on this, but given the party had recorded 'their lowest share of the vote in a general election in Scotland in more than 150 years' (*Herald*, 5 March 2016), any talk of electoral revival was generally given short shrift by the media.

At the Scottish elections of 2016, however, the role of the Conservatives was far more influential, as by this point their unionist message was far more coherent, developed and refined. Aiming to build a group to act 'as a bulwark against a second independence referendum' (*Aberdeen Evening Express*, 1 May 2015) had been a stated aim even before the election of 2015, but it was not until 2016 that the Scottish Tories could see them-selves becoming the official opposition in Holyrood. This was hailed as an 'historic result' and a 'seismic shift' in the press (*Daily Record*, 6 May 2016); for the first time since Davidson's election as leader in 2011, the Scottish Conservatives had shown themselves to be an electoral force in Scottish politics once again.

Leapfrogging Labour to become Holyrood's principal opposition party further enhanced Davidson's profile in the media, particularly as a result of her regular debates and exchanges with First Minister Nicola Sturgeon. The result – despite Davidson's party still lagging far behind the SNP in terms of overall support – helped demonstrate the effectiveness of campaigning on a unionist message, while at the same time showing others that the Tory revival might indeed be a genuine phenomenon. This latter narrative, which was of course largely attributed to Davidson, was further vindicated by the 2017 general election. Buoyed by poll results and aided by data modelling (*Daily Mail*, 23 April 2017), the Scottish Conservatives claimed 13 seats in Scotland, their strongest general election showing in several decades.

Unprecedented gains in Scotland had essentially 'saved' Theresa May's government, following the latter's ill-advised snap general election and resultant loss of an overall Tory majority in the Commons. Much was made of this unexpected electoral dynamic, with the contrast between the fortunes of the Scottish Conservatives (regarded as on the rise) and their UK party (seen to be losing electoral support) regularly highlighted in the media, a factor which inevitably saw Ruth Davidson's star rise even further in the weeks and months following the 2017 general election.

Amie Gordon (*Daily Mail*, 8 June 2017) described Scotland as 'now the one bright spot for the beleaguered Tories', while George Osborne viewed Davidson as 'the heroine of the party' (*Independent*, 12 June 2017). The apparent debt owed to the resurgence of the Conservatives in Scotland for this 'electoral lifeline' (*Financial Times*, June 2017) further boosted Davidson's profile beyond Scotland. She and her party were hailed as having 'saved the bacon of Theresa May's increasingly unpopular government' (*Scotsman*, 7 July 2017), with some speculating that Davidson would now wield considerable influence over the main UK party (Simpkins 2018a), a theme to which we shall return to later.

Having 'miraculously rehabilitated the party in the eyes of voters' (*Vogue*, 26 April 2018), Davidson's media standing peaked in the aftermath of the 2017 election, with commentators continuing to talk up her potential influence at Westminster. For example, it was stated that 'Mrs May will find that Ruth Davidson can also be bloody difficult' (*Daily Mail*, 10 June 2017), many believing her more moderate stance on Brexit was likely to have some impact on the UK Government's negotiating process. Even though there was (and has subsequently been) little evidence for this assertion, it remained a remarkably popular opinion, framing Davidson as a UK Conservative Party heavyweight.

George Osborne, then editor of the *Evening Standard*, also supported this point, stating on the *Andrew Marr Show* that 'if the Ruth Davidsons of the world are starting to flex their muscles, in my view that can only be a good thing' (*Independent*, 11 June 2017), while Davidson's colleague (and one-time leadership rival) Murdo Fraser said he believed the Scottish Conservatives 'can have a tremendous amount of leverage' (*Independent*, 10 June 2017). Describing her position as 'nigh unassailable', Tom Peterkin would also comment on Davidson's apparent ascendancy within the party: 'Barely a day goes by without her being tipped as a possible successor to Prime Minister Theresa May. Ms Davidson's breezy, good-humoured and earthy style has become a breath of fresh air for the UK party activists brought up on plummy public school accents' (*Scotsman*, 19 October 2017).

Peak Davidson, however, did not last long, with differences between the Scottish and UK Conservative parties over Brexit and the future of the Union gradually undermining claims regarding Davidson's influence on the party leadership in London. In particular, despite paying lip service to the 'precious' Union, as Alex Massie would note, Scottish unionists ended up 'wondering if they're actually the last true believers in an old-time religion that's suddenly become deeply unfashionable. They worry, with increasing reason, that they have been abandoned by people they mistakenly considered their co-religionists' (*Spectator*, 28 August 2019).

This gap between the priorities and values of the Scottish and UK parties was further highlighted during the 2019 Conservative leadership election, which culminated in Boris Johnson becoming UK party leader and therefore Prime Minister. As Daisley would argue of Davidson: 'It's her party that holds her back, and now it too faces being weighted down by its overbearing older sibling' (*Scottish Daily Mail*, 22 July 2019). Despite the gains experienced under her leadership, all was apparently not well in the upper reaches of the party, and so when Davidson announced her resignation in late August 2019 it was not wholly unexpected. Indeed, in May that year she had observed that 'binary constitutional referenda are enormously divisive', adding that she 'would happily never fight another one in her life', perhaps her clearest public indication that she was contemplating resignation (*Andrew Marr Show*, 5 May 2019).

Ruth Davidson's Resignation

Davidson's resignation was, as one journalist had it, 'an understated affair' (*Spectator*, 29 August 2019), with her message to the gathered media brief, stoic and guarded in equal measure. Another commented that there 'were no jokes, no customary vinegary asides aimed at her pinched First Minister opponent. Not even a flash of that signature smile' (*Daily Mail*, 30 August 2019). The tone and content of her speech generated little controversy; rather, what was highlighted was the lack of any direct challenge to Boris Johnson, despite the fact that his election to leadership of the party and therefore Prime Minister – not to mention his recent prorogation of Parliament – were considered factors in Davidson's decision to stand down.

This (missing) aspect of Davidson's speech drew praise from Chris Deerin, who said that it 'was telling that, even at the death, she refused to turn her gun on Johnson and his government. Loyalty – to the Union and the party – has been a hallmark of her leadership' (*New Statesman*, 29 August 2019). Some brief attention was devoted to speculating to whom Davidson was referring when she spoke of politicians who had 'failed to lead', with Darren Hunt seeing this as 'a guarded swipe at Scottish First Minister Ms Sturgeon' (*Express*, 29 August 2019), but James Forsyth asserting that her intended target was actually David Cameron: 'it wasn't hard to work out who she was talking about' (*Spectator*, August 2019).

In the days following Davidson's resignation, her stated decision to stand down for family reasons generated considerable discussion among commentators. Much of this opinion was, of course, understanding and empathetic, echoing the positive reaction from mothers who supported her decision as 'resulting from the pressures of being a new parent' (*Daily Mail*, 29 August 2019). Having heard Davidson admit in her speech that the pressures of her job had negatively impacted on various personal relationships, several journalists were at pains to provide an understanding perspective, with Deerin asserting that 'every parent knows the inner rewiring that comes with the birth of a child, the resettling of priorities and the fresh emotional imperatives' (*New Statesman*, 29 August 2019).

This theme – of maternal and professional demands influencing a sudden re-evaluation of priorities (*Spectator*, August 29 2019) for the outgoing Tory leader – also prompted pieces by journalists who shared her experiences (*Guardian*, 31 August 2019; *Daily Record*, 30 August 2019). Others drew attention to the fact Davidson had come in for criticism for (in the minds of some) implying that women could not combine motherhood with a demanding professional life. In a similar vein, she would also be used as an example of how issues of parenthood tended to be discussed differently when referring to male or female politicians, with the latter being seen as having to excuse choices and actions not expected of a man (*Guardian*, 31 August 2019).

Several commentators blamed Davidson's demise on her Westminster colleagues. As Alex Massie opined: 'Ruth Davidson's success was made possible by her opponents and her demise has been brought about by her erstwhile friends and colleagues. She is a victim of both Brexit and the UK Conservative party's undeniable shift to the right' (*Spectator*, 28 August 2019). Stephen Daisley also observed how the hard Brexit stance of many UK Conservatives had seen Davidson 'thrown into conflict with her party'

(*Scottish Daily Mail*, 29 August 2019). In this context, Davidson was often framed as having been underappreciated or undermined, with her own record seemingly beyond reproach.

Gerry Hassan drew attention to how the whole affair of Davidson's resignation indicated 'the strategic weakness of Scottish unionism and the limits of its influence in both the UK and Tories' (OpenDemocracy, 30 August 2019), a point repeated by Ian Swanson, who predicted the Tory revival would be halted if the Scottish Conservatives were to take a more extreme right position (*Edinburgh Evening News*, 2 September 2019). Perhaps the most colourful analogy came from Chris Deerin: 'On reflection, it's hard to avoid the feeling that Davidson, in the end, felt much like Geoffrey Howe: sent to the crease only to find that, before the first ball is bowled, her bat has been broken by the team captain' (*New Statesman*, 29 August 2019).

In engaging with this discourse as a whole, one cannot help but detect an overtone of bitterness, with several commentators (particularly those with established Tory sympathies) evidently bemused that the UK party could have allowed the Union's most experienced and recognised campaigner (and by extension the Union itself) to end up playing second fiddle to Brexit. The UK's decision to leave the European Union in June 2016 (and the majority Remain vote in Scotland) had long caused Davidson problems, though these were mitigated by claims of her ameliorating influence post-2017. Criticising her record, Sean Bell perceptively observed: 'Those who have watched Brexit's troubled evolution will be hard-pressed to specify what impact any of her vaunted interventions had on the whole tawdry process' (CommonSpace, 29 August 2019).

Few in the media were blind to the reality that Boris Johnson assuming office had been a major factor in influencing Davidson's decision to step down (*Washington Post*, 29 August 2019; *Guardian*, 29 August 2019). Much was made of Davidson and Johnson's interactions, with their divergent positions on Brexit leading to descriptions of their relationship as 'strained' (*Independent*, 29 August 2019). They had first clashed publicly during the 2016 debate, with Davidson describing Johnson as displaying a 'brazen, chauvinistic style' (*Courier*, 21 June 2016), even 'calling him a "liar" to his face' (OpenDemocracy, 30 August 2019). As Bill Perrigo would write, 'her distaste for Johnson was no secret' (*TIME*, 29 August 2019).

A series of tributes appeared in the wake of Davidson's resignation, some of which bordered on the sycophantic. For example, Daisley would describe her as 'not another run-of-the-mill leader who put on a brave face and managed the party's decline. She was transformative, resurrecting a political force long thought spent and reshaping Scottish politics in the process' (*Scottish Daily Mail*, 29 August 2019), while Amie Gordon said Davidson had 'become a tour de force in Scottish politics' (*Daily Mail*, 29 August 2019). The most glowing reviews tended to come in pieces which explicitly referenced Davidson's impact in relation to unionism within Scotland, but even commentators not normally recognised as sympathetic to the Tories granted praise to Davidson, such as Gerry Hassan's observation that Tory unionism had gained 'a new tone and attitude under Davidson. It was less apologetic, more populist, campaigning and challenging, and more prepared to mix it with the Scottish nationalists' (OpenDemocracy, 30 August 2019).

As had been the case for several years – during the period in which Davidson was being built up by large sections of the media – attention was once again drawn to the ex-leader's background and distinctiveness from the conventional 'Tory' image. The fact she was not perceived as a typical Conservative (*The Conversation*, 30 August 2019) received positive comment from various observers, with Sarah Smith stating that 'Ruth Davidson's unique selling point has always been that she doesn't look like and doesn't sound like a Tory' (BBC News online, 29 August 2019). Explicit allusions to her background were invoked to solidify this characterisation, with her secondary school being described as 'bog-standard' by Daisley, who would further highlight how Davidson 'was not born into privilege as so many prominent Tories are' (*Scottish Daily Mail*, 29 August 2019).

Described as a 'prominent campaigner against independence' (*Financial Times*, 29 August 2019), Davidson was also seen as having played an important part in the victory for the 'No' side in 2014 (*TIME*, 29 August 2019), with Andy Maciver concluding that it was in that year she 'became the right person, in the right place, at the right time' (*Scotsman*, 30 August 2019). That this narrative – which obviously contained a degree of truth but still exaggerated Davidson's actual importance to the 2014 outcome – gained traction in the media owed something to her own version of events. Davidson's resignation statement, for example, cited her involvement in the successful No campaign as her proudest political achievement (*Daily Mail*, 29 August 2019; BBC News online, 29 August 2019). Boris Johnson would also speak to this theme, responding to her resignation by insisting that 'her passionate support for our union was crucial to the [2014] result' (*Independent*, 29 August 2019).

Of course, some commentators challenged that dominant narrative. Sean Bell noted the irony that 'Davidson sought to finally end constitutional discourse in Scottish politics, and now leaves it discussing little else. If this is a legacy, it is a legacy of failure' (CommonSpace, 29 August 2019). Such negative portrayals of Davidson's legacy were not isolated to critiques of her supposed role in the 2014 decision, however, with her record (and the manner in which it was being reported) also drawing critical comment.

Dani Garavelli, for example, said of Davidson that what she 'saw was a woman who was photo-opportunity heavy and policy-lite, and who passed up every chance she had to be an ally to her sisters' (*Scotsman*, 31 August 2019). The media's role in building up Davidson to a standing which was perhaps beyond her actual achievements was also commented upon, with Bell describing the coverage as being 'so homogenous in style and opinion that it probably would have saved time if Scotland's columnists had simply got together and released a hasty cover of "Candle in the Wind"' (CommonSpace, 29 August 2019).

Hassan provided some explanation for this phenomenon, pointing to London-based commentators who were ignorant of both Scottish politics and the limits of Davidson's actual achievements:

> Davidson has been regularly hailed as an 'election winner', 'box office dyna-mite' and the saviour of the Tories, when the story is a little more qualified: a politician of populist touch who . . . took [the Scottish Tories] from fourth place to second place in votes. (OpenDemocracy, 30 August 2019)

Such appraisals of Davidson did not appear in a vacuum, as discussion of her diminishing importance (both in her own party and in wider UK politics) had appeared for several months before her eventual resignation.

'How quickly a political star can fade,' observed Massie (*Spectator*, 28 August 2019), with Deerin commenting how Davidson had become 'something of a ghost figure in Scottish politics, less often seen and heard' (*New Statesman*, 29 August 2019). That the media itself had played an integral role in creating a particular image of the Scottish Tory leader was rarely remarked upon in any self-reflective manner, though Massie's observation that 'as more than one Scottish cynic suggested, no politician was ever half as good as the Ruth Davidson some people imagined they could see' might have been more accurate than most (*Spectator*, 28 August 2019). The words of Hassan are also relevant here, in that he related Davidson's legacy to wider changes within political communication and deliberative democracy, saying that Davidson's departure left a variety of questions 'about the role of celebrity and personality in politics; of the role of the media in reporting on media savvy types; and how hype breeds hype and a politics of superfi-ciality' (OpenDemocracy, 30 August 2019).

Davidson's more general political legacy aside, there was a greater degree of uniformity of opinion in discussing Davidson's role in the revival of unionism in Scotland, it being apparent to both her supporters and detrac-tors that her resignation would certainly have an impact on the nature of the constitutional debate in Scotland. As Andy Maciver noted, 'she relegated the

Tory brand to the small print, pushing instead the Unionist identity and herself. Why? Because she knew the Tory brand had not recovered and was not a vote winner, whereas she and Unionism are' (*Scotsman*, 30 August 2019).

Others drew attention to the impact Davidson's departure would have on the Scottish Conservatives, unanimously seen as a blow to the party (*Spectator*, 29 August 2019; *Washington Post*, 29 August 2019), with Hassan predicting they would 'have to get used to politics as a more bumpy ride, without the protective shield of the Davidson leadership' (OpenDemocracy, 29 August 2019). Judged of far greater importance, however, was how the defence of the Union would be weakened without her leadership. Commenting on this, Daisley said the Union had lost its 'doughtiest defender' and its 'hardiest, most energetic champion' (*Scottish Daily Mail*, 29 August 2019).

Lamentations regarding Davidson's resignation, meanwhile, were most prevalent among journalists at conservative outlets, with Massie describing how 'Davidson's departure is a boon to the independence cause and a grievous blow to Unionism' (*Spectator*, 28 August 2019). Deerin echoed this sentiment in anointing Davidson the UK's 'most compelling and prominent advocate north of the border', adding that she was 'a proper star, of the kind that are all too rare in politics' and that there was now 'no obvious figure in any party to take her place' (*New Statesman*, 29 August 2019).

This latter point, that in the event of a second referendum there would likely be a lack of leadership on the 'No' side (*Scotsman*, 30 August 2019), was also widely discussed, reflecting the unique position Davidson (with the assistance of several branches of the media) had fashioned for herself in contemporary Scottish politics. In several pieces discussing her resignation and its potential impact on the future of the Union, one is struck by an evident sadness, disappointment or frustration at Davidson's decision, with there being something akin to the outpouring of grief from fans when a football team suddenly loses its star player. As Bell put it, so 'fulsome were some of the tributes, one might be forgiven for thinking their writers were in mourning not just for Davidson's leadership, but for all that they had invested in that project' (CommonSpace, 29 August 2019).

Overall then, the media response to Davidson's resignation as leader of the Scottish Conservatives was to frame it in terms of the impact it would have on popular support for unionism, a reaction entirely in keeping with the dominant narrative anchors which had characterised coverage since the referendum. Davidson was only ever truly relevant in Scottish politics as a result of her stance on the constitutional issue, and the extensive coverage of her resignation clearly demonstrated the perception of how integral to the future of the United Kingdom she had become.

Conclusion

The main conclusion to draw from this overview of media coverage of Ruth Davidson is that the former Scottish Conservative leader had something of a special niche in the Scottish press and broadcast media, an interaction which was not necessarily symbiotic, but was at the very least mutually beneficial on the whole. With the majority of Scottish newspapers (often explicitly) unionist in their constitutional preferences, they found in Davidson an acceptable champion for a cause they sought to promote. Rarely off-message and reliable for soundbites and photo opportunities, she could often rely on them for positive coverage (particularly during and after the 2014 referendum).

Though Davidson's immediate future is unclear, she will continue as an MSP and there is every likelihood that she may yet feature prominently in a second independence referendum. Should she decide to return to front-line politics in this capacity, it is likely she would find a relieved response from the Scottish media, many of whom seem increasingly worried and pessimistic about how the Scottish Tories (and, more importantly, the Union) may perform in the years ahead.

EIGHT

The Conservative 'Territorial Code' under Strain

Richard Hayton

Introduction

The Conservative Party, the late Jim Bulpitt (1982: 169) argued, 'is the party of central autonomy'. And while the nature of that central autonomy might have varied over time, its pursuit has, Bulpitt suggested, remained the defining feature of the Conservatives' 'territorial code' since the late nineteenth century. The party leadership has prioritised elite control over the main fields of 'high politics' in order to defend Conservative interests through the exercise of national power and to demonstrate governing competence as part of its electoral statecraft (Bulpitt 1986).

This chapter argues that since returning to power at Westminster in 2010, Conservative statecraft has broadly followed Bulpitt's schema. However, it also suggests the party's territorial code has come under increasing strain, as the political and constitutional consequences of the independence referendum in Scotland and the EU referendum vote have unfolded. The primary focus of the chapter is on the Conservative Party as a state-wide actor, namely through governments led by David Cameron (2010–16), Theresa May (2016–19), and Boris Johnson (2019–). In terms of statecraft and territorial politics, it concentrates on devolution and the centre's dealings with Scotland, as well as the place of Scottish conservatism – revived under the leadership of Ruth Davidson – in relation to its UK counterpart.

Sovereignty, Unionism and Devolution in Scotland

The defining principle of the United Kingdom's constitution is parliamentary sovereignty, which for Conservatives is 'the cornerstone of the nation'

(Aughey 2018: 33). The Conservatives are also commonly regarded (and have regarded themselves) as the party of the Union, a position embedded following their merger with the Liberal Unionists in the early twentieth century, and encapsulated by the change of name to the Conservative and Unionist Party in 1909. If, as its official historian Lord Lexden (*Spectator*, 2 May 2015) has asserted, 'the supreme object of the Conservative Party is the preservation of the nation', this has been understood via a defence of the twin pillars of the Union and parliamentary sovereignty.

Conservative opposition to Labour's plans for devolution, vigorously articulated by John Major at the general elections of 1992 and 1997, and then by William Hague during the 1997 devolution referendums, was rooted in this worldview. This 'high unionism', as Aughey (2018: 92) terms it, continues to prevail in much of the Conservative Party, even as proponents increasingly acknowledge a conflict with the party's electoral interests. The Conservatives' unionism could, as Seawright (1999) put it, be understood as an 'important matter of principle', although it was one that not all the party, especially in England, remained strongly attached to.

For Gamble, alongside the unionism that dominated the party in the twentieth century, an older tradition of English Toryism can also be identified, which has seen a revival in Conservative circles since devolution to Scotland and Wales in the late 1990s. For the English Tories, any accommodation with devolution was difficult, given 'What mattered most for Tories was that the principle of undivided national sovereignty – Crown-in-Parliament – should be upheld. This meant a strong, centralised executive authority whose writ could not be challenged within the territory of the British state' (Gamble 2016: 362). So, while 'English Tories have always considered the Union to be desirable', it is a secondary concern, behind their desire to preserve and defend the sovereignty of the Anglo-British state (Gamble 2016: 360). While the leadership of the UK-wide Conservative Party has retained a unionist stance, Gamble detects that this 'makes less and less sense to many party members and MPs, and the political logic is leading the party away from defending the Union as a priority' (Gamble 2016: 361). These sentiments have also found expression in influential elements of the Conservative commentariat and intellectual circles, for example in the writings of journalist Simon Heffer and philosopher Roger Scruton (see English et al. 2009).

As Wellings (2012) has convincingly demonstrated, the Conservative attachment to parliamentary sovereignty inhibited the rise of English nationalism, which instead found its primary expression via Euroscepticism. This Anglo-Britishness rose to further prominence in the 2016 referendum on EU membership and shaped much of the ensuing debate over how Brexit ought to be fulfilled (Wellings 2019). The strength of ideological commitment in the Conservative Party to the reassertion of sovereignty through Brexit was starkly illustrated by polling of members which found that more than half (54 per cent) prioritised it over the survival of the party, while almost two thirds (63 per cent) favoured leaving the EU even if it meant Scottish independence and Irish reunification (YouGov 2019).

Devolution to Scotland prompted Conservatives such as Heffer (1999) to call for English independence. This was not a position entertained by the Conservative hierarchy at Westminster who, in the words of Lord Strathclyde, regarded English nationalism as 'of no serious intellectual interest to Conservatives, who are a United Kingdom Party' (quoted in Hayton 2012: 85). Given their initial hostility to the proposed Scottish Parliament, 'the Conservative approach to territorial management has proven surprisingly flexible' (Randall and Seawright 2012: 107). William Hague (1998) claimed that devolution struck 'at the heart of the constitutional arrangement that has held our Union together for hundreds of years', but also acknowledged that the Conservatives could not hope to 'unscramble the omelette' and instead had to find new ways to bolster the Union while accommodating devolution.

Conservative attention at Westminster then turned to considering possible mechanisms for 'English votes for English laws' (Hayton 2012: 84–9). The Scottish Conservatives missed the opportunity, floated by some figures, radically to embrace devolution by endorsing full fiscal responsibility for Scotland (Torrance 2012). For John Curtice, by advocating a 'no/no' in the 1997 referendum, the party found itself 'on what proved to be the wrong side of the devolution debate', with lasting negative consequences for its electoral prospects in Scotland (Curtice 2012: 117). Holyrood did, nonetheless, provide an institutional platform for the party in Scotland, and helped ensure its survival (ibid.).

Returning to Bulpitt's framework: in spite of initial opposition, the Conservatives were able to accept New Labour's devolution arrangements as they did not threaten central autonomy (Convery 2014a). Indeed, they arguably reinforced the dual polity, as the activities of the devolved institutions were confined to matters of low politics (Bradbury 2006), meaning that in 2010 the Conservatives 'inherited a set of arrangements which did not involve making painful concessions. Centre autonomy in terms of devolution had largely been achieved' (Convery 2014a: 29). Conservative Unionism, articulated forcefully by David Cameron as Leader of the Opposition between 2005 and 2010, focused on the benefits it brought to all parts of the United Kingdom in terms of the centre's capacity for high politics, whether that be national security, foreign policy or economic prosperity (Randall and Seawright 2012: 109; Aughey 2018: 92–3). The constitutional arguments were however, far from settled, as Cameron would discover in office.

The Cameron Premiership, 2010–16

David Cameron's commitment to the Union was seemingly heartfelt and pragmatic, yet his premiership encompassed two referendums which threw its continued existence into doubt. Cameron's pragmatic unionism was illustrated by his decision not to attempt to unravel the Barnett formula (Randall and Seawright 2012: 109), and the implementation, via the Scotland Act 2012, of the Calman Commission's recommendation to grant further powers to the Scottish Parliament (Convery 2016a: 29). In his assessment of the state of Conservative unionism elsewhere in this volume, Alan Convery convincingly portrays Cameron as the 'supreme recent interpreter of the pragmatic approach' (Chapter 9). His acquiescence to the SNP's desire to hold an independence referendum following their victory at the 2011 Scottish Parliament elections can also be seen as integral to this outlook. While acknowledging that a referendum was a 'massive gamble', Cameron (2019) justified the decision in his memoirs: 'Denying it would merely be delaying it; and delaying it would ignite a level of grievance that made independence inevitable.' So as much as unionists might dislike it, a referendum on the unambiguous question of 'yes' or 'no' to independence had become, in Cameron's view, the only way to secure the Union's long-term future.

The very occurrence of the 2014 referendum on Scottish independence illustrated how much unionism had shifted in the last few decades. Discussing the debate on devolution in the 1970s, Richard Rose contrasted the position in Northern Ireland vis-à-vis that on the British mainland:

> Whereas in Ulster the Westminster Parliament is ready to allow Northern Ireland to secede unilaterally, the 1974–9 devolution debate showed Westminster's adamant view that under no circumstances would Scots or Welsh be allowed to vote about independence in a referendum. Westminster is not prepared to admit that Scotland or Wales has the unilateral right to withdraw from the United Kingdom, should a majority there wish to do so. (Rose 1982: 129–30)

After more than a decade of devolution and the ascent to majority government of the SNP in Scotland, such a position would have been, as Cameron correctly calculated, untenable. So, while the UK Government insisted its Scottish counterpart needed permission to legally hold an independence referendum, it did not dispute its democratic legitimacy in doing so. The limitations on the capacity of the centre to use parliamentary sovereignty to uphold the territorial integrity of the United Kingdom were therefore laid bare. Sovereignty, it appeared, rested with the 'Scottish people', as Scottish nationalists of various hues had long argued. Yet, allowing the referendum to take place posed a clear threat to high politics and Conservative statecraft, prompting some in the party to fiercely oppose the decision (Cameron 2019). While the Conservatives could accept devolution, given it did not pose a threat to central autonomy, the break-up of the Union would be an entirely different matter, prompting multiple complex issues for Westminster to resolve.

In the end, Cameron's gamble paid off and the threat to the Union was averted with a solid, if far from crushing, 'No' vote (55 to 45 per cent). However, while opponents of independence won the ballot, they arguably lost the campaign (Moran 2017: 81). The largely negative case posited against independence, stressing the economic risks and financial uncertainty it could bring, was effective but did not appear to signal a rejuvenation of unionist sentiment. Panicked by tightening polls in the dying days of the campaign, the leaders of the main unionist parties at Westminster – Cameron, Nick Clegg and Ed Miliband – made a 'vow' to the people of Scotland to deliver maximal devolution if they voted to remain part of the United Kingdom. And, in a move he later conceded was poorly timed (Cameron 2019), on the morning the referendum result was declared, the Prime Minister declared that 'England must also be heard' and that 'English votes for English laws' (EVEL) should be introduced at Westminster (Hayton 2015).

Together, the decisions to endorse further devolution and EVEL signalled the extent to which Conservative territorial statecraft had been transformed. The traditional Westminster view of the United Kingdom as bound together by parliamentary sovereignty and a political union – a British political union – was being irreversibly altered. The central autonomy model had always meant that Conservatives were comfortable with the idea of the UK as a union, rather than a unitary state. However, the English doctrine of parliamentary sovereignty meant that, as Keating (2018: 161) put it, the 'one thing unionism could not accept was the existence of parliamentary institutions in the component nations, arguing that, precisely because these were nations, such institutions would inevitably assume sovereignty rights themselves'.

But this was now self-evidently the case. The Scotland Act 2016, which implemented 'the vow', acknowledged the permanence of the Scottish Parliament in the UK's constitutional arrangements, and further stated that it could only be abolished if the Scottish people provided their consent via a referendum. The Act also gave statutory recognition to the Sewel Convention. The ambiguities inherent in the UK's constitutional arrangements had long meant they could be viewed rather differently from alternative vantage points, with English Tories able to retain their Dicean view of sovereignty while unionists north of the border could maintain that this did not hold true in Scottish constitutional law (Keating 2018). However, what Convery (Chapter 9) characterises as the 'ultra-unionist' view had seemingly become an historical anachronism as the UK morphed into a quasi-federal state.

In Ruth Davidson, Cameron (2019) felt he had found someone who embodied 'the pro-devolution, anti-independence, modern, compassionate Conservative Party' that he wanted to see across the UK. Davidson's charisma and political skill as leader of the Scottish Conservatives was showcased in the EU referendum campaign, and undoubtedly helped fuel an unexpected revival in the party's fortunes in Scotland (see Chapter 2 in this volume). Davidson's success in presenting unionism as a positive alternative to separatism suggested the Conservatives had, finally, found a way to reconcile their commitment to the Union with a positive approach to devolution, championing further powers for Scotland within the UK. This revised territorial code was, however, formulated in the context of UK membership of the European Union, which had, as Keating (2018: 168) noted, 'provided an important external support system for the devolution process, compensating for its incompleteness'. Cameron's decision to hold an in–out referendum on Europe, therefore, brought the sustainability of this territorial code into question.

Cameron's justification for holding a referendum on EU membership in 2016 echoed the reasoning he gave for consenting to the plebiscite in Scotland in 2014. He felt that the pressure to hold a referendum 'was strong and growing', and that if he did not promise to do so, a future government would – quite possibly a Conservative administration recommending a vote to leave (Cameron 2019). It was therefore better to grasp the nettle and have more control over the process than to allow further anti-EU resentment to build. In short, a referendum, he believed, 'was not only necessary to achieve the changes we required to secure Britain's interests *within the EU*; it was needed to settle this issue *within the UK*' (Cameron 2019, original emphasis). Of course, the idea that complex constitutional questions could be settled by way of a deceptively simple binary question was naive at best, the shifting sands of the devolution 'settlement' since 1997 being a case in point. Little, if any, consideration appears to have been given to the implications for territorial politics in the decision to hold a referendum on EU membership. The decision was instead largely driven by party political considerations related to internal management and the potential electoral threat posed by the UK Independence Party (UKIP). Given the presence of just one Conservative MP representing a constituency north of the border, the Scottish dimension hardly figured in this calculation. It would be left to Cameron's successor, Theresa May, to grapple with the territorial fallout from this fateful decision.

The 'precious bond' under Strain: Theresa May, 2016–19

In her very first statement as Prime Minister, Theresa May reaffirmed her party's long-standing attachment to the Union, observing that:

> not everybody knows this, but the full title of my party is the Conservative and *Unionist* Party, and that word 'unionist' is very important to me. It means we believe in the Union: the precious, precious bond between England, Scotland, Wales and Northern Ireland. But it means something else that is just as important: it means we believe in a union not just between the nations of the United Kingdom but between all of our citizens, every one of us, whoever we are and wherever we're from. (May 2016a)

Like her predecessor, May's commitment to the Union was heartfelt. It was integral to her understanding of Conservatism, and of the vocation of the Conservative Party to which she had dedicated so much of her life. May was a practising Christian and, as Aughey (2018: 35) noted, her statement of unionist belief had an almost religious quality to it, 'much like the reaffirmation of a vow, of keeping faith with the sacramental rights of party tradition'. Seeking to stay faithful to this unionism while also pursuing what she regarded as the central mission of her premiership – delivering Brexit in a form that satisfied an English Tory yearning for the reassertion of national sovereignty – would ultimately prove to be a contradiction May could not reconcile.

Perhaps inevitably, like most Conservatives May displayed an essentially English understanding of unionism. From this vantage point, the United Kingdom becomes in essence an extension of England, 'an England with appendages' (Aughey 2018: 38). The issue of Brexit would bring the neglected inconsistencies in unionist thinking to the forefront of national political debate. While it is possible to trace a tradition of Euroscepticism on the left of British politics, the Brexit project was very much the child of the right, emerging from a long-standing and often bitter debate in Conservative circles regarding the UK's place in the European integrative project.

These tensions could be traced to an ideological shift that took place in the Conservative Party during the Thatcher era, when the English Tory view of Crown-in-Parliament national sovereignty reasserted itself (Hayton 2012: 62). The displacement of a more pluralist 'One Nation' Conservatism with this exclusivist view of sovereignty reflected the influence of Powellite thinking on Thatcherism. Enoch Powell was, of course, a fierce opponent of devolution to any part of the United Kingdom, believing the integration and integrity of the whole state, including Northern Ireland, were imperative to resist 'other threats to British nationhood' such as the EEC (European Economic Community) (Corthorn 2012: 969). Unsurprisingly, then, under Margaret

Thatcher the Conservatives' previous flirtation with Scottish devolution under Edward Heath was shelved. The Conservatives' journey from being the 'party of Europe' to the party of Brexit thus began in the Thatcher era, as the debate about European integration came to be framed in terms of this understanding of national sovereignty. The tagline of the 2016 Leave campaign, 'Take back control', reflected this traditionalist Westminster-model view of the United Kingdom as a unitary state (Keating 2018).

This was a view May embraced in her understanding of what 'delivering' Brexit entailed. Although she was widely ridiculed for the soundbite 'Brexit means Brexit', which she coined during her party leadership campaign, May did have a clear view of what Brexit meant, which she spelled out repeatedly. As she told the Conservative Party conference in October 2016:

> Whether people like it or not, the country voted to leave the EU. And that means we are going to leave the EU. We are going to be a fully-independent, sovereign country, a country that is no longer part of a political union with supranational institutions that can override national parliaments and courts. And that means we are going, once more, to have the freedom to make our own decisions on a whole host of different matters, from how we label our food to the way in which we choose to control immigration. (May 2016b)

As the Prime Minister repeatedly stated, her objective in negotiating Brexit was 'taking back control of our borders, money and laws', an aphorism that became the title of a government command paper justifying the Withdrawal Agreement made with the EU in November 2018 (HM Government 2018). 'Borders', in this context, referred primarily to immigration, which had been a major driver of the Leave vote, and the government's policy of ending the free movement of people to and from the EU. But it was the specific territorial issue of the border between Northern Ireland and the Republic of Ireland, where both sides professed a commitment to avoiding a hard border, 'including any physical infrastructure or related checks and controls' (European Commission 2017: 7), that would become the key sticking point for May in her efforts to secure a deal.

The UK Government and the EU agreed a 'backstop' position was needed to ensure an open border on the island of Ireland, in the event that the future trade relationship between the bloc and the UK (to be negotiated post-Brexit) could not guarantee this. The initial backstop proposal was for Northern Ireland to remain in the EU Customs Union and Single Market, which would have necessitated a customs and regulatory border in the Irish Sea (Institute for Government 2019). Such a solution would have effectively maintained central autonomy by leaving Westminster free to pursue alternative trade and regulatory policies for the rest of the UK, and would have been consistent with the long-term strategy of disengaging Britain from Northern Ireland pursued by both Conservative and Labour governments over the previous three decades. In the 1993 Downing Street Declaration, for example, the UK Government had stated explicitly that it had 'no selfish or strategic interest in Northern Ireland' – in effect, official recognition by John Major's administration that the bond between Conservative and Ulster Unionism had been broken some time before (Gamble 1995: 15). However, May found herself unable to accept this solution, declaring it a threat to the 'constitutional integrity of the UK' (quoted in Institute for Government 2019).

In truth, May's hands were tied following her disastrous 2017 general election campaign, which left the Conservatives without a majority at Westminster. Following this, her government was dependent upon support from the Democratic Unionist Party (DUP) of Northern Ireland. For the DUP, any proposal dividing Northern Ireland from the rest of the UK was unacceptable, and the idea was dismissed. Following this, the backstop included in the Withdrawal Agreement included a UK-wide customs territory. However, this proved unacceptable to hard-line Eurosceptics on the Conservative benches, who argued it limited UK sovereignty by potentially tying the UK to the EU for an indefinite period. In short, a compromise between the desire to assert national sovereignty and manage the territorial questions posed by Brexit could not be found.

For virtually all Conservatives, including May, the decision to leave the European Union was one that 'the country' as a singular entity took. The fact that two of the nations of the United Kingdom, Scotland and Northern Ireland, voted Remain was of no greater consequence than the fact that a region within England (London) did so. The government therefore rejected the suggestion that the consent of the devolved administrations was required. However, this desire to uphold this principle of undivided national sovereignty brought the Conservative territorial code into question, undermining the party's unionist credentials by bringing Westminster into direct conflict with Scotland in particular.

In pushing through the EU Withdrawal Act 2018 in the face of a refusal by the Scottish Parliament to grant legislative consent, May's government defied the Sewel Convention, reasserting Westminster sovereignty (a position upheld in 2017 by the Supreme Court). In essence, as Convery (Chapter 9) argues, the UK Government adopted an 'ultra-unionist' position. Although this arguably strengthened the power of the central state in constitutional terms, it weakened the revised central autonomy model pursued by David Cameron, which had been built on 'respect' for the UK's non-English nations and their democratic institutions, as well as shared consent for any constitutional changes. In short, whether May intended it or not, the primacy in her party of English Toryism was asserted. This was a direction of travel that would continue under her successor, Boris Johnson.

'Do or die': Boris Johnson, 2019–

If David Cameron and Theresa May could both plausibly be thought of as conforming to a tradition of Conservative and Unionist leaders who took seriously, as the latter put it, both elements in their party's name, the same could not be said for Boris Johnson. Johnson's carefully constructed political persona of bumbling, caddish, public school-educated amateurism embodied the new English Toryism identified by Gamble (2016), as did his previously expressed views on the Union. In one of his *Daily Telegraph* columns for example, just a couple of years into the process, Johnson argued that devolution was 'causing all the strains that its opponents predicted, and in allowing the Scots to make their own laws, while free-riding on English taxpayers, it is simply unjust . . . I propose that we tell them to hop it' (*Telegraph*, 1 February 2001).

During the 2019 Conservative Party leadership election, Ruth Davidson made clear her unease regarding a possible Johnson premiership, endorsing at first Sajid Javid, then Michael Gove and, in the final run-off, Jeremy Hunt, over the eventual winner. Davidson was joined by a majority of Conservative MSPs in backing Hunt, whom they praised for his willingness to prioritise the protection of the Union above everything else, even Brexit (*Scotsman*, 27 June 2019). For Johnson, by contrast, Brexit represented 'do or die', a sentiment that resonated with the majority of (largely English) Conservative members who had backed him by a margin of two to one in the final all-member ballot.

In a wide-ranging reshuffle following his arrival at Number 10, Johnson sacked the Secretary of State for Scotland, David Mundell, who tweeted that he would (from the backbenches) hold the new Prime Minister to account 'on his commitments to the Union'. Mundell, like Davidson, had favoured Remain in the EU referendum, and his apprehension regarding Johnson centred around his insistence that the Conservatives must back a 'no-deal' Brexit if an agreement could not be reached before the deadline of 31 October 2019. A no-deal Brexit, Mundell had warned during the leadership election, would fuel Scottish nationalism and put the future of the Union in peril (*Guardian*, 6 July 2019).

Davidson had expressed similar sentiments and indicated that she would not back a no-deal outcome, which raised the prospect of every political party at Holyrood opposing the position of the Westminster government on the biggest issue facing the country in decades. Her resignation as Scottish Conservative leader, barely a month into Johnson's premiership, was driven by the conflict of loyalties she found herself facing, unable to commend to the electorate a Prime Minister she feared threatened the Union, the defence of which had become strongly associated with her political persona (*New Statesman*, 29 August 2019).

These unionist fears were not without grounds. One poll conducted during the Conservative leadership election campaign gave Johnson an approval rating of minus 37, and indicated a 6 percentage-point lead for 'yes' in a hypothetical independence referendum held under his premiership (*The Times*, 23 June 2019). Analysis of the polling evidence showed a consistent uptick in support for independence during 2019, the source of which was an increase among voters who had backed Remain in the EU referendum, 51 per cent of whom now favoured independence (up from 47 per cent a year earlier). Amongst Leavers, 64 per cent continued to oppose independence (Curtice 2019).

For all her insistence that 'no deal would be better than a bad deal', Theresa May's cautious unionism made the chances of her ever sanctioning it remote. The unexpected revival of the Scottish Conservatives at the 2017 general election also meant their voice (and votes) could potentially have been decisive should such a scenario have arisen under May. Johnson's determination to push for a general election if his pathway to Brexit continued to be blocked by the House of Commons, however, altered that dynamic and opened up the possibility of the Conservatives campaigning for no deal against what it would portray as a 'Remain alliance' of assorted opposition parties. Importantly, the Scottish Conservatives, under Davidson's interim successor Jackson Carlaw, U-turned and pledged support for a no-deal Brexit during the UK Conservative Party conference (*Herald*, 29 September 2019).

It is worth remembering that for all the focus on the possibility of a no-deal Brexit under Johnson, he repeatedly stated that it was not his preferred outcome, describing such an eventuality as 'a failure of statecraft' (*Guardian*, 2 October 2019). In rejecting the Withdrawal Agreement negotiated by his predecessor, Johnson eventually displayed some willingness to treat Northern Ireland differently, allowing it to align certain regulations with the Republic in order to ease cross-border trade. A proposed 'veto' for Stormont also indicated a desire to shift matters to the periphery. Tariffs, however, were to be reserved as a matter of 'high politics', Brexiteers such as Johnson considering the capacity for the UK to negotiate its own trade deals as central to their vision of a 'Global Britain' (Daddow 2019). Compromising UK territorial integrity, in that sense, was not something they were willing to countenance.

Conclusion: Strained to Breaking Point?

The consequences of the 2016 vote to leave the European Union continue to reverberate throughout the British political system. And as the chief architects of Brexit, the Conservatives found themselves struggling to devise, articulate or implement an effective statecraft response to the multiple challenges it produced. Nowhere was this truer than in the field of territorial politics, where the party's operational code came under intense strain. The pro-devolution unionist position the party had arrived at under the leadership of David Cameron and Ruth Davison provided for central autonomy and sub-state national differences in politics and policy, while sidestepping more profound questions regarding national sovereignty.

As an instinctive unionist Theresa May initially sought to uphold this framework, but was unable to find a path through the competing demands she faced from different wings of her party. Brexit found the 'English Tory' view of parliamentary sovereignty in the ascendency, most obviously when Boris Johnson became premier, and led to the reassertion – at least temporarily – of Westminster primacy over the whole of the United Kingdom and its devolved institutions. This undermined central autonomy by drawing the UK Government into conflict with the devolved institutions and into the quagmire of the Irish border issue, which had been effectively depoliticised via the 1990s peace process.

A so-called 'soft' Brexit, with the UK remaining in the European Single Market and Customs Union, was initially favoured by Ruth Davidson as the best way to safeguard the future of the Union. While it would certainty have circumvented many of the territorial issues that arose, it proved incompatible with an English Tory mindset which came to dominate the Brexit debate both within the Conservative Party and beyond. On the other side of the equation, it was difficult to avoid the conclusion that a no-deal Brexit would make the break-up of the United Kingdom more likely, possibly leading to a vote on Irish reunification and raising demands for a second independence referendum in Scotland.

While Johnson suggested he would refuse to sanction any such request from Holyrood, such a strategy seemed likely to further fan the flames of Scottish nationalism (Kenny and Sheldon 2019a: 11). Brexit might, on the other hand, make the practicalities of Scottish independence all the more complex, as the border question in Ireland could be writ large between England and Scotland if the latter was to remain part of the EU while the former departed. In short, the territorial politics of the UK remained highly unstable. As Bulpitt (1982: 144) remarked, 'for the Conservative Party the

United Kingdom is, and always has been, a particularly difficult piece of political real estate to manage'. Whether the party could navigate Brexit and devise a new territorial code to hold the Union together was far from clear. If it could not, then it would likely constitute the greatest failure of traditional Conservative statecraft.

NINE

The Scottish Conservative Party and the Three Unionisms

Alan Convery

Introduction

If there is one thing all Scottish Conservatives can agree on, it is their commitment to the Union. No other issue unites the party in quite the same way. However, there are many ways for Scotland to remain part of the United Kingdom and the party's unionist thinking has had to evolve to accommodate both devolution and the independence referendum of 2014. Brexit also presents new challenges to conceptions of unionism and the type of union Scotland can expect if it continues to reject independence.

This chapter suggests that Conservative unionist thinking can be broadly split into three camps: the ultra-unionists, the devo-pragmatists and the radical reformers. First, there are the *ultra-unionists*. This group broadly accepts the existence of the Scottish Parliament but insists that nothing has changed in terms of the sovereignty and supremacy of Westminster. Second, there are the *devo-pragmatists*, who represent the majority of Conservatives in believing that devolution fundamentally altered the British constitution but the priority is to find a practical accommodation with this new reality rather than trying to design or codify a new settlement. The task now is rather: how can the old and new British constitutions (Bogdanor 2011) rub along with the minimum of fuss? David Cameron was the archetypal devo-pragmatist. Ruth Davidson also arrived (via a circuitous route) at a devo-pragmatist position that she was able to exploit for electoral gain. Finally, the *radical reformers* believe not only in the transformational effect of devolution, but also that the Conservatives should be proposing a more codified and explicitly federal British constitution. This group is currently outside the Conservative Party mainstream.

This chapter argues that ultra-unionist thinking gradually gave way to pragmatic accommodation during the Conservatives' period in opposition (1997–2010), particularly under David Cameron's leadership. The further devolution reforms of the Coalition Government (2010–2015) and the Conservative Governments (2015–), including the decision to grant permission to hold an independence referendum, represent the best of this pragmatic Conservative tradition. However, under the pressures of Brexit, the Conservative Party has displayed an atavistic tendency to reach back to its previous ultra-unionism. It is unclear whether this regression represents a fundamental shift or a temporary response to a difficult situation. Ruth Davidson's resignation as leader in 2019 may in time come to be seen as the bookend on a period of pragmatic adaptation that finally allowed the party to embrace both the Scottish Parliament and a steadfast commitment to the Union. The radical reformers remain marginal (including in Scotland) but their thinking, it is suggested, shows the only long-term response to preserving the United Kingdom.

Unionism in the Scottish Conservative Party after 2014

The Conservative Party used to boast a popular and sophisticated brand of unionism. Its genius lay in its ability to reconcile a commitment to the UK state with a commitment to Scottish distinctiveness. The Conservatives created the Scottish Office at the end of the nineteenth century and steadily increased its powers over the course of the twentieth. This policy of gradual 'devolution' of responsibility to the Scottish Office formed the basis of the Scottish Parliament's powers in 1999. The Conservatives thus established the idea of 'administrative devolution' (Mitchell 2003) at the heart of their thinking about the accommodation of Scottish distinctiveness. This process allowed the Conservative Party to unselfconsciously continue to use the Westminster model as its organising perspective for British government.

For Mitchell (1990: 8), unionism has three aspects: 'as a social and cultural meaning, as an expression of Scotland's constitutional position within the United Kingdom, and a jurisprudential meaning as the sovereignty of parliament'. The social and cultural meaning of unionism in Scotland, linked to religious sectarianism and the remnants of the union with Ireland, at first declined and then largely disappeared. In expressing Scotland's position within the United Kingdom, unionism, particularly in the Conservative Party, came to prize preservation of the Union above Scottish distinctiveness. This aspect of unionism came to be taken for granted, rather than articulated afresh for a new century without Ireland or Empire.

Finally, in paying such close attention to parliamentary sovereignty, unionism in Scotland placed limits on the scope of its own constitutional thinking. In his speech to the 1994 Conservative Party conference, for instance, Ian Lang said the argument about a 'democratic deficit' was 'essentially a separatist one, amounting as it does to a rejection of the sovereignty of the United Kingdom Parliament' (Lang 1994: 232). Both Lang and Michael Forsyth articulated the view that devolution would lead inevitably to separation (Lang 1994: 236; Forsyth 1995: 248). Unionism therefore subscribed to a conception of the British state with Parliament at its centre (Mitchell 1990: 9–11).

We may add to these three a fourth strand of Conservative unionist thinking that became particularly important in the 1980s and 1990s: the idea that Scotland needed to be saved by Westminster from its left-wing self (Mitchell and Convery 2012). Thus, Forsyth argues that attempts in the 1980s to resurrect devolution were made by 'leftist politicians hoping to ring-fence Scotland's collectivist and interventionist establishment and protect it from the free-market reforms of the Conservative Government' (Forsyth 1995: 246). Similarly, Baroness Thatcher's article in the *Scotsman* urging Scots to vote 'no' in the 1997 referendum argued that true devolution to the Scottish people would come through cutting government expenditure. She warned, however, that this 'is the last thing which so many still socialist-minded Scottish politicians want' (*Scotsman*, 9 September 1997). The implication was that devolution for Scotland would reverse the hard-won economic gains of the previous 18 years.

But as voting patterns in Scotland and the rest of the Union began to diverge in the late 1950s, the Conservatives failed to see the logical end point of the system they had created. As Mitchell (1990: 12) argued, 'the problem for Unionism has been that, in maintaining a distinctive Scottish aspect, the danger always existed that a demand to incorporate a democratic component would be made'. The 1993 government paper, *Scotland in the Union: A Partnership for Good* (HM Government 1993), marked both the final and most sophisticated exposition of Conservative unionism without devolution (Kidd 2008: 35). And the result of the 1997 general election, which left them without a single MP in Scotland, ensured the Conservatives would have to think again.

However, the Conservatives also failed to renew their unionism in opposition (1997–2010), both in Scotland and at a UK level. In Scotland, they settled on a grudging acceptance of the Scottish Parliament and generally avoided thinking about how it might be improved. At the UK level, the party also accepted the Scottish Parliament and devolved further powers from Westminster to Holyrood (Convery 2014a), but it did not engage in any debate as to the future structure of an asymmetrically devolved UK. The UK party's most significant move was a 2010 manifesto commitment to implementing the recommendations of the Calman Commission (2009) on Scottish devolution, which for the most part became law via the Scotland Act 2012.

In government, the Conservatives were surprised by the Scottish National Party's victory at the 2011 Scottish Parliament elections. Almost immediately afterwards, the Scottish Conservative Party elected Ruth Davidson as leader. Davidson strongly opposed Murdo Fraser's (arguably more imaginatively unionist) proposals for a separate Scottish party of the centre-right to replace the damaged Conservative brand. She also declared during her campaign that the Calman proposals constituted a 'line in the sand', and that she would not support further devolution.

The main strategy of the Conservatives at a Scottish and UK level following her election, however, was to extricate the party from this 'line in the sand' as elegantly as possible. David Cameron declared in his speech to the Scottish Conservative Party conference in March 2012 that he was 'open-minded about the transfer of more powers' (Cameron 2012). Davidson then fully reversed her position in March 2013 and commissioned Lord Strathclyde to produce a report on the future of devolution in Scotland (Scottish Conservative Party 2014b). She endorsed its conclusions (BBC News online, 2 June 2014), which included the devolution of all income tax rates and bands to the Scottish Parliament.

During the campaign to keep Scotland in the United Kingdom, Conservative politicians were forced to confront more explicitly their (hitherto perhaps largely instinctive) conception of the Union. Conservative unionism now appeared to rest on more practical supports. In particular, Cameron emphasised the economic benefits of working together: 'we're the oldest and most successful single market in the world, and with one of the oldest and most successful currencies in the world' (Cameron 2014). Much like the EU, Scotland was depicted as a member of a UK trading and currency club that pooled economic risk and lowered transaction costs (see also HM Treasury 2013a, 2013b, 2014). However, there was still a strong cultural and social aspect to this conception of the Union: according to Cameron, the people of the islands of the UK are connected and alike. The social and cultural meaning identified by Mitchell (1990) is linked to business and family: 'Our human connections – our friendships, relationships, business partnerships – they are underpinned because we are all in the same United Kingdom, and that is number one reason why we are stronger together' (Cameron 2014).

However, the promise of more powers for the Scottish Parliament from not only the Scottish Conservatives but Scottish Labour and Liberal

Democrats too were couched within the parameters of the existing model of devolution and did not imply moving away from parliamentary sovereignty. Thus, the Conservative unionism outlined by Cameron and Davidson may be considered 'bi-constitutional' in the same manner as New Labour's attitude to the constitution (Flinders and Curry 2008). It was happy to tolerate the more consensual arrangements of the devolved administrations while maintaining the majoritarian logic of government at Westminster. It did not envisage any changes to the centre. Thus the parliamentary sovereignty element of Conservative unionism remained intact. Those who support federalism necessarily reject this conception of the union based on parliamentary sovereignty at the centre. For them, the logic of devolution and the maintenance of devolution require changes to the centre.

In a previous volume, Mitchell and Convery (2012) argued that the Scottish Conservatives' unionism was 'prisoned in marble', their reluctance to concede any ground to the SNP having prevented them from thinking imaginatively about the future of the Union. The 2014 independence referendum, however, finally prompted the party to fully to come to terms fully with devolution. Thus, the Strathclyde Commission stated that:

> When these actions are taken within the context of Conservative policies on empowering individuals and decentralising power throughout the rest of the UK, it is clear that empowering the Scottish people to shape their own nation within the security of a United Kingdom is not just something we are willing only grudgingly to accept, it is something that sits at the very heart of what it means to be a modern Scottish Conservative. (Scottish Conservative Party 2014b: 3–4)

The proposals of the Strathclyde Commission were, in fact, more radical than the reforms proposed by the Scottish Labour Party. The parties' respective proposals, however, came together in the Smith Commission and its conclusions were implemented in the Scotland Act 2016. The Scottish Conservatives' version of unionism therefore evolved to incorporate a more fiscally autonomous Scottish Parliament, as well as the idea that devolution should be more formally recognised as a permanent part of the British constitution.

Luckily for the Scottish Conservatives, their conversion to devo-pragmatism coincided with the rising salience of unionism as an issue in Scottish politics. They were thus able to capitalise on the idea that they were comfortable with devolution (and a UK Conservative Government had a proud record of facilitating much more of it) but also resolutely against revisiting the independence question after 2014. At the 2016 Scottish Parliament elections, the party campaigned on a policy-light manifesto and instead emphasised its commitment to unionism (no second independence referendum), strong opposition to the SNP in the Scottish Parliament, and the attractive leadership of Ruth Davidson. They were able to contrast their forthright unionist approach with the Labour Party's (at times) apparent open-mindedness on the issue of a second independence referendum.

Such a strategy was even more in evidence during the 2017 general election in Scotland, when the issue of a second independence referendum was more prominent, in light of the vote for Brexit in 2016. Internal Conservative analysis suggested that the common issue among likely Conservative voters was opposition to a second independence referendum (Hassan 2018: loc.6160). Thus, the Scottish Conservatives again emphasised their commitment to the Union at every opportunity. Indeed, Nicola Sturgeon commented during that campaign that 'Ruth Davidson is going around saying that I talk about nothing other than independence. She talks about it so much that I don't get a chance' (Hassan 2018: loc.4585).

Unfortunately for the Scottish Conservatives, just as they were settling down into this pragmatic accommodation of two facets of their ideology, the ground started to shift beneath them. The implementation of the UK's withdrawal from the EU put the UK's devolution settlement under extreme strain, forcing answers to previously fudged questions about where power lies and when or if Scotland might be allowed a second independence referendum. The Scottish Conservatives once again found themselves pulled in two directions by their unionism. For instance, the party campaigned strongly for a Remain vote in the EU referendum and 62 per cent of Scots agreed with them. Loyalty to the UK party dictates, however, that the Scottish Conservatives should support a Conservative Prime Minister's efforts to deliver Brexit. It is, at best, an awkward situation. Similarly, having just supported the Scotland Act 2016 that put the Sewel Convention 'on a statutory footing', the Conservatives had to defend the UK Government's decision to ignore the fact that the Scottish Parliament declined to give its consent to the EU Withdrawal Bill. The Scottish Conservative Party once again found itself isolated and in an uncomfortable position when it came to key constitutional questions.

These unsettled times prompted the Scottish Conservatives to try and balance 'standing up for Scotland' with a commitment to promoting the United Kingdom as the best constitutional option. However, this chapter suggests that these day-to-day reactions to events stem from three broad logics of unionist justification.

The Ultra-Unionists

The uncompromising or 'ultra' strand of unionist thinking is essentially unchanged since 1997. At its heart is a conception of parliamentary sovereignty that cannot be diluted. The Scottish Parliament exists but should not be accorded any special status within the constitution. It is to be managed rather than embraced. This pre-1997 hangover hampered Scottish Conservative Party leaders until 2014 in their attempts to show the party had 'accepted' devolution (Convery 2016a).

The creation of the Scottish Parliament and the subsequent increase in its powers might have been enough to extinguish this line of thinking as a serious proposition. However, the 'ultra' point of view has never gone away and its continued relevance was demonstrated most starkly in the British Government's arguments during the Miller v Secretary of State for Exiting the European Union case in the Supreme Court in 2017. The Advocate General (and Scottish Conservative peer), Lord Keen, represented Her Majesty's Government for the devolution parts of the case. These centred on whether the Sewel Convention (that the Westminster Parliament will not 'normally' legislate on devolved matters without the devolved legislatures' consent) applied to the legislation enacting the UK's notification of EU withdrawal ('Article 50').

Not content with arguing that the Convention did not apply to matters of foreign affairs, of which EU withdrawal was one, Lord Keen went further. Referring to the specific language of the convention as written in the Scotland Act 2016, he stated that attention would have to be paid to 'what is meant by "recognised as" or what is meant "by regard" to, but ultimately it will be for Parliament to decide whether or not it adheres to the convention as interpreted by the court'. For the UK Government, the Sewel Convention was a 'legal irrelevance' (Keen 2016: 105–6). Even if it could be established the Sewel Convention applied in the case of triggering Article 50, Parliament is the sole interpreter of what 'normally' means, so might choose to ignore it anyway.

Thus, a key part of the UK's emerging territorial constitution was dismissed as a procedural device for administrative convenience. The Westminster Parliament is sovereign in all matters and may overrule the devolved legislatures as it sees fit at any time. Such an interpretation of the constitution is firmly of the 'ultra-unionist' mindset. Instead of trying to come to an accommodation with devolution, one simply declares that nothing has changed.

Of course, it may be argued that such an interpretation was always beneath the surface of all of the changes made since 1999. Some may argue that devolution was never intended to place limits on parliamentary sovereignty – indeed, that is explicit in the Scotland Act 1998, even as amended. There is a neat logic to this position. However, sticking doggedly to such a legalistic reading of the nature of devolution has profound consequences for the type of political vision unionists can articulate for Scotland's position in the UK. It leads to the conclusion that no entrenchment of the rights of devolved institutions will ever be possible. If adherence to the Sewel Convention is purely a matter of convenience, then what else might Westminster choose to ignore in future? The ultra-unionist thus prioritises neatness over pluralism and presents a much narrower vision for the future of devolution, believing there to be no merit in a discussion of federalism. However, this line of uncompromising thinking has been challenged by the Conservative devo-pragmatists.

The Devo-Pragmatists

The supreme interpreter of the devo-pragmatic approach to territorial politics was David Cameron. For those such as the former Prime Minister, the Scottish Parliament has fundamentally changed the British constitution, rendering the ultras' quaint Westminster model interpretation both untenable and unhelpful. However, they also believe the task of neatly codifying or providing a coherent philosophy for the new settlement is best left to academics and think tanks. The practical work of politicians who believe in the Union is to make it work by sheer force of British pragmatism, balancing the demands for Scottish autonomy with wider UK concerns.

Oliver Letwin (then Chancellor of the Duchy of Lancaster) articulated the devo-pragmatist view in oral evidence to the House of Lords Constitution Committee in 2016:

> The test of these things is not whether in some common room or lecture room it looks as if it is a neat and clearly defined system, but, rather, whether it guarantees what, to my mind, constitutions are there to guarantee: namely, the liberties and rights of individuals to live in a liberal democracy under the rule of law. (Letwin 2016: 4)

Letwin also argued that intergovernmental arrangements work well when ministers in Westminster and the devolved institutions can simply pick up the phone and have a reasonable discussion about overlapping policy issues (Letwin 2016: 3). There is therefore little need for more formalised intergovernmental institutions. Such a pragmatic approach can accommodate both the granting of permission to hold a referendum in Scottish independence in 2014 and the devolution of further powers in the Scotland Act 2016. It is not concerned about asymmetry and believes there are more important things to be getting on with than trying to impose order on something that already works. Problems are dealt with as they arise and there is no objection in principle to greater powers for the devolved legislatures.

Such a cast of mind is also more attuned to the importance of conventions (both practically and symbolically) in a system that prioritises informal working. Thus, for example, when the Scottish Parliament declined to give its consent to a part of the UK Government's welfare reforms in 2015 that affected devolved powers, the UK Government revised the legislation and later secured the Scottish Parliament's consent. Holyrood's permission was also sought and granted for both the Scotland Act 2012 and the Scotland Act 2016. Whether or not the Sewel Convention was justiciable was a question that did not need to be answered, for the Convention had been observed.

The Scottish Conservatives also derived electoral benefits from this devo-pragmatic approach. In 2016, their commitment to oppose a second independence referendum helped them to secure a higher share of voters who voted 'No' to independence in 2014 (Curtice 2017a). In 2017, the party found that the issue most potential Conservative voters could agree on was opposition to a second independence referendum (Cowley and Kavanagh 2018: 291). Finally, however, there are Conservatives who are not content to keep muddling through and instead, to use Letwin's words, seek a 'theoretical underpinning' (Letwin 2016: 3). This group might be labelled the 'radical reformers'.

The Radical Reformers

The doyen of the radical reformers is Welsh Conservative Assembly Member David Melding. For him (2012: 14), any Conservative who is serious about the preservation of the Union needs to fundamentally reconsider how the UK is governed: 'without a firm constitutional settlement, where the powers of the UK state are set out and enshrined, Unionism is destined to fail'. A federal solution is therefore attractive because 'there is something in the British political tradition that is especially conducive to the federal form' (William Riker, quoted in Melding 2012: 30). Melding's plan proposed an incremental approach, starting with a new Act of Union and allowing English self-government to develop organically.

Similarly, for Murdo Fraser MSP, the mechanics of the type of institutions that would constitute a federal United Kingdom are less important than the grand narrative. Thus, in relation to the problem of the size of England, he believes it is:

quite possible to sketch out the start of what could develop in time into [English] federal sub-states. Transplanting a US, Canadian, Australian or even German model of federalism onto the UK is never going to be a simple or straightforward process, but the history of the development of the UK constitution has been one of a series of messy, but working, compromises, which in theory make very little sense, but in practice hang together very well. There might just be signs of a very British solution to a historic problem. (Fraser 2014)

Federalism is therefore an idea that combines the best of both worlds: 'federalism within the UK, if it were workable and could be achieved, is a solution which could unite both unionists, and many nationalists, and provide a secure framework for the future' (Fraser 2014). In the same vein, Torrance argues that federalism is 'the only constitutional model that would give adequate and coherent expression to the delightfully messy status quo' (2014: 97).

David Marquand (2006) considers the British attitude to federalism 'neurotic', concluding that misconceptions and myths blind British political elites to its potential benefits. There is a British tradition of placing the label 'federal' on systems that are, strictly speaking, devolution. At the same time, British elites are content to ignore the (quasi-) federal implications of governing arrangements that politicians insist are merely devolution (Gamble 2006; Flinders 2010). In the context of the European Union, meanwhile, 'federalist' is a term of abuse in the Conservative Party.

It is therefore important to be clear about what federalism does and does not mean. Federalism involves two central principles: a formal division of sovereignty between two levels of government, and a guarantee that the division of powers between the federal government and sub-state governments cannot be altered without the latter's permission. Thus: 'In a federal system of government, sovereignty is shared and powers divided between two or more levels of government, each of which enjoys a direct relationship with the people' (Hueglin and Fenna 2006: 32–3). This differs from a unitary state under which powers given to sub-state tiers of government may be withdrawn by the central government at any time.

In practice, this basic definition can be broken down into three uses of the term (Elazar 1987). First, the word 'federalism' can be used in a normative sense to mean broad support for a system of government that includes areas of regional self-rule and central–regional shared rule. This is federalism as ideology. Second, the term 'federal political systems' describes those countries that exhibit such features in their governing arrangements, including, for instance, devolved unions, quasi-federations and indeed federations (Watts 2007: 240–1). Third, the term 'federation' refers specifically to those countries in which

> neither the federal nor constituent units of government are constitutionally subordinate to the other; that is, each has sovereign powers derived not from another level of government but from a constitution that is not unilaterally amendable by either level of government; each is empowered to deal directly with its citizens in the exercise of its constitutionally assigned legislative, executive and taxing powers; and each is directly elected by its citizens. (Watts 2007: 240)

Thus, when radical reformers propose a 'federal UK', what they are referring to is the third definition. They want to see the UK become a formal federation. Instead of incrementally travelling along a path where the UK may in time exhibit more features of a 'federal political system', they want a decisive break that fundamentally re-establishes the UK as a federation. That is what separates them from those who refer loosely to a more federal UK as desirable or incremental.

This distinction is very important because the UK's present devolution arrangements display clearly some of the features of federal political systems. One scholar argues that they are in fact 'quasi-federal' in nature (Bogdanor 2001, 2003). Although theoretically there is nothing to stop the Westminster Parliament from unilaterally abolishing the devolved legislatures in the same manner that Margaret Thatcher's government abolished the Greater London Authority (or indeed Edward Heath's government did the old Parliament of Northern Ireland), it is almost impossible to imagine the circumstances under which it would do so. In practice if not in legal theory, sovereignty has been *divided* between Westminster and Belfast, Cardiff and Edinburgh.

However, the UK Government still officially maintains that 'devolution does not cede ultimate sovereignty' (HM Government 2007). An attempt to maintain parliamentary sovereignty is a central component of the UK's devolution arrangements. Thus, the 1997 white paper *Scotland's Parliament* stated unequivocally that the UK Parliament 'is and will remain sovereign' (HM Government 1997: vii). According to Campbell (2011: 100), when discussing these proposals with the Cabinet, the then Secretary of State for Scotland, Donald Dewar, stated: 'we're putting the whole package firmly within the context of the UK and the sovereignty of the UK Parliament'. The principal architects of devolution were determined to preserve the reassuring appearance of the continuation of the doctrine of parliamentary sovereignty. Such a commitment is incompatible with plans for a formally federal United Kingdom.

However, the history of federalism in Britain is much more complicated than the present arrangements and attitude of the British Government suggest. There exists a British tradition of federalism (Burgess 1995). During the negotiations over the Act of Union between Scotland and England, for instance, various authors proposed schemes they labelled 'federal'. In particular, Hodges and Fletcher produced pamphlets that argued for a federal union, rather than the incorporating union that was proposed and ultimately adopted (Kendle 1997: 6).

During the late nineteenth and early twentieth centuries, meanwhile, there were various proposals to create a British Imperial federation. Again, however, there was conceptual confusion as to what federalism actually meant. The Imperial League certainly wanted closer ties between Britain and its Empire, but they did *not* want a system that would be recognised as federal (Burgess 1995: 50; Kendle 1997: 48). The UK also had to deal at this point with the Irish Question. Various quasi-federal schemes were proposed, in particular the idea of 'Home Rule all round'. F. S. Oliver, for example, was a leading proponent of Conservative federalism in the early twentieth century (Mitchell 1990: 39). The difficulties of territorial management meant that ideas about federalism never disappeared for long. In the 1970s, the Kilbrandon Commission casually dismissed federalism thus: 'the United Kingdom has for centuries been governed in a spirit of unity and co-operation, and even if this unity is now being questioned, it would hardly be satisfactory to adopt a legalistic system intended for a much earlier stage of constitutional development' (Royal Commission on the Constitution 1973: para 526).

The official position of the Liberal Democrats is the creation of a federal UK. However, as Evans (2014) notes, their lack of thinking in this area means they might be viewed as 'federalist in name only'. In the Conservative Party itself, the position of Scotland has in the past prompted more radical considerations of the future of the UK. In a pamphlet published in 1967, the 'Thistle Group' (which included Michael Ancram, Malcolm Rifkind and Peter Fraser among its members) published a pamphlet advocating a Scottish Parliament which raised its own revenue and remitted a portion of it to a federal UK treasury (Mitchell 1990: 54). Such a position never found widespread support in the Conservative Party. It is instructive that it took until 2014 for the Scottish Conservatives to propose substantial new tax-raising powers for the Scottish Parliament.

We may draw two central conclusions from this brief history. First, consideration of federalism is neither particularly alien nor novel in debates regarding the UK's constitution. Second, there is a tendency to misunderstand federalism and especially to confuse federalism with other systems of government, particularly the devolution of power away from the centre. States can be devolved and unitary without being federal. The powers envisaged in the most radical proposals for further devolution to Scotland, for instance, could be devolved to Scotland without the need for the UK to become a formally federal state. In the most recent debate about Scottish independence, the British tradition of confusion about the term 'federalism' continued: it became shorthand for devolving substantially more powers to Scotland.

Even the UK Independence Party briefly supported a 'federal' future for the United Kingdom (*Irish Times*, 12 September 2014). In considering federalism, therefore, Conservative radical reformers need to be clear about the problem they are attempting to solve, and about why they feel they need to go beyond merely devolving more powers, as in the past. Paradoxically, in the context of Scotland, 'federalist' is taken to mean further decentralisation of power; in the context of the European Union, it is taken to mean further centralisation of powers. However, the idea of a 'federal superstate' is, as Henig (2007: 9) argues, 'totally without meaning – by definition a federal state can only be the complete opposite of the superstate'.

A Conservative plan for federalism therefore faces a difficult task. It must not only confront conceptual confusion and long-standing hostility; it must also give Conservatives a convincing reason to abandon their attachment to the Westminster model of British Government, and in particular the central notion of parliamentary sovereignty. The fundamental problem for the radical reformers is that they are attempting to make explicit something that the pragmatists are (for good reason) content to fudge: has Westminster's sovereignty been divided or not? Gormley-Heenan and Sandford (2018) refer to this conundrum as 'Schrodinger's Devolution'.

Unfortunately, the process of implementing Brexit has forced Westminster to give an answer to this question and it has not been helpful for the radical reformers' project. Westminster flunked the first substantial test of devolution. First, its arguments in the Miller case in the Supreme Court demonstrated a hostile attitude to any kind of revisionist interpretation of the constitution. Second, in order to make abundantly clear where power lies, the UK Government then unilaterally overruled the Scottish Parliament when it declined to give its consent to the EU Withdrawal Bill.

Thus, the central question the federalists must contend with is this: if Westminster cannot even concede the most basic principle of legislative consent, how on earth do you suppose that it is going to pass an Act of Parliament to formally divide its sovereignty? And, if your version of federalism does not involve such a codified division, then how is it any different from the arrangements that pertain at the moment? Until they find a way out of this difficulty, the radicals' proposals are imaginative but impractical. Indeed, if they do not envisage any formal division of sovereignty where one level of government cannot unilaterally overrule the other, it may be questioned whether what they are proposing is 'federalism' at all.

Conclusion: Union at What Cost?

This chapter has identified three broad categories of unionist thought in the Conservative Party since 1997. Having finally abandoned the dead-end of ultra-unionism under David Cameron, a pragmatic accommodation (in the best conservative tradition) for the most part held sway. The Conservatives became committed devolutionists and could point to some notable successes in managing territorial politics, including the 2014 independence referendum and the Scotland Acts of 2012 and 2016. Under Ruth David-son's leadership, meanwhile, the Scottish Conservatives were able to exploit their new position to appeal to unionist voters across the political spectrum. A radical fringe argued for a bolder approach, but never made much progress in a party which preferred to deal with day-to-day problems rather than creating overarching narratives.

The process of implementing Brexit, however, forced the Conservatives to make a series of quick decisions that fundamentally departed from their devo-pragmatic approach. They began the process in pragmatic mode, having just devolved further powers to Scotland through the Scotland Act 2016. Theresa May promised to work closely with the devolved governments and legislatures. However, as the costs of unionism increased, the Conservatives fell back on an 'ultra-unionist' interpretation of the constitution which prioritised central power over territorial accommodation. It may be that this was an anomalous period borne of intense pressure, but the whole process has been damaging for those in the party who support a more pragmatic or radical approach to devolution. It has placed the Scottish Conservatives in a very awkward position.

There are many arguments against having an uncodified constitution. However, one of its principal advantages in relation to devolution is that it allowed tricky questions to be fudged while politicians got on with the practical business of governing. It was in many ways a very conservative arrangement. Moreover, EU membership also provided a common framework of rules that allowed further powers to be devolved without having to think about creating more formal institutions to govern overlapping policy areas.

In the absence of these arrangements, Conservatives will need to think again about what type of unionism they believe in. A radical federalising reform would probably provide the most secure footing for the long term, but is unlikely while Westminster elites balk at theoretical underpinnings and insist upon the sanctity of parliamentary sovereignty. Ultra-unionism is a neat answer and has a long pedigree in the party, but leads to a rather depressing vision for the future of the Union in which Scottish aspirations are always firmly secondary to UK concerns (and in which delivering Brexit comes first). Finding its way back towards devo-pragmatism is therefore probably the best the party can hope to achieve. However, even if the Scottish Conservatives stick to such an approach, there is no guarantee the UK party will resist the attraction of a more centralising ultra-unionist stance.

TEN

Scottish Conservatism and Northern Ireland: Mapping an Ambivalent Relationship

Jonathan Evershed

Introduction

Since the term was coined in the wake of the 2014 independence referendum by the journalist Aidan Kerr, there has been some debate about the extent to which politics in Scotland has been 'Ulsterised' (Kerr 2014). The many and impassioned rejoinders to David Torrance's suggestion – following the SNP's victory, the Tories' resurgence and Labour's collapse at the Scottish Parliamentary election in 2016 – that the 'Ulsterisation of Scottish politics [was now] complete' (*Herald*, 8 May 2016) strikingly revealed the political-cultural and emotional resonances of the term and the consternation it could evoke (see, e.g., *Guardian*, 11 May 2016; *Herald*, 15 May 2016; *Herald*, 10 May 2016).

At stake were a series of overlapping questions: Has the cleavage between unionism and nationalism become so dominant politically as to render all other questions marginal or even irrelevant?[1] To what extent is this cleavage marked by particular kinds of ethno-sectarian division, prejudice and conflict? And is such a division necessarily haunted by the spectre of violence? For as Geoghegan has suggested, 'Ulster' is all too often taken as 'shorthand for atavistic violence, bitterness and division. A toxic politics where ethnicity trumps all else' (Bella Caledonia, 10 May 2016).[2]

In direct contradistinction to more than 30 years of armed conflict in Northern Ireland, the politics of the national question in Scotland have been marred during the twentieth and early twenty-first century by only intermittent and fairly tokenistic violence (Brooke 2018: 17–44). It is also the case that Irish unity – the primary issue around which political division in Northern Ireland hinges – is in many respects a fundamentally different prospect to that of Scottish independence. The SNP are not Sinn Féin in much the same way that, as I discuss further below, the Scottish Tories are not the Democratic Unionist Party (DUP): they have different motivations and different histories.[3]

Scotland's political culture is different from Northern Ireland's, and there is some justification for the suggestion that any overly close comparison between the two is necessarily misconceived. However, as Graham Walker has asserted,

> The suggestion that Scottish politics has become 'Ulsterised' has triggered fierce rebuttals, so fierce in fact that conclusions might be drawn about raw nerves being touched. The blanket condemnation of those who have dared to see something pertinent in the term threatens to create a situation in which legitimate explorations of Scotland's many connections with Northern Ireland – and yes, some are political – are frankly discouraged. (*Scottish Review*, 18 May 2016)

There are, in arguments both for and against the 'Ulsterisation' thesis and in the fears it evokes, implicit (mis)characterisations of the nature and legitimacy of the conflict in the North of Ireland, and a will to deny that Scotland could succumb to what is (dis)regarded or (mis)understood merely as a sort of incomprehensibly sectarian pathology which afflicts its near neighbour. In this regard, and as I explore in greater depth in this chapter, the 'Ulsterisation' debate maps and mirrors broader attempts to draw a cordon sanitaire around Northern Ireland and keep it out of Scottish politics. This has often come at the expense (1) of deeper understandings in Scotland about the politics of Northern Ireland, and (2) of a deeper interrogation of the political entanglements between Northern Ireland and Scotland which have shaped relationships within and between them. These relationships have been and remain shaped by contradictory forces: by solidaristic sentiment *and* profound antipathy; sameness *and* difference; constitutional principle *and* political expediency.

In this chapter, I explore some of these shifting and contradictory dynamics as they have manifested themselves in the relationship between Scottish Conservatism and Ulster Unionism. I provide a brief overview of the history of this relationship – which was, as identified by Walker and Officer (1998), Burness (2003), Jackson (2012a), Mitchell and Convery (2012) and Torrance (2012), among others, highly salient in the consolidation of Conservatism as a political force in Scotland during the twentieth century, but which has become more ambiguous as understandings of 'Union', processes of secularisation, patterns of integration and differentiation, and the nature of centre–periphery relations in Northern Ireland and Scotland have increasingly diverged. I also examine how this relationship has continued to be reshaped into the twenty-first century by a potent mix of political forces which has included the Irish peace process, the Scottish independence referendum and Brexit. This examination includes some assessment of claims about the place of an 'Ulster' connection in general and an 'Orange vote' in particular, in the (apparent) revival of Conservatism in Scotland under Ruth Davidson.

The Irish Question

As Farrington and Walker (2009: 138) note, historically 'the term "Unionist" in Scotland referred to the Union with Ireland and it was this meaning that was carried in the name used by the Conservative Party in Scotland until 1965'. Scottish Unionism emerged as a distinct political formation in the nineteenth and early twentieth centuries. It took its cue, and was in large part derived from, Irish Unionism, with the 'unions of most relevance [being] the 1603 Union of Crowns and the 1800 Union with Ireland, rather than the 1707 Union of Parliaments' (Mitchell and Convery 2012: 174). According to Mitchell and Convery (ibid.), the Scottish Conservatives' 1912 rebranding as the Scottish Unionist Party represented 'the ultimate act of communion with Ulster Unionists' in the context of the perceived threat to the Union posed by the passage of the Third Home Rule Bill and the 'Ulster Crisis' it had precipitated (see Stewart 1967; Parkinson 2012).

Pledging to resist Irish Home Rule by any means necessary (and foreshadowing some of the Tory rhetoric about 'Parliament versus the people' during the vexatious debate surrounding the UK's withdrawal from the European Union) then Conservative Party leader Andrew Bonar Law made the extraordinary and pseudo-revolutionary proclamation that 'there are things stronger than parliamentary majorities' (Law, quoted in *New Statesman*, 4 September 2019). His 1912 pledge that he could 'imagine no length of resistance to which Ulster [could] go in in which [he] would not be prepared to support them' (quoted in *Dublin Review of Books*, October 2019) spoke to the extent of the familial, political-cultural and economic connections between Ulster and Scotland which he himself embodied.[4] These connections were deeply felt, and were underpinned and mobilised by the Grand Orange Lodge of Scotland (Walker 2016: 8; see also Gallagher 1987; McFarland 1990). As Mitchell and Convery (2012: 174) have noted, they continued to shape (and be shaped by) Scottish Conservative politics into the mid-twentieth century, with 'the Scottish Tories' core support among Protestants with family ties across the Irish Sea contribut[ing] to the continuing relevance of this very real imagined community'.

However, as Jackson (2012a) and Arnott and Macdonald (2012) have demonstrated, Scottish Unionism was never *just* about Ireland. From its inception, it had a distinctly Scottish identity and was also (even primarily) concerned with matters closer to home, including that of the perceived threat of socialism. Jackson (2012a: 24) has also identified that even in the 1910s there was a certain distaste among Tories in Scotland for some of the more 'flamboyantly' militaristic and 'Orange' manifestations of Unionism as associated with Ulster. As discussed further below, not wanting to be seen to be openly associated with Orangeism has become an increasingly key concern for Scottish Conservatives, with mixed consequences for their electability.

Above all, the role played by 'mainland' Conservatives during the Home Rule Crisis was as strategic and tactical as it was principled, Bonar Law's primary aim having been to weaken Asquith's Liberal government and force an election to return a Conservative government (Smith 2001). As Edward Carson, the Dublin-born barrister and MP who had led the Ulster Unionist Party (UUP) in its resistance to Home Rule, famously lamented in 1921, 'I was only a puppet, and so was Ulster, and so was Ireland, in the political game that was to get the Conservative Party into power' (HL Debs 14 Dec 1921 Vol 48 c44). This political game culminated, after the First World War, in the Tories' complicity in the 'betrayal' of three of Ulster's nine counties, which were ceded to the new Irish Free State in 1921–2 (see Mulvenna 2016: 20–1). As Aughey and Gormley-Heenan have noted, ultimately, 'it was the very failure to win the argument on Ireland's place in the Union which helped to secure the Conservative electoral interest at Westminster, with the removal of the Irish Party complemented by continuing Ulster Unionist representation and novel success in Scotland' (Aughey and Gormley-Heenan 2016: 433).

Thus, while Scottish Unionists were certainly motivated in the early to mid-twentieth century by sincere feelings of affinity with their (Northern) Irish fellow travellers, it is nonetheless arguable that this affinity was 'elective' (see Aughey and Gormley-Heenan 2016: 438) and even fairly equivocal from the outset. The opening of a devolved Northern Ireland Parliament and the signing of the Anglo-Irish Treaty in 1921 removed 'Ulster' from the front line of British politics for the best part of half a century and, arguably, permanently stunted its ability to motivate or drive Conservative politics. The apparent resolution of the Irish Question helped to cultivate among Tories what Aughey (2018: 61), following Richard Rose, called an 'unthinking unionism', one which may occasionally have paid lip service to the integrity of Northern Ireland's place within the Union, but which habitually saw the borders of the British state as coterminous with those of the island of Great Britain. While Northern Ireland's sectarian divisions were echoed in some forms of Scottish popular culture, including the notorious 'Old Firm' rivalry between Celtic and Rangers, this was of limited *political* consequence, even after the outbreak of the Troubles in 1969 (Rosie 2004: 4, 10–11).[5] Thereafter, a primary concern of Scottish politicians of all hues was the insulation Scotland against any potential overspill of violence (Walker 2016: 15–21). In this endeavour, they were broadly successful.

The escalating violence on the other side of the Irish Sea contributed to a decline in the Tories' willingness and ability to engage in 'popular Unionism' or play the 'Orange card', insofar as either had (still) existed prior to 1969 (Walker 1995; Gallagher 1987). Tensions between the Orange Order (and the wider 'Loyalist' community) and the Conservative Party in Scotland first (re)emerged with the suspension of Stormont in 1972 and during the 1973–4 Sunningdale experiment in power sharing – whereupon UUP MPs at Westminster resigned the Tory whip, severing what institutional links then remained between Ulster Unionism and 'mainland' Conservatism; again during the referendum on Scottish devolution in 1979 – in which the Order advocated a 'Yes' vote, in opposition to the Conservative position; and finally, and most dramatically, after the Thatcher government's signing of the Anglo-Irish Agreement in 1985 (Walker 1995: 156–8).

Walker (2016: 20) has suggested the latter represented a final 'rupture between the Conservatives and militant Protestant and "Loyalist" voters that had been developing for decades', contributing (albeit as only one among a series of factors) to the Scottish Tories' declining electoral fortunes in the 1980s and 1990s. The Labour Party (which, as explored in more depth below, had at any rate always had its own healthy 'Orange vote') was the key beneficiary. But the 1994 Monklands imbroglio also demonstrated that the SNP – long held in suspicion by Catholic voters – had its own stake in the complex dynamics of political sectarianism in Scotland, and some capacity to attract a working-class Protestant vote (Walker 1995: 34–8; Bradley 2004: 248).

Crucially, as Walker (1995: 158) intimates, Scots of all political stripes consistently demonstrated they were quite ready to abdicate responsibility for managing the conflict in Northern Ireland to London. Scottish Tories were really no different from their English and Welsh counterparts in finding the Troubles in equal parts perturbing, confusing and, eventually, boring. First the violence and, latterly, the peace process in Northern Ireland reinforced a sense that it was a 'place apart': a place outside of 'normal' British politics in which – with enduring consequences discussed further below – Scotland had and demanded little to no real stake.

Combined with, inter alia, the decline of religion, in general, and Protestantism, in particular, as a mobilising force in Scottish politics; Scotland's increasing diversity and multiculturalism; the move towards devolution under New Labour; and the deep existential questions raised about the future of the United Kingdom by the end of Empire and the growth of Scottish Nationalism, the Troubles contributed to shifts in the centre of Scottish Conservatism's political gravity and of the loci of Scottish Tories' political identity (cf. Rosie and Hepburn 2015: 151; Ascherson 2019). By the beginning of the new millennium, rather than indicating a position on the Irish Question, 'the "Unionist" in the Scottish Conservative and Unionist Party name was emphatically a reference to the 1707 Union' (Mitchell and Convery 2012: 177). This has become all the more categorically the case as a result of the 2014 independence referendum and in the wake of the 2016 EU referendum.

Integration and Differentiation

As well as mirroring changes in the wider British political landscape, the diminishing centrality of the 'Irish Question' to Scottish Conservative and Unionist politics since 1912 speaks to something of a deeper and more enduring truth. To put it bluntly, Scotland is an integral part of the Union in a way that Northern Ireland is not, and Scotland matters far more to Ulster Unionism than Northern Ireland matters to Unionism anywhere on the British 'mainland'.[6] Irish (re)unification – per the terms of the 1998 Belfast/Good Friday Agreement's 'principle of consent' and its provisions for a border poll – and the final repeal of what remains of the Union of 1800 could be undertaken without undermining the fundamental integrity of the British state. The same is not true of the Union of 1707.

In 1993, John Major conceded that the British Government had no 'selfish strategic or economic interest in Northern Ireland' (DFA 1993: 1). While Major did himself also acknowledge that 'no nation could be held irrevocably in the Union against its will' (HM Government 1993: 5), it remains difficult (though perhaps decreasingly so) to conceive of a UK Prime Minister making so emphatic a claim about Scotland's lack of strategic or economic importance.[7] Similarly, in the event of any forthcoming poll on Irish unity, it is hard – Theresa May's claims about the Union's 'preciousness' during her tenure as Prime Minister, and Boris Johnson's self-appointment as 'Minister for the Union' notwithstanding – to picture a British elder statesman or -woman imploring Northern Irish citizens to vote to remain in the United Kingdom with anything like the passionate intensity demonstrated by Gordon Brown during the 2014 Scottish referendum.[8] And while it may be increasingly *difficult* – following the political upheavals that have reshaped Scottish politics during and since 2014 and 2016 – to imagine a future Prime Minister of the

UK representing a Scottish Parliamentary seat, it is (and long has been) entirely *impossible* to imagine one hailing from any constituency in Northern Ireland.

Farrington and Walker (2009) argue that contemporary differences between Scots and Ulster Unionism(s) reflect and, in part, stem from the divergent patterns of integration which have enrolled Northern Ireland and Scotland into the British political ecosystem on these radically different terms. In particular, they point to Scotland's full integration into British party politics vis-à-vis Northern Ireland's distinct and separate party system. Throughout the twentieth and early twenty-first century, Scotland played a full and significant part in the 'normal' Labour–Conservative/left–right politics of the Union (Walker 2016). By contrast, and as Coulter (2015) has documented, attempts to integrate Northern Ireland more fully into mainstream British politics – an aspiration espoused over the course of the twentieth century by an eclectic mix of political groups and individuals including the British and Irish Communist Organisation (BICO) and Enoch Powell, among others – have foundered on the rocks of 'mainlander' reticence, Ulster Unionist mistrust and insecurity, and profound political-cultural differences between Northern Ireland and Great Britain.

A formal electoral alliance between the UUP and the Conservative Party was formed during David Cameron's tenure as party leader, ahead of the 2010 general election.[9] But this experiment – which went under the clumsy and roundly ridiculed banner of 'UCUNF' (Ulster Conservatives and Unionists – New Force) – ended in dismal failure[10] (see Tonge et al. 2019). The Northern Ireland Conservatives have continued to contest subsequent elections, consistently failing to establish a presence in Northern Ireland which can hold a candle to that which the Tories have maintained in Scottish politics, even at their lowest electoral ebb (see Smith 2011: 13–15, 129–33). Where the Scottish Conservatives (appear to) have succeeded, particularly since 2014, in largely capturing and owning the 'Unionist' label, the Conservative Party in Northern Ireland has been singularly unsuccessful in its attempts to do the same. As David Cameron reflected in his memoirs, while the party might have 'failed to modernise . . . along with the UUP in Northern Ireland', Ruth Davidson, he believed, 'really would make us a New Force in Scotland' (Cameron 2019: 316).

Evidence provided by Tonge et al. (2014: 178–9) might suggest that members of the DUP – the near hegemonic force, electorally, in contemporary Ulster Unionist politics – feel 'closer' to the Conservatives than to any other 'mainland' party, but this 'closeness' is decidedly tepid. It is qualified by key social and economic policy differences and, more profoundly, by the warning contained in Edward Carson's 1921 lamentation about his being used as a 'puppet'. A deep uncertainty remains among Ulster Unionists about the Tories' steadfastness in their commitment to defending Northern Ireland's place in the Union. This uncertainty draws on lived experience of the Sunningdale (see McCann and McGrattan 2017) and Anglo-Irish (see Cochrane 1997) Agreements and, more recently, the fiasco over the post-Brexit Irish border backstop (RTÉ News, 20 October 2018). 'There can be few indices that have captured quite so graphically the unionist community's distrust of the British state,' suggests Coulter (2015: 411), 'as the sequence of lost deposits suffered by the Northern Ireland Conservatives.'

As Farrington and Walker note:

> An obvious contrast, historically, between Northern Ireland and Scotland is the absence in the latter of the sense of perceived internal threat felt by the majority in the former to their identity. [Ulster Unionists] have sought security from Irish Nationalism, and their relationship to the Union has been shaped by the varying degrees to which that desire has been met or frustrated at different points in time. Scottish frustrations, on the other hand, have focussed on perceived English neglect of, or indifference to, the essential concept of partnership. (Farrington and Walker 2009: 139)

Even in those parts of Western Scotland where Ulster Unionist hopes, fears and prejudices resonate most deeply, similar experiences of ontological insecurity have historically been offset by a different orientation to – and deeper involvement in – 'mainstream' British political culture than generally pertains in Northern Ireland (see Bradley 2004: 258–9; Walker 1995: 184; Walker 2016: 87). While this may now be in flux following the 'indyref', interpretations of the Union – its nature, purpose or *telos* and perceptions as to what constitutes a risk to it – are still quite different either side of the North Channel (cf. Keating 2019).

These differences – reflected, for example, in the divergent histories and experiences of the Scottish and Northern Ireland Conservatives – have flowed from differential processes of political integration since 1921,[11] but these differential processes of integration are also a result of profound and *prior* differences. To wit, meanings, experiences and expressions of the Union, 'Britain' and 'Britishness' in Scotland and Northern Ireland have always been different,[12] becoming ever more so over one hundred years of profound political and social change in both jurisdictions (see Jackson 2012b). This has contributed to shaping the ambivalence, incongruity and instrumentalism which define contemporary political interactions between Scottish Conservatism and Ulster Unionism, two political movements whose priorities and political cultures – despite claims to the contrary – have become increasingly distinct and disparate.

Hands across the Water?

As Aughey (2018: 153–4; see also Simpkins 2018) notes, the Tories' disastrous performance in the snap 2017 general election was 'marked by a twofold irony':

> The first was that only the success of the party in Scotland . . . secured the party's majority position at Westminster . . . Ruth Davidson had more than delivered for the UK leader. The second was that her impressive achievement became almost immediately eclipsed by May's decision to achieve a 'confidence and supply' arrangement with the Democratic Unionist Party.

Formal talks between the Conservative Party and the DUP were announced on 9 June 2017. On the same day, Davidson tweeted, 'As a Protestant Unionist about to marry an Irish Catholic, here's the Amnesty Pride lecture I gave in Belfast', along with a link to the keynote lecture on marriage equality she had delivered at Belfast Pride in 2016. The subtext of her tweet was quite clear, and it reflected something of the political-cultural distance between the types of Conservatism and Unionism that were now electorally ascendant in Scotland and Northern Ireland.

The DUP's opposition to marriage equality had consistently thwarted attempts to extend it to Northern Ireland. Ironically, given the party's own 'blood red line' of 'no regulatory divergence' between Northern Ireland and Great Britain in the context of Brexit (*News Letter*, 14 March 2018), this made Northern Ireland the only part of the UK (and, for that matter, these islands) in which same-sex marriage remained illegal. Davidson was keen to ensure any Tory–DUP deal would not signal a roll-back on LGBTQI rights in Scotland, England and Wales, and to use it as an opportunity to press for the extension of such rights to Northern Ireland (BBC News online, 9 June 2017).

Sheldon and Kenny (2019) have demonstrated how Brexit and the Conservative–DUP confidence-and-supply agreement (eventually concluded between the two parties on 26 June 2017) functioned to produce forms of rhetoric and posturing around the Irish backstop reminiscent of the Tories' role in the Home Rule Crisis. It might reasonably be speculated that – like their English and Welsh counterparts – some of the 2017 intake of Scottish Conservative MPs might have developed new links with the DUP, thus explaining their voting behaviour. In July 2019, the House of Commons was given the opportunity to vote to extend same-sex marriage legislation to Northern Ireland in the event that the devolved power-sharing executive was not restored by the end of October 2019.[13] Five Scottish Tory MPs voted against, while six also voted against the extension of abortion rights to Northern Ireland on the same terms (*The National*, 10 July 2019).

While opposition to the kind of social conservatism represented by the DUP might be popular and even dominant in contemporary Scottish Conservatism, it is evidently not hegemonic. The fault lines and divisions in 'Team Ruth', including on issues of conscience and particularly on Brexit, have mirrored those in wider contemporary Conservative politics (BBC News online, 27 March 2019). It is also noteworthy that a clandestine donation to the DUP during the 2016 Brexit referendum, amounting to some £435,000, was brokered by a former vice chair of the Scottish Conservative Party. Around £200,000 of this 'dark' money was used by the DUP to pay for a two-page wrap-around advert for the Vote Leave campaign in the *Metro* newspaper (which does not circulate in Northern Ireland) (OpenDemocracy, 19 May 2017). Shaped by the complex and deeply divisive politics of Brexit, and wilfully obscured in places, the precise nature of contemporary relationships between the DUP and Scottish Conservatism are hard to chart or measure with any great accuracy.

Nonetheless, as Scottish Conservative leader, Davidson generally set out her political stall as one which deliberately disclaimed any such relationship. As Graham Walker (interview with author, 2019) notes, when Davidson visited Belfast in 2016, it was 'very much in the context of supporting same-sex marriage. And she made it clear that she was here for that purpose. I don't think she made contact with any leading Unionists when she was over here. And that speaks volumes I think'. This is all the more striking when juxtaposed to Boris Johnson's calculated (though ultimately abortive) flirtation with the DUP.[14] According to Walker (ibid.), Davidson's leadership style was of

> a very singular kind . . . And her impact has been a complex phenomenon . . .
> But I would say for certain that she has not dabbled in what you might call the
> old kind of 'popular Unionist' politics, which would have made a thing about
> Ulster and 'kith-and-kin' kind of appeals of one kind or another.[15] She's studiously avoided that. Though that has not been a feature of Conservative politics more generally since the 1960s. It really hasn't. You could even talk about
> the impact of the Troubles in Scotland as being quite limited, in terms of any
> political support given from Scotland to the Unionists. So, it's not really that
> surprising. But she does seem to have given this another dimension, in that
> she has publicly set herself up *against* things that the DUP are identified with.

Tentative claims that the Scottish Tory 'fightback' under Davidson was based in part on a resurgent Conservative 'Orange vote' (see, e.g., *Spectator*, 6 May 2017) should be read against her deliberate eschewing of the trappings of Orangeism.

As Walker (interview with author, 2019) intimates, many of the Westminster seats won by Scottish Conservatives in 2017, such as those in Perthshire and Aberdeenshire, are not historically home to an 'Orange vote' at all. And while there have been 'mutterings' about its 'return' in Glasgow and parts of west-central Scotland, 'the days when the Tories were simply the Protestant/Loyalist party are surely long gone. The fact that working-class voters appear to be returning in significant numbers to the Conservatives is a testament to Ms Davidson's ability to detoxify the Tory brand' (*Herald*, 6 May 2017).

It is far from clear that what recently renewed Protestant working-class support there has been for Conservative Party as a result of this project of 'detoxification' can endure beyond Davidson's tenure as leader. As suggested by one senior Tory in Dumfries and Galloway (interview with author, 2019), there is serious concern that Boris Johnson's old-Etonian foppishness and his reckless approach to Brexit will do serious damage to the Tories' standing in this section of Scottish society. There is also a suggestion that, even by 2017, Labour remained the (residual) electoral preference of Orangemen. According to Jim McGarg, then Grand Master of the Orange Lodge of Scotland, 'most of the Protestant Order's members are Labour supporters', with five of the estimated six Lodge members elected as councillors in 2017 standing as Labour candidates (*Herald*, 7 May 2017).

Attempts under Davidson's leadership to distance contemporary Scottish Conservatism from more emphatically 'Orange' forms of Unionist culture and politics mirrored the official No campaign's shunning of Ulster Unionism during the independence referendum. As Walker (2016: 68–9) notes, there were 'attempts by some Unionist politicians in Northern Ireland to intervene in the "Indyref" campaign, but the alarmist nature of their comments played badly in the Scottish media, and the "No" side made it clear that they did not need or welcome such assistance'. Sidelined by 'Better Together', the Orange Order in Scotland established its own 'British Together' campaign, the flagship of which was a large, pro-Union demonstration in Edinburgh a week before the referendum (in which many Orange Order members and bandsmen from Northern Ireland participated). Somewhat contrary to received wisdom, there is some suggestion this parade might not have been particularly damaging for the 'No' argument, and may even have acted as a form of damage limitation (see Geoghegan 2015: ch. 3; Walker 2016: 70–1).

In crafting their economistic 'Project Fear', 'Better Together' deliberately sought to avoid emotive appeals about 'Britishness', thereby alienating a section of Scottish society for whom issues of identity are of deep emotional significance (see Geoghegan 2015: ch. 3). The 'British Together' parade, combined with Gordon Brown's late-stage intervention and barnstorming defence of the Union, provided something of an emotional hook, shoring up ailing working-class support for the 'No' side. Following the 'indyref', Davidson continued to draw from the 'Better Together' playbook in her effort to turn the Scottish Conservatives into the premier pro-Union party. And in so doing, she may have replicated the ways in which the No campaign risked speaking over the heads of sections of its potential support base. Insofar as Orange support has meaningfully and sustainably (re)emerged for the Conservatives – and it is not clear that it has – this may have been in spite rather than because of the party's electoral strategy.

Furthermore, where Davidson sought to employ more 'popular' Unionist tropes in her campaign rhetoric, this was generally less than convincing. For example, when she tweeted on 14 May 2017 that 'Corbyn's spokesperson saying Jeremy wasn't on the side of the IRA, but simply seeking peace is offensive to anyone who's worn the uniform', and 'Quite simply, Corbyn & Co. wanted the IRA to win', she was roundly mocked, including by some former British soldiers (CommonSpace, 15 May 2017). Smacking of insincerity, these comments appeared petty and wilfully divisive, an exercise in opportunistic point-scoring which at any rate failed to resonate electorally (cf. Shipman 2017: 328–9). Critics also contended that these tweets signalled Davidson's willingness to play fast and loose with Northern Ireland and its peace process where it was perceived that this might serve Scottish Tory political interests.

This type of criticism was levelled all the more emphatically when, in 2018, Davidson and her long-term ally and then Secretary of State for Scotland, David Mundell, threatened to resign their posts if a Brexit deal resulted in the creation of a 'border of any kind' in the Irish Sea (see *The National*, 18 October 2018). The DUP had insisted that any new regulatory or customs checks on goods entering Northern Ireland from Great Britain under the terms of a Brexit backstop would represent a threat to the UK's constitutional integrity (RTÉ News, 20 October 2018),[16] and Davidson and Mundell's intervention could arguably have been read as an expression of support for the embattled position of Unionists in Northern Ireland on this issue.

However, it ultimately, and quite explicitly, had far more to do with shoring up their own party's position vis-à-vis its SNP adversaries than with expressing solidarity with the DUP (see *Financial Times*, 17 October 2018). As Walker intimates:

> If one part of the UK gets special treatment, then that sets a dangerous precedent which could be pounced upon by the SNP. The Tories are very aware of this argument that 'Scotland and Northern Ireland voted remain,

whereas England and Wales didn't', but if you go down the road of opt-outs and special treatment on that basis, then you are leading to the break-up of the UK. It's important for them to stick to the point of principle that it was a UK-wide vote. So that is why they have been quite robust about their opposition to the backstop, but I don't think it's really to do with any great fellow feeling with Unionists in Northern Ireland. (interview with author, 2019)

Conclusion

The degree of instrumentalism that defined Ruth Davidson's politicking around the backstop is perhaps the ultimate expression of the ambiguities which have – as explored in this chapter – long shaped Scottish Conservative attitudes towards Northern Ireland in general and Ulster Unionism in particular. Expressions of support for Unionists across the North Channel, and claims about 'defending' what remains of the Union of 1800, are useful for Scottish Conservatism insofar as they bolster more meaningful attempts to protect the Union of 1707.

There is certainly still a section of the Scottish population for whom feelings of solidarity with their Northern Irish 'kith and kin' continue to run far deeper, and in which these feelings remain central to people's lived experience. But it is not clear that this has been integral to – or even widely catered for by – the rebuilding of the Scottish Conservatives since 2014. The vote the Tories husbanded in Scotland since the independence referendum was undoubtedly *Unionist*, but it was far from overwhelmingly *Orange*. Thus, while the Scottish Question may, as Walker (2016: 78) suggests, have 'spilled over into the intricately patterned Orange and Green rivalries spawned by the Irish question and Irish population settlements in Scotland', it remains unclear what precisely this might mean for voting patterns and wider politics in Scotland in the longer term. At the time of writing, it is too soon to accurately pronounce the Labour Party's 'Orange vote' dead and buried, to determine what capacity the SNP retains to attract working-class Protestant votes[17] or to predict what precise role Brexit might come to play in fundamentally reshaping the Scottish political landscape.

Contemporary Scottish Conservative ambivalence towards Northern Ireland is, ultimately, emblematic of a deeper issue reflected in the 'Ulsterisation' controversy with which this chapter opened, namely, that there is a gap in Scottish understanding of Northern Ireland, and a lack of appreciation for its political complexities. Across all of Scotland's political parties, sustained engagement with the Northern Irish peace process has been notably lacking. As Walker notes:

If 'Indyref' was notable for the healthy level of grassroots engagement with debate, it can be said to have been excessively self-referential and neglectful of the impact of the vote on relationships within the British Isles ... It would, for instance, have helped the case for independence if its advocates had outlined how the new Scotland might contribute to the uneasy peace in Northern Ireland that any fracturing of the Union would have been likely to put under threat. (interview with author, 2019)

Walker has also noted that, despite its base in Edinburgh, the British–Irish Council (BIC) – 'the most significant part of the East–West strand of the Good Friday Agreement' – has not been mobilised effectively by subsequent Scottish Governments and has largely been left to 'languish in obscurity' (Walker 2016: 80). This is all the more striking when juxtaposed to Scotland's bilateral (para)diplomatic efforts in the context of Brexit, including in relation to the Republic of Ireland. As noted by one Fine Gael member of Seanad Éireann (Irish Senate):

What is interesting is the very overt, increased engagement of the Scottish Parliament and the Scottish parties in everything Irish. There are two Scottish 'Innovation Offices' in the EU and we've a *very* proactive one here in Dublin ... Nicola Sturgeon has been here a couple of times, Fiona Hyslop has been here as well. There's constant engagement, and when they're here they reach out politically. And they work hand in glove with the office here. Calling it an 'Innovation Office' is the biggest ruse ever! It's a mini-Embassy, really. (Interview with author, 2018)

Contemporary bilateral relations between Scotland and Northern Ireland are primarily of a technical nature, and have been shaped as much (if not more) by European as by British frameworks (McCall 2007). Such institutionalised links as do exist across the North Channel, including under the auspices of the EU's INTERREG programme (which groups together Northern Ireland, the border counties in the Republic of Ireland, and the West of Scotland), face potential disruption as a consequence of Brexit (Todd 2015; Soares 2016: 842).[18] Politically, as Walker (2016: 81) argues, Scotland has 'many years of silence on the Northern Ireland situation to make up for, and no amount of obsessing over Old Firm antagonisms will ever be a substitute for positive interaction and thoughtful engagement'. With politics across these islands in a state of Brexit-induced flux which looks unlikely to settle in the short to medium term, and with all the risks to peace in Northern Ireland that this has brought with it, the need for such engagement has perhaps never been greater.

Acknowledgements

I am grateful to Graham Walker and Joe Webster for their help and guidance in the writing of this chapter. Research presented here was conducted under the auspices of the ESRC-funded project 'Between Two Unions: The Constitutional Future of the Islands after Brexit'. I would also like to acknowledge the support of the Economic and Social Research Council and the project team.

ELEVEN

The Scottish Conservatives and Europe: The Reluctant Brexit Party

Anthony Salamone

Introduction

After the 2016 referendum, Brexit became *the* defining issue of British politics. Its multifaceted yet largely introspective arguments stemmed from a lack of consensus regarding the United Kingdom's place in Europe and the world, and an acute difficulty in realising, or indeed accepting, its declining geopolitical significance. In Scotland, Brexit competes for attention with the independence debate, although the clear immediacy of the former surely warrants its priority. Scottish politics has, between these two issues, been preoccupied with the constitution for some years, often at the expense of much else. The devolution era in Scotland, which in May 2019 passed its twentieth anniversary, has at the same time fostered a distinct political culture, notable for its continental European features – a hemicycle parliament, coalition governments and multi-party budgets (Dardanelli 2006). European Union membership was embedded into the devolution settlement and European integration has found consistent cross-party support in the Scottish Parliament.

The Scottish Conservative and Unionist Party has been on a journey of evolution over those two decades, as have all the parties at Holyrood. While the SNP transformed from a fringe party at Westminster to the party of government in Scotland, and Scottish Labour fell from its position as the titan of Scottish politics to the third party (or worse), the Scottish Conservatives have more recently become the principal party of opposition, seemingly detoxified and second only to the SNP (albeit by some distance). A political party must be continually cognisant of its surroundings in order to survive. Having navigated the aftermath of the 2014 referendum, the Scottish Conservatives successfully shaped a cogent narrative against independence. The question of Europe, by contrast, has been – and will continue to be – a serious challenge to the Scottish party's electoral revival.

Scotland has proven much more at ease with Europeanism than England, its mainstream politics quite comfortable with both the European Union and membership thereof (Keating 2015). As a consequence of the independence debate, Scotland is also accustomed to discussing high-level constitutional issues. Indeed, Europe was a major part of the 2014 independence referendum: not whether to join the EU, but how to do so and how long it would take. Despite the opposing views on those questions, the clear implication from that particular dialogue was the accepted importance and normality of EU membership. After 2016, the Scottish Conservatives were compelled to decide how to balance their response to Brexit, their connection with the UK Conservatives and their relationship with Scotland's voters. In whatever measure the Scottish party has managed to attract new voters by overcoming difficulties around its connection with and perceived responsibility for the UK party, Brexit – and its implications for devolution and the independence debate – could reverse that progress.

No status quo or 'normal' situation exists to which Scotland or the UK could return. The UK will necessarily continue to debate its relationship with Europe and the rest of the world for years to come and, even outside of the EU, it will always be affected to a degree by European policies and decisions. The Scottish Conservative Party will have to adapt to the realities of this persistent uncertainty in the near future. This chapter considers the impact of Brexit on the Scottish Conservatives during the leadership of Ruth Davidson in four dimensions: Brexit's distinct Scottish political context, its electoral consequences, the conduct of Brexit within the UK, and the Brexit negotiations themselves. It concludes with reflections on the future prospects for the Scottish party in light of all four.

Brexit in the Scottish Context

Scotland did not vote for Brexit. While the EU referendum was a UK-wide contest, that reality has defined post-2016 political developments in Scotland. The 62/38 per cent Scottish result, although not an 'overwhelming majority' as some have claimed, was a decisive victory for Remain. Unlike in England and Wales, where support for EU membership was predominantly concentrated in certain urban areas, every local authority in Scotland was majority Remain. Notwithstanding sizeable minority support for Leave and some well-known opposition to the EU, principally in fishing communities in the North East (McAngus 2018), the political picture in

Scotland was overall pro-European. The EU referendum result in Scotland has also served as an anchor of legitimacy for the Scottish National Party and others to articulate resistance to Brexit and to advocate constitutional responses ranging from federalism to independence.

The Scottish Conservatives were not a party of Brexit enthusiasts. While hosting its share of Eurosceptics, and likely the largest proportion in the Scottish mainstream, the party was not replete with veterans of the decades-long anti-EU backbench campaigns waged by English Conservatives like Sir William Cash, John Redwood and Sir Bernard Jenkin. Were it not for David Cameron's Bloomberg speech and his decision to legitimise both an EU referendum and thus the idea of leaving the EU, the Scottish party would likely have remained comfortable with the Holyrood consensus in favour of EU membership.

During the EU referendum campaign, the Scottish Conservatives supported Remain, in contrast with the officially neutral UK party. Ruth Davidson was a passionate and high-profile spokesperson for continued EU membership. At the BBC's 'Great Debate' at Wembley in June 2016, Davidson proclaimed Remain the best option, saying: 'I know the EU isn't perfect, but the benefits far outweigh any costs. And the Britain that I know, the Britain that I love, works with its friends and neighbours. It doesn't walk away from them' (BBC News online, 22 June 2016). In campaigning to stay in the EU, the Scottish Conservatives were on the same page as the other four parties at Holyrood.

The mixed EU referendum result left the Scottish Conservatives, and indeed the other Scottish unionist parties, in a quagmire. Mainstream Scottish politics, including the Conservatives, was successful in convincing the Scottish electorate to reaffirm EU membership. However, unionists were by definition committed to the UK Union, and therefore to endorsing the UK-wide decision to leave the EU, despite clear opposition to Brexit in Scotland.

In the immediate aftermath of the EU referendum, the political atmosphere was febrile. David Cameron had abruptly resigned and the UK's Leave result surprised many in Scotland. For a brief period, there appeared to be a degree of consensus and the Scottish Parliament's first post-referendum motion calling on the Scottish Government to explore options to 'protect Scotland's relationship with the EU' passed by 92–0. The Conservatives abstained, yet their decision not to oppose the motion was significant. Thereafter, the party moved to opposing nearly all 'pro-EU' resolutions from the SNP or others. The SNP's calls for a second independence referendum to be placed 'on the table' had undoubtedly sharpened the Scottish Conservatives' political calculus.

Ultimately, the Scottish Conservatives supported the UK (Conservative) Government's efforts to implement the result of the EU referendum. This was never much in doubt, and it was grounded in four principal reasons. First was the primacy of honouring the results of referendums; second was embracing the UK-wide nature of the ballot – propositions such as requiring support from all four nations, while compatible with federalism, were not compatible with how the Scottish and UK Conservative parties had defined unionism; third was consistency between the Scottish and UK Conservatives; fourth (more by happenstance than design) was the defining of a distinct political position on Brexit. In the end, the Conservatives became the only mainstream Scottish party to support 'delivering Brexit'.

Having settled on this after the referendum, the Scottish Conservatives attempted, largely unsuccessfully, to advocate for a 'softer Brexit' – that is, closer association with the EU, for instance through remaining part of the European Single Market. Ruth Davidson originally argued for an 'open Brexit', a distinct option on the Brexit menu comprising close trade links and openness on immigration. In the aftermath of the 2017 UK general election, Davidson said: 'We must, in my view, seek to deliver an open Brexit, not a closed one, which puts our country's economic growth first' (Reuters, 12 June 2017). In all circumstances, the Scottish party called for leaving the EU *with* a deal.

The party's original support for a soft Brexit put it on the same page as much of Scottish opinion (to either remain in the EU or pursue a soft Brexit), but in a minority in terms of the UK Conservative Party. The Scottish Conservatives ended up largely as bystanders as the Westminster debate moved swiftly on to a 'hard' Brexit (leaving the Single Market and Customs Union), and later to a 'no-deal' Brexit (exiting the EU with no planned arrangements). In response, the Scottish party retreated from its soft Brexit position to simply arguing that the UK must leave the EU with a (any) deal. Despite private opposition to the UK's eventual Brexit path, publicly Scottish Conservatives closely matched the UK party, a trajectory which became self-reinforcing. Once it accepted Brexit and, subsequently, a hard Brexit (however reluctantly), it would have been very challenging to reverse course.

Electoral Consequences of Brexit

Brexit has reshaped British politics by introducing Remain and Leave electoral fault lines. In Scotland, Brexit and the independence debate have become deeply intertwined. For those opposed to Brexit, Scotland already has the option of becoming a separate state, as demonstrated by the 2014 independence referendum. Moreover, the SNP and its allies have continued their pursuit of independence throughout the Brexit process, laying the groundwork for a future referendum with opposition to Brexit and a posited disconnect between Scotland and the rest of the UK on Brexit, devolution and the future direction of the state. Writing to Theresa May in her ultimately failed bid in March 2017 for a second independence referendum, Nicola Sturgeon argued that, as a consequence of Brexit, 'the people of Scotland must have the right to choose our own future – in short, to exercise our right of self-determination' (BBC News online, 31 March 2017).

Equally, the Scottish Conservatives' response to Brexit has also been largely defined by the independence debate. For instance, during the Brexit process Ruth Davidson disavowed referendums for their purported divisiveness, saying she 'would happily never fight another constitutional referendum again in my lifetime' (*Scotsman*, 3 May 2018). However, if another independence ballot had not been an immediate prospect, might Davidson have been able to support a second EU referendum? As Ireland among others has demonstrated, a second referendum on the same topic is not an inherent democratic outrage, and indeed can prove constructive (see Barrett 2017). While the existence of a viable independence movement rendered that prospect impossible, in different circumstances the Scottish Conservative Party might have been able to articulate its pro-European sentiment more concretely.

The post-2014 electoral revival of the Scottish Conservatives has been largely attributed to its success in consolidating unionist support (Simpkins 2017). Its party brand comprised a distinct Scottish identity, detoxification from its association with the UK Conservatives and a reinforced message on unionism. The Scottish Conservatives have not avoided independence; indeed, their opposition to it has been the central aspect of their message and electoral campaigns (Scottish Conservative Party 2016). The party's position on Brexit also became a core part of its distinct offer. The Conservatives are the only mainstream party in Scotland to support implementing Brexit. Scottish Labour prevaricated on Brexit for some time like its UK party, but eventually aligned with the SNP, Scottish Greens and Scottish Liberal Democrats in supporting a second EU referendum and remaining in the EU. Accordingly, the Scottish Conservatives could build an electoral strategy that occupied a unique political space: opposition to independence combined with support for Brexit.

In contrast to the UK party, the Scottish Conservative message was less about enthusiastic endorsement of Brexit and more about fulfilling the EU referendum result. Davidson made it clear she was not 'flying the flag for Brexit' (BBC News online, 11 September 2017). Her preferred framing was achieving a 'sensible' Brexit through a 'good' deal for Scotland and the UK. In addition to attracting moderate Brexit supporters and ardent Brexiteers, it could also appeal to voters who simply wanted Brexit to be concluded. While this pro-UK, pro-Brexit position has some potential to be successful, it also carries major limitations. The Scottish party's support of Brexit was grounded in at least achieving a Brexit deal, and preferably a closer relationship with the EU. However, it was very difficult to argue for an open Brexit when the UK Government did not pursue such a policy. By taking a clear pro-Brexit stance, the Scottish Conservatives found themselves competing on that front with the Brexit Party, which would easily endorse a no-deal Brexit. In a worst-case scenario, the Scottish Conservatives could lose both Brexit enthusiasts and pro-Europeans and be left with a smaller base of mainly moderate Brexit supporters.

Moreover, support for the UK Union and Brexit together was not the prevailing view in Scottish public opinion, as evidenced by the strong support for EU membership in the 2016 referendum and subsequently. The other two main unionist parties, Scottish Labour and the Scottish Liberal Democrats, both opposed Brexit and favoured remaining in the EU. Although the electoral weakness of these parties (especially Labour) played a part in the Scottish Conservatives' electoral revival, they might not remain weak indefinitely, and could end up offering an alternative path for unionist voters to support closer EU links rather than the Scottish Tory line of honouring Brexit.

Indeed, the two major electoral contests in Scotland since the EU referendum up to the end of Davidson's leadership delivered mixed results for the Scottish Conservatives. First, the 2017 snap UK general election allowed the party to consolidate its anti-independence and Brexit support, capitalising on disaffection with the SNP's pro-EU response to Brexit and its perceived hasty push for another independence referendum. The Conservatives displaced the SNP in parts of the North East and Central Scotland, where opposition to the SNP's approach was strongest. Second, the 2019 European Parliament election (which was ostensibly not supposed to take place in the UK) was less encouraging for the party. While it retained its single MEP, compared with 2014 it dropped from third to fourth place and its share of the vote declined by more than 5.5 per cent. The Brexit Party replaced UKIP (UK Independence Party) as the fringe anti-EU party and came second in the election, demonstrating a clear challenge for the Scottish Conservatives on the question of Europe.

In between those two elections, Theresa May's Withdrawal Agreement failed to get through Parliament, exit day was extended and there was increased speculation regarding a no-deal Brexit. The SNP also shifted to back unequivocally a second EU referendum, and while the Scottish Conservatives maintained their pro-Brexit position, their preferred 'soft' Brexit option receded. Future elections in Scotland would pose a challenge for the party, having strong Brexit *and* independence dimensions.

The Scottish Conservatives will compete with Scottish Labour and the Scottish Liberal Democrats on unionism, and with the Brexit Party on Brexit. If Scottish public opinion continues to harden against Brexit, the Conservatives may feel it necessary to rely more on their anti-independence stance instead of their Brexit position. However, should the UK's politics continue to be weakened further by Brexit uncertainty, the Scottish party may well find itself dealing with rising unpopularity with Brexit as well as increased pressure on the UK Union.

Conduct of Brexit within the UK

Brexit was to a significant extent more about ongoing political debates *within* the UK than actual negotiations with the EU 27 members. Internal disagreements over how or whether to leave the EU were the major hurdles to reaching a Brexit finality, rather than the EU27–UK dialogue itself. Moreover, the process of Brexit – how it was conducted within the UK – had implications for the UK's governance arrangements. For Scotland, Brexit had an impact upon both intergovernmental relations (i.e. relationships between the UK and Scottish Governments) and devolution (the powers of the Scottish Parliament and Government).

The UK Government's approach to Brexit was not inevitable, particularly in respect of intergovernmental relations. In contrast with Theresa May's initial commitments as Prime Minister to agree a common way forward on Brexit with the devolved administrations, the Scottish and Welsh governments (Northern Ireland not having had an executive since March 2017) had relatively limited involvement in the UK's internal Brexit negotiations and preparations. Whether the UK side of the Brexit negotiations themselves, or major moments like May's Lancaster House speech and Article 50 activation letter, the devolved administrations were on the outside. The Joint Ministerial Committee, the UK's main intergovernmental forum, was seen by the Scottish and Welsh governments to be insufficient for handling Brexit (Scottish Government 2019).

The impact of Brexit on the devolution settlement, meanwhile, was a core component of the Scottish debate. Questions of which powers 'returning from Brussels' should be placed with Holyrood or Westminster, how those choices should be made, and how the UK and Scottish governments should develop 'common frameworks' to work together on former EU areas consumed a significant amount of Holyrood's attention (Salamone 2018b). The EU Withdrawal Act 2016 altered some areas of competence which the Scottish Parliament already held, and Holyrood's related EU Continuity Bill attempted to set a different path on retaining EU law after

Brexit. Brexit and the Withdrawal Act certainly challenged the previous convention that the transfer of powers from London to Edinburgh was generally one way (Salamone 2018a). Debates on devolution took place at both the Westminster and Holyrood levels, although the Scottish Conservatives had a stronger independent identity at Holyrood.

Its response to these devolution issues were measured. It acknowledged concerns about post-Brexit devolution but sought to downplay notions of Brexit causing totemic challenges to devolved governance. At Holyrood, the Scottish Conservatives agreed with the other four parties on some principles, but voted against the EU Continuity Bill and related motions. This stance set it apart once again from the other unionist parties. Scottish Labour and the Scottish Liberal Democrats both supported the Scottish Government. Accordingly, the Conservatives have been able to adopt a position defined by reasonability – not giving in to apparent nationalist pressure.

At the time, the Conservative constitutional relations spokesperson Adam Tomkins called the Continuity Bill 'an invitation to make bad law and to make law badly. To that invitation, we politely say no thanks. Scottish Conservatives will not be supporting this ill thought through bill' (*Telegraph*, 1 March 2018). Indeed, most of the aspects covered by common frameworks and the EU powers debate were technical and esoteric, and less dramatic than opponents portrayed them. In keeping with its approach to Brexit, the Scottish Conservatives largely – though not fully – aligned with the UK Conservative Party, pursuing opposition to independence, support for Brexit and moderation on devolution.

Brexit Negotiations and Strategy

The UK Government's attempts to carry out Brexit, through negotiations with the EU27 and domestic preparations for withdrawal, were fraught with challenges, contradictions and changes of course. Even the most ardent supporter of Brexit would have found it difficult to argue that everything went well. In the negotiations, the UK Government set conditions, such as on financial commitments and citizens' rights, and then ultimately agreed the EU position anyway. It accepted the principle of an Ireland backstop, which it later attempted to reject, and took nearly two years from the referendum to set out its first paper on the future EU–UK relationship. Ultimately, its original withdrawal agreement was rejected three times by the UK Parliament.

Theresa May compounded her Brexit difficulties by not seeking cross-party consensus (if it was to be had) at the start of the process, holding an unnecessary general election in which she lost her small working majority, and setting seemingly indelible negotiating red lines without agreement from Cabinet, party or Parliament (despite being a minority government after June 2017). In her Lancaster House speech, May announced her decision to leave the EU Single Market and the Customs Union, as well as her objective to negotiate the future relationship before leaving the EU: 'I believe the framework I have outlined today is in Britain's interests. It is in Europe's interests. And it is in the interests of the wider world' (May 2017). The subsequent course of Brexit tested that assertion to breaking point.

After the 2017 snap election, the Scottish Conservatives increased their Westminster cohort to 13 MPs (McGowan 2018). A major argument thereafter was that this group of Scottish Tory MPs could have a significant influence on the UK Conservative Party (*Guardian*, 11 June 2017). However, across the major moments of Brexit, before and after that election – from the Lancaster House speech (announcement of a hard Brexit) and activation of Article 50, to the negotiations themselves, the joint report and the draft Withdrawal Agreement – it was difficult to point to substantial political or policy victories achieved specifically by the 13 MPs. By virtue of David Mundell's relationship with Ruth Davidson, the Scottish party also had space for indirect influence through the Scotland Office, yet the department was not at all central to the UK Government's Brexit strategy. While the Westminster group may have achieved collective influence elsewhere, it was not apparent on Brexit. By contrast, another group of a comparable size – the Democratic Unionist Party (DUP) – had pivotal influence on the government and its Brexit policy, through providing its working majority via a confidence-and-supply agreement.

Nevertheless, in the absence of a differentiated arrangement (namely, a fully separate party or caucus), the Scottish Conservative Westminster cohort faced several challenges. First was the lack of a common, distinctive position on Brexit. While the Westminster group was generally loyal to Ruth Davidson, members took different positions on Brexit, with some actively supporting a hard Brexit and aligning with the European Research Group (ERG). Second was the fact May concentrated her efforts on persuading the hard-line ERG and the DUP to back her approach and eventual deal. Given the majority of the Scottish Conservative group held middle-ground Brexit views, it would not have been a natural focus for May in any case. Third was the closed decision-making style which May practised. Her Brexit strategy and nearly all major policy decisions were decided by a very small team around the Prime Minister. As a result, it was difficult for anyone outside of that circle to have substantial influence on Brexit policy, even 13 Scottish Conservative MPs.

Neither the Westminster group nor the Scottish Conservative Party as a whole had much influence on the UK Conservatives' approach to Brexit. In

addition to attempting to steer the government towards a successful negotiated Brexit, Ruth Davidson and David Mundell tried to impress upon the
UK leadership the potential for Brexit to affect the Scottish independence
debate. During the 2019 Conservative leadership contest, Mundell wrote
that the new Prime Minister would need to '[deliver] a Brexit that works for
the whole UK, including Remain-voting Scotland. It also means ensuring
that, from top to bottom, the UK government is geared towards strengthening the union. It will require a change' (*Guardian*, 6 July 2019).

Despite being of the same party, Scottish and UK Conservative views
continued to diverge. Immigration was a particularly noteworthy example.
The UK Government proposed a post-Brexit regime of a high minimum
salary threshold, limiting numbers of permits for agricultural workers and
points-based restrictions for EU citizens. The Scottish Conservatives, and
Ruth Davidson in particular, disagreed with these positions given their possible impact on Scotland (they also lacked much aversion to the free movement of people). Nevertheless, the UK Government made no clear change
of course as a result of their interventions.

With the failure of May's Withdrawal Agreement, the delays to Brexit,
her eventual resignation and the resulting leadership contest, the passing of the premiership to Boris Johnson brought a distinct change of
dynamic which, on balance, was largely negative for the Scottish Conservatives. Alongside his swashbuckling rhetoric and aggressive politics,
Johnson wholeheartedly accepted a no-deal Brexit and became fixated
on leaving the EU on 31 October 2019, whatever the costs. In his first
speech on the steps of Downing Street, Johnson both accepted 'no deal'
and began to shift (future) blame onto the EU, declaring that the UK
must 'prepare for the remote possibility that Brussels refuses any further
to negotiate and we are forced to come out with no deal not because we
want that outcome – of course not – but because it is only common sense
to prepare' (Johnson 2019).

The increasing likelihood of a no-deal Brexit caused significant unease
in the Scottish Conservative Party. Johnson's leadership style and approach
to Brexit also seemed finally to provide the boost for independence some
had awaited (or feared) since the day after the EU referendum. The Scottish
party leadership was also cut off from the UK Cabinet upon the replacement of David Mundell as Secretary of State for Scotland with Alister Jack,
who was not close to Davidson. Johnson, like May, also concentrated Brexit
decision-making on a small team at Number 10 and the Cabinet Office,
making it even more difficult for the Scottish party to make its voice heard.

Johnson's first trip to Edinburgh as Prime Minister, especially his meeting
with Nicola Sturgeon at Bute House, looked like the visit of a foreign dignitary,

the optics of which were questionable from a Scottish Conservative perspective. One potential source of optimism for the party was Johnson's initial pledge to strengthen the UK Union and engage more actively in Scotland, even if it were to mean bypassing the Scottish Government. Given the primacy of Brexit and the relative marginality of Scotland to Westminster politics, however, that pledge might yet prove more rhetorical than real, and could easily backfire if not presented tactfully.

With the heightened chance of a no-deal Brexit and the added strains between the Scottish and UK parties, the Scottish Conservatives arguably found themselves in a worse position under Johnson than under May. In the run-up to the 31 October 2019 Brexit deadline, the Scottish party focused its rhetoric on continuing to argue for leaving the EU with a deal and supporting the Prime Minister's renegotiation efforts, at least until interim leader Jackson Carlaw's widely publicised U-turn prior to the Conservative Party's 2019 autumn conference:

> Another extension, another three months, with nobody really agreeing on what they would do during that [time] or what the outcome would be, is far more damaging for Scotland, for the United Kingdom and for business, for everybody, than finally getting to a point where we resolve this issue and move on. (BBC News online, 30 September 2019)

Reports suggested Carlaw had failed to inform the Scottish Conservative shadow cabinet of this change in policy, provoking 'cold fury' among some colleagues (*Telegraph*, 30 September 2019).

Future of the Scottish Conservative Party and Brexit

Brexit and the UK's relationship with Europe will remain core aspects of British and Scottish politics for years to come. The UK will continue to be part of the EU's orbit – simply from a position on the outside, and with minimal influence. And since relations with the EU will remain politically salient, they will continue to influence Scotland's other debates on independence and devolution. The fundamentals of public opinion on the EU will surely remain. Scotland's pro-European sentiment will not go away – in fact, it has increased since the EU referendum (*Holyrood*, 15 August 2018). For the Scottish Conservatives, a particular worry will be the emerging convergence between support for Europe and support for independence (*Financial Times*, 20 June 2019). While this trend, if it develops, may not affect the party's now Brexit-focused voter base, it may make a sustained majority for Scottish independence more likely.

The UK-wide EU referendum result obliged the Scottish Conservatives to take a position on Brexit consistent with its views on the British and European unions. In the end, the party adopted a pro-Brexit position, even though it had not previously advocated for that outcome. While the Scottish party was initially successful at gathering pro-Union and pro-Brexit support, it remained in question how far that combined constituency would take it. The party seems unlikely, for example, to achieve a hypothetical majority in the Scottish Parliament on an anti-EU message. Moreover, it has become isolated on the issue of Brexit, and it would be difficult for the party in future to return to a pro-EU position. Looking ahead to the 2021 Holyrood election and in the aftermath of the 2019 Westminster election, Brexit will be centre stage and the Scottish Conservatives will continue to be associated with the UK Government's handling of the issue. If Scottish public opinion in favour of Europe increases, and if the UK Conservatives are blamed for Brexit failings in Scotland, the Scottish Conservatives might end up being concerned with retaining their existing seats rather than any hope of gaining more.

Brexit demonstrated the difficulty the Scottish Conservatives faced in influencing the UK party on certain matters. While Brexit did not cause this difficulty, it made it more visible and pronounced. And given the Scottish party's prior history in debating greater autonomy or independence from the UK party, it may well look again to other political parties and arrangements in Europe. The German CDU–CSU model provides a clear example of separate parties in permanent coalition, with space for the CSU to differentiate within Bavaria yet have more influence at the federal level in terms of profile and policy (see Frymark 2018).

Such a model might yet prove viable for the Scottish Conservatives. The party already has considerable autonomy within Scotland, so the main benefit would be to achieve distance from the UK party's legacy and record. A fully separate party would be more effective at Westminster only if the parliamentary group had sufficient numbers. The Scottish party could in such circumstances secure policies, funding or even ministerial posts, and have greater visibility for its distinct achievements. In reality, federations and unions can accommodate various party structures. A separate party would also enable the Scottish Conservatives to articulate a different policy on Brexit and its aftermath, which might better suit their long-term electoral prospects.

On the other hand, Brexit raised the profile of the independence question, which might be beneficial for the Scottish Conservatives' anti-independence campaigning, but it also gave rise to circumstances which have and might further still increase support for independence. The Scottish Conservatives, perhaps now a reluctant Brexit party, defined their post-referendum Brexit stance at the cost of their interpretation of the UK Union. Throughout the Brexit process, the Scottish Conservative and Unionist Party largely found itself reacting to UK Government decisions and strategy. As Brexit continues to play out in Scotland and the rest of the UK, it may continue to find itself in a similarly uncomfortable position.

TWELVE

A Tale of Two Nationalisms: Scottish Nationalism and Unionism in the Age of Disruption

Gerry Hassan

Introduction: The Coming of Boris Johnson

A few days after Boris Johnson became Prime Minister, Ian Blackford, the SNP's Westminster leader, said he had 'no mandate' for a 'No Deal Brexit' and that he had not 'been voted in by the people of Scotland. He has to respect Scotland's wishes to remain in the EU' (BBC News, 29 July 2019). In a similar vein on social media, pro-independence voices called Johnson 'an unelected PM' who represented the 'continuing undemocratic rule of [Westminster] Tories over the people of Scotland' or 'Prime Minister of Englandshire'. Upon the appointment of Alister Jack as Scottish Secretary, Douglas Chapman, an SNP MP, said it represented 'posh boy dictatorship'.

Scottish Conservative and other centre-right voices responded to this criticism with a barrage of counter-charges. These included branding the SNP and independence 'the politics of grievance', claiming that 'the SNP hates Britain and its traditions' and that 'hatred of England can lead to self-destruction', while characterising the party as the 'unconstitutional undemocratic SNP' and 'nation wreckers'. 'The SNP's latest tool to divide the country even further – class hatred,' stated Miles Briggs, a Tory MSP: 'as if 12 years of SNP grievance and division hasn't done enough' (29 July 2019). Another claimed that 'the SNP are really bad losers', the argument being that it had not honoured the results of the 2014 and 2016 referendums.

Just a normal set of exchanges in any week of Scottish post-2014, one might say. But this had an extra frisson in the early days of Boris Johnson's premiership. It followed the turbo-charged high-wire politics Scotland had become used to – of insult, incomprehension of opponents' views and challenging the legitimacy of those with different opinions: a kind of mental trench warfare, a slow war of attrition in which each side attempted to wear down the other.

Scottish nationalism and Scottish Tory unionism are supposedly two irreconcilable forces, two sworn enemies fighting to the bitter end over the future of the nation. This is, of course, how they both want to see themselves and each other, but there is more to it than that. For much of Scotland's existence as part of the Union, these two supposedly opposing forces have actually coalesced in what has been accurately called 'unionism–nationalism', a politics of autonomy and distinctiveness within the union (Morton 1999; Kidd 2019).

This chapter will explore the limitations of this bifurcation of Scottish politics, as well as the shortcomings of the politics it articulates, and in doing so will address the dynamic between the two and the degree of co-dependency and mutual self-interest they share. It will also do so in the context of Ruth Davidson's eight-year tenure as Scottish Conservative leader from 2011 to 2019, assessing how her leadership was perceived in light of the above, how it framed and reframed that bifurcation, and what the future prospects for the Scottish Conservatives might be.

A Short History Lesson: Scotland before 1979

Politics were not always as they are today. Scottish unionism has at times celebrated its Scottish credentials and traditions, including its defence of national distinctiveness in the 1940s and 1950s when it stood against Labour centralisation. At the same time, Scottish nationalism has not always been synonymous with anti-Toryism and the centre-left, flirting with the centre-right and Conservative support in the post-war era. That period overlapped with Labour's long antagonism towards Scottish self-government which only ended in 1974, and in terms of attitude took well into the 1980s to disappear entirely.

The basic tenets of what is being discussed here should be examined, namely the underlying assumptions of Scottish nationalism and unionism. The former is a minority nationalism in the UK, competing with the official, majority nationalism of the UK state. It comes in numerous forms – civic, non-civic, cultural, political – with the political variant mostly but not completely associated in recent times with the campaign for self-government and, increasingly, independence.

Scottish unionism, meanwhile, is the belief that the union between Scotland and England is beneficial to the people of Scotland as well as the rest of the UK. Unionism, however, is also a form of nationalism – British state nationalism – an expression of the UK's 'official' nationalism. What this brings forth is that a large part of Scottish politics, in particular during and

since the independence referendum, has become a tale of competing nationalisms – one of which is relatively open about it, understands itself and is
seen by others as 'nationalism' (Scottish), while the other does not see itself
in such terms and feels slighted whenever others identify it as such (British).

This dynamic between minority and majority nationalisms, between
non-official and official nationalisms, is one repeated the world over. What
this does, despite its prevalence in Scotland, is diminish the bandwidth of
politics and shrink the vibrancy and veracity of other political traditions
and, because of this, the quality and substance of political debate. Hence,
political traditions with deep roots in the Scottish body politic – conservatism, liberalism and social democracy – have all been diminished by an
environment defined by competing nationalisms.

For whatever the degree to which conservatism has become associated
with unionism (or more recently, social democracy with Scottish nationalism), these ideologies have separate existences and rationales beyond
constitutional politics. Both these philosophies have rich intellectual traditions, and yet their ballast and mindsets have become atrophied and con-
strained by their restriction within the parameters of Scotland's ongoing
constitutional debate.

Was 1979 Really Scotland's Year Zero?

Scottish nationalism and unionism have meant different things at different
times but a distinct dynamic set in after 1979 with the election of the first
Thatcher government. Then, the Conservatives gained 31.4 per cent of the
vote in Scotland to Labour's 41.5 per cent, and 22 seats to Labour's 44 (Butler
and Kavanagh 1980). More fundamentally, the media and public discourse
surrounding this result was not couched in terms of Scottish self-government
and 'no mandate' – all that was to follow, therefore redefining 1979 as a kind
of 'Year Zero'. Instead, contemporary headlines concerned the exhaustion of
Labour, the end of the Callaghan government, the energy of Thatcher and the
need for change.

With this caveat, the immediate post-1979 period initially defined
Scottish politics in terms of left versus right, which then slowly retreated
and gave way to the 'Scottish dimension'. By 1983, the left-versus-right
axis began to be superseded by the constitutional question, and at the
1987 general election – held against the backdrop of 'high Thatcherism' –
this transformation was nearly complete. There were still references to left
and right, but these were now portrayed through a constitutional lens,
talk of 'the Doomsday scenario', 'no mandate' and the idea of Scotland
becoming a Tory-free zone (Stewart 2009; Torrance 2009).

Thatcher herself instinctively knew Scotland was different, and becoming more so during her premiership. Charles Moore, her official biographer, put his finger on one critical element in his examination of the political terrain following the 1987 election. He identified how the traditional tropes of patriotism played out differently north and south of the border, and to the Conservatives' disadvantage in Scotland:

> As a patriotic political campaigner without rival, Mrs Thatcher found it disturbing that in Scotland she could not play that card without being trumped by parties from the left. A right-of-centre party which lacks dominant patriotic appeal tends to reduce to a fairly small middle class party of business. (Moore 2019: 18)

So, Scottish politics was reframed between 1979 and 1997 around the campaign for a Scottish Parliament, self-government and the constitutional question (Hassan 2012, 2014). The legacy and influence of this has grown into a Scottish consensus – one with a popular and elite basis – which took institutional form in the official account of devolution and the Scottish Parliament (Mitchell 2014). This was informed by the electoral decline of the Scottish Conservatives, who went from 31.4 per cent of the vote in 1979 to 17.5 per cent in 1997, and from 22 seats to zero, making the long-predicted 'Tory-free' Scotland a reality (at least in terms of parliamentary representation) as the twentieth century drew to a close. Thereafter, the Scottish Tories often adopted an apologetic demeanour in an attempt to mitigate the reality that it was perceived by many voters as a pariah party cut adrift from the pro-Home Rule Scottish consensus.

Devolution Stories and the Rise of the SNP

A significant shift occurred when the SNP won the 2007 Holyrood election and formed their first devolved government. Over the next four years, this minority administration (led by Alex Salmond) sought occasional support from the Scottish Greens and informal assistance from Annabel Goldie, leader of the Scottish Conservatives since the resignation of David McLetchie. Labour belatedly attempted to make this a live issue, using it to resurrect the 'tartan Tory' charge against the SNP, but it had little traction.

The SNP's landslide victory in 2011 resulted in a majority government, a commitment to an independence referendum and a new Scottish Conservative leader, Ruth Davidson. These last two factors would contribute to improving the fortunes of Scottish Toryism. Davidson brought the Tories back in from the cold, while the referendum allowed her party to re-inhabit their natural political terrain and make a genuine, heartfelt stand for their core belief – the case for the Union – and do so in a way which the other opposition parties, the Liberal Democrats and Labour, could not.

Ruth Davidson embodied a modern, forward-looking conservatism, very different from the tweeds and twin sets and pearls of Scottish Tory legend (Liddle 2018; Davidson 2018a). She was irreverent, funny, challenging, good at communications and media. She spoke to a younger generation for whom 1979 and even Thatcher was part of the distant past (often overlooked), and was profoundly urban in her language and demeanour, which mattered in a party that had virtually disappeared from all Scotland's major cities.

Davidson also carved out a niche position in relation to the UK Conservative Party, signalling her opposition to what some said was an Islamophobic campaign against Sadiq Khan at the 2016 London Mayoral election, and in the European referendum of the same year. In the latter, Davidson placed herself in a political space directly opposed to Boris Johnson and the Leave campaign, although the logic of this became more questionable in the years that followed; first, when Leave won, and second, when Johnson became Prime Minister in July 2019. This constituted a major political headache for Davidson, challenging her strategy of detoxifying Scottish Toryism and contributing to her resignation as party leader in August 2019.

The independence referendum campaign, however, had played a pivotal part in the reintroduction of the Scottish Tories to the political mainstream. Davidson led an energetic, populist defence of the Union, one that the once-dominant Scottish Labour Party proved incapable of making. Its case for the Union, led by Gordon Brown, was qualified and conditional, stressing 'pooling and sharing' within the UK. The Conservatives, on the other hand, believed in it as an article of faith.

This continued to benefit the Scottish Conservatives post-2014 as politics divided into independence versus the Union, with the primary advocates of each – the SNP and Conservatives – squeezing out, in particular, Scottish Labour (Johns and Mitchell 2016). As the Scottish Tories revived following the 2015 'tsunami' at the 2016 Scottish and 2017 Westminster elections as the main opposition to the SNP, they gathered an increasing plurality of 'No' voters, becoming the main anti-independence party and even outpolling Labour (Hassan 2018; Convery 2016a).

This led to a growing fan club centred around Ruth Davidson. This had roots in Scottish Tory circles but also reached into the opposition parties and large swathes of the media commentariat, many of whom had no previous record of Tory sympathies. It also, tellingly, stretched into the corridors of the UK Conservative Party as it – led by David Cameron and subsequently

Theresa May – struggled to find a credible voice to articulate what they said was compassionate, modern conservatism. While it lasted, the Davidson phenomenon was an unusual state of affairs for members of the Scottish Conservative Party, who had grown used to being treated as outcasts. Now they had a popular celebrity leader who was causing political waves, was talked about in glowing terms, and even dared to appear on non-political programmes such as *Have I Got News for You* and *Celebrity Bake Off*.

Davidson's emergence as a much-talked-about Scottish politician in London circles had some similarities with the way in which Nicola Sturgeon's star had burned brightly during and after the 2015 UK general election. Then, many centre-left commentators had indulged in a fantasy politics where someone of Sturgeon's talents transformed the British left through a different type of leadership. The Davidson obsession, like its Sturgeon equivalent, was partly the attractiveness of a distant star which they (London-based commentators) could only semi-understand and observe via their London telescope. It also revealed the sad condition of UK political leadership – Labour's Ed Miliband in the case of Sturgeon, and the Conservatives' Theresa May vis-à-vis Davidson.

At the same time, Ruth Davidson became a lightning rod and hate figure for many independence supporters. She was, after all, a Tory – unapologetic, unflinching and effective – and the widespread abuse and abrasive comment directed at her was, although it probably did not feel like that, a sort of compliment. These independence supporters were saying that Davidson had influence and impact, and that she mattered; the same voices had not felt and acted in the same way towards David McLetchie and Annabel Goldie.

The Rise and Fall of Ruth Davidson

The rise of Ruth Davidson and the over-the-top commentary about her riding to the rescue of the Union, becoming First Minister of Scotland in 2021, or stopping a hard-line Brexiteer becoming leader of the UK Conservatives post-Cameron or May, always bordered on the ridiculous. Nevertheless, this attitude reached the highest echelons of the party, according to Martin Kettle (*Guardian*, 3 May 2019). He revealed the existence of a Cameron plan (when Prime Minister) to bring Davidson into his Cabinet as Defence Secretary, give her a seat in the Lords, and then bide his time before moving her into the Commons via a safe seat. Even after Cameron resigned as Prime Minister, he still harboured high hopes for Davidson, writing in his memoirs that with 'the phenomenal Ruth Davidson at the helm, I don't doubt that we could become the biggest [party]' at the 2021 Holyrood elections (Cameron 2019: 557).

At the same time, some anti-Tory commentators tried hard to deny the basic facts that Davidson *was* popular with voters and *had* overseen a revival of the Scottish Conservative Party, such was their detestation of all things Tory. And when Boris Johnson's ascent to the premiership brought a sudden crash in Davidson stock, some previously sympathetic pundits repudiated their previous investments. 'Project Ruth', meaning the remaking of the Scottish Tories under her tutelage, 'is over', proclaimed Kenny Farquharson (*The Times*, 31 July 2019).

All of these judgements were based on little hard evidence in terms of polling. Ruth Davidson, when she resigned in August 2019, had seen eight years of consistently positive ratings with the public, and whatever happened in the future to the party she had once led, this was a significant record and achievement for any leader of an opposition party, let alone the leader of the Scottish Conservatives.

The Longer Crisis of Scottish Unionism Following Two Referendums

The rise and fall of Ruth Davidson can only be understood in the context of the febrile state of Scottish and UK politics post-2014 as well as the fragile composition of unionism. During the 2015 general election, for example, the Conservatives launched a series of posters depicting the Labour leader Ed Miliband in the breast pocket of Alex Salmond, who was planning a return to the House of Commons. As Nicola Sturgeon's profile rose during the campaign, her image replaced that of her predecessor. This was directed at soft UKIP (UK Independence Party) voters in England who might be scared into voting Conservative, horrified at the prospect of a weak Labour government 'held to ransom' by a powerful SNP contingent (Butler and Kavanagh 2015).

This strategy appears to have had some effect, with the Conservatives winning a slender parliamentary majority rather than the hung Parliament many expected. At the same time, it was seen by some pro-unionist voices as an assault on the fundamental tenets of unionism. Hence, numerous observers felt Davidson was being hung out to dry for the sake of defending marginal seats in England. More explicitly, Hugo Rifkind viewed it as a willingness to weaken the case for the Union for short-term electoral advantage. Demonising the SNP's potential influence at Westminster and casting Scottish representation as somehow questionable was not, he felt, a convincing pro-Union message:

> Remember all those decades when there was a Tory PM and almost no Scottish Tory MPs? Remember the way they'd shrug and explain that this was just how

a union works, and that the reverse could as easily be true? Call me a mug, but I actually thought they meant it. They don't want a partner, these people, but a pet.

This sad state, Rifkind continued, had led to 'Tories abandoning unionism for their own self-interest (while pretending they haven't) and Labour cleaving to it for theirs (while pretending they aren't)'. This was, he argued, a fundamental shift with potentially huge consequences:

> It is not the SNP who are the real threat to Britain, for all their swift and startling resurgence. It's their secret English allies, who are many and various and hiding in plain sight. And they pretend to oppose the Scottish separatists, and the Scottish separatists pretend to oppose them, but both are giggling behind the backs of their hands. (*Spectator*, 21 March 2015)

This commentary neatly anticipated the arrival of Boris Johnson as Prime Minister in July 2019 and the related prospect of a no-deal Brexit. Ruth Davidson had long been an opponent of both, even launching an internal initiative known as 'Operation Arse' in October 2018, the aim of which was to prevent Johnson becoming UK party leader and thus also premier. But in the early days of the Johnson administration, the new Prime Minister went out of his way to pull the rug from under Davidson and her case for moderate conservatism and unionism.

Not only did Johnson sack David Mundell, a Davidson ally, as Secretary of State for Scotland against her explicit advice, but he undermined Davidson's standing within the wider UK party. As he postulated and pontificated about a no-deal Brexit, it became clear Davidson had no real authority over the 13 Scottish Conservative MPs in any critical parliamentary votes. Hence, it was hardly a bolt from the blue when, just over a month into Johnson's occupancy of Downing Street, Davidson resigned as Scottish Tory leader.

The bigger picture was even more serious. Johnson's professed unionism was characteristically rhetorical – 'the awesome foursome' was how he described the UK on his first day as Prime Minister. By his statements and actions, however, it appeared he had little grasp of the delicate tapestry and ecology that comprised the Union he professed to love. Johnson may have gone on a grand tour in his first week, visiting Scotland, Wales and Northern Ireland, but in none did he meet with a uniformly positive response, or seem to understand the way in which Brexit had exacerbated pressure points within the 'awesome foursome' he now led.

This was a unionism which had no real grasp of or interest in the history, practices and traditions of the union state, and instead went through the motions, pretending it understood the three non-English nations of the UK. This had become an English nationalism that was, to all intents and purposes, showcasing the demise of any coherent and popular unionism. This was particularly acute in Northern Ireland, where the new government was seemingly insensitive to the Good Friday Agreement. Despite this, in early 2020 power sharing was restored at Stormont.

In Scotland, while a plausible case could be made against the SNP and its arguments for independence, what was missing from Johnson's Conservative Party (or indeed any alternative pro-Union viewpoint) was a positive and strategic case for Scotland and the Union, or any offer which might attempt to reset the terms of the debate north of the border. Scotland appeared to be viewed like Northern Ireland and Wales: faraway countries of which they knew nothing.

Thus, British Toryism under Johnson ended up promoting very unconservative values (more Rousseau than Edmund Burke), continually invoking the inalienable mandate of popular sovereignty of 17.4 million voters in pursuit of an absolutist, indivisible notion of authority that brooked no compromise. In this, the Tory tradition had forgotten its own history and the humiliation of the British state when it has previously embraced absolutist sovereignty – the loss of American colonies in 1775–6, or Irish independence in 1921–2.

In both cases, the British authorities, first under Lord North in relation to America, and second, the Tory response to Irish Home Rule in 1911–14, deliberately refused compromise and reform, and instead stood firm on the basis of 'no surrender'. Fast forward to Boris Johnson in his first months as Prime Minister referring to a 'do-or-die Brexit', and describing the Benn–Burt attempt to extend the deadline for leaving the European Union on 31 October 2019 as a 'Surrender Bill'.

Scottish Conservatives beyond the Current Claims of Two Nationalisms

Scottish nationalism's claim to be a centre-left and anti-Tory force could in future come under more scrutiny and question. Similarly, the perception of Scottish Toryism as being opposed to all things associated with Scottish nationalism might not always make sense in the world of Brexit Britain. The simplistic dichotomies of recent decades – of Scottish nationalism as centre-left and Scottish unionism as centre-right – might not always hold true, certainly if history is any guide (see Kidd 2019; Jackson 2012b).

One of the key dimensions in this respect will be the crisis of unionism across the UK and how this plays out in Scotland, and Labour unionism as much as Conservative (on the former, see Edgerton 2018; Hassan and Shaw 2019). As explored above, the reductive match-up of the constitutional question along left-versus-right lines has deprived of political oxygen and attention political traditions that exist beyond that framing, chiefly conservatism, social democracy, liberalism and even – to an extent – environmentalism.

The fate of the Scottish Conservatives is thus tied up with the consequences of Brexit, while the party also has to develop a credible policy prospectus for the 2021 Scottish Parliament elections, sans Ruth Davidson as leader. The Tory MSP Murdo Fraser has observed that the SNP in power has 'been vociferous about devolution from Westminster to Edinburgh, but whilst complaining about London power-grabs, they themselves have been all too happy to grab power away from local councils' (Fraser 2019: 274). This is good as critique, but demands a proactive programme – so far lacking – by way of a response.

Also, might there be space for a political party which gives voice to the one million Scots who voted Leave in 2016 and have mostly been left unrepresented by Scotland's MSPs and MPs? The Scottish Conservatives could lay claim to this mantle, despite most of its elected national politicians campaigning for Remain, and have the advantage over the Brexit Party of having numerous MSPs and MPs, whereas the latter have none. The other obvious space is continuing to give voice to the 55 per cent who opposed independence in 2014. Not only does this (at the time of writing) have the benefit of representing a majority of voters in Scotland, but the Conservatives have proven themselves more comfortable (and credible) doing so than Labour or the Liberal Democrats.

These two communities – Brexit and the Union – demonstrate the existence of a distinctive terrain for the Scottish Conservatives, although neither is without risk. There are obvious tensions between the two and the reality that membership of the Union in 2014 was predicated on Scotland and the rest of the UK remaining in the EU, whereas the 2016 result has led to Scotland leaving the EU against its majority will. Scotland voted in those two referendums to stay in both unions it was part of, but is only being allowed to remain in one – the UK.

Conclusion: An Indian Summer?

Ruth Davidson's eight years as Scottish Tory leader were a period of uplift for the party and, in retrospect, an Indian summer. The party became the main advocate of the case for the Union, saw its poll ratings and representation rise and, in a sense, came in from the wilderness. Yet this has to be qualified. For the party in this fortuitous period did not attempt to remake its appeal and raison d'être. Rather, it relied upon the politics of personality. As James Mitchell has observed, 'Davidson failed to detoxify the label but adopted Murdo Fraser's [2011] strategy by dropping the name. Her error was to personalise and not institutionalise the change – the 'Ruth Davidson Party' rather than some alternative' (*Sunday National*, 1 September 2018). In this respect, Davidson's period as leader was one of qualified success, but filled with missed opportunities.

This brings us back to the Scottish constitutional question and the realities of a small nation in close proximity to a much larger neighbour with whom it shares a state. This will continue as a set of evolving relationships, related to but not entirely synonymous with the constitutional debate and the state of self-government. Through the uncertainty and fluidity which characterise the age we live in, and a politics of the Union and unionism in long-term crisis, the competing claims of the two nationalisms under discussion have shown their limits. Maybe it is possible, looking beyond this, to discern a politics of the future which is not only about sovereignty and statehood.

While it is not possible to return to the classic mid-twentieth-century traditions of conservatism and social democracy, it is possible to imagine a politics which inhabits renewed versions of these ideologies and adapts them for the challenges of twenty first-century capitalism, society and the complex demands of sovereignty, voice and power in an age of interdependence. This would involve difficult choices beyond Scotland in terms of the English dimension and how the UK positions itself geopolitically after Brexit, although perhaps the tensions between being the 'unionist' and 'English' Conservative parties are increasingly too wide to bridge (Aughey 2018: 149).

William Waldegrave, a Cabinet minister during the Thatcher and Major eras, believes his party's illusions run the risk of losing Scotland and Northern Ireland, resulting in a 'smaller kingdom of England and Wales' whereby 'England without Scotland would run the risk of an even worse bout of the disease of English nationalism than has so far emerged around the Brexit debate' (Waldegrave 2019: 116–17). What does Scotland have to do to both navigate the wreckage of the disaster nationalism which British Toryism and unionism has collapsed into, while at the same time developing a politics of self-government which does not pretend that Scottish nationalism has all the answers? How can it progress a politics of the near future which does not become the prisoner of debates, claims and counter-claims belonging to the past 40 years? And how can it develop political ideas that acknowledge the Scottish desire for difference and autonomy, while being honest about the limitations and constraints of such autonomy?

Chapter 1

1. Davidson had spent a year running Annabel Goldie's office at Holyrood prior to the 2011 elections, an unusual posting for a regular candidate. There were also considerable – and controversial – moves to ensure Davidson was top of the Glasgow regional list, a ranking which virtually ensured her election to the Scottish Parliament. On declaring her candidacy, her opponents' campaign teams suspected party HQ of supplying Davidson's team with private member mailing lists (Convery 2014b; private information). John Lamont, who initially put himself forward with Davidson's backing, was also viewed in one account 'as a stalking horse for her candidacy' (Liddle 2018: 114).

2. This campaign also allowed the Scottish Conservatives to acquire the contact details of around 70,000 pro-Union supporters, a database that would prove crucial at the 2016 Holyrood election (Liddle 2018: 9).

3. That said, the Scottish Conservative vote increased at European Parliament elections held in June 2014, albeit on a low turnout. But given the fact UKIP's vote doubled in Scotland (enough to elect one of five MEPs), this was considered to be a good result.

4. The former Scottish Conservative MSP Nick Johnston said he would vote 'Yes', while the Independent Conservative councillor Peter de Vink and historian Michael Fry (who had left the party in 2007) formed a centre-right, pro-independence group called 'Wealthy Nation'.

5. 'I think the Scottish Conservatives could potentially have the largest Holyrood group we have ever seen next year' (*Aberdeen Evening Express*, 1 May 2015).

6. A Scottish Conservative tax commission reported in January 2016, *A Dynamic Scotland* restating opposition to tax increases but proposing a new 'middle band' of income tax (ICCFTS 2016). Initially, Davidson had suggested new taxes could be lower, but dropped this line when it became clear the numbers did not add up (Liddle 2018: 217).

7. At the 1987 UK general election, the Scottish Conservatives polled 24 per cent or 713,081 votes, while in the 2016 Scottish Parliament elections it managed 22 per cent in the constituency vote (501,844) and 22.9 per cent (524,222) on the regional list. The SNP's comparison, of course, took no account of differential turnout and the party's further electoral decline between 1987 and 2016.

8. David Cameron had raised this prospect following the 2015 general election. Asked whether he saw Davidson as a potential successor, he replied: 'Well, indeed. I don't put a limit on her ambition, I think she is extremely effective' (Liddle 2018: 187).

9. Convery believed it was 'time for the Scottish Conservatives to start parking their tanks on unexpected lawns' (Convery 2016b), just as its sister party had in Wales after 2011 (Convery 2016a).

10. Most assumed the Ravenscraig result was a new development, but due to the introduction of the single transferable vote in 2007, the Scottish Conservatives had gained a councillor in that same ward 10 years earlier. It was then lost in 2012 but regained at the 2017 election.

11. Davidson responded in kind: 'I have never had a problem standing up to the alpha males in my party. I wonder whether the First Minister has always been able to say the same' (Official Report, 22 May 2019).

12. Even after her resignation, the Scottish Conservatives sent out mailshots featuring Ruth Davidson's picture and a personal plea to back the party. 'In effect, the Scottish Tories want to pretend that Davidson is still their leader and hope that the voters forget she stood down in part because of her disagreements with Boris over Brexit,' wrote Stephen Daisley. 'It's a bizarre strategy, but these are bizarre times' (Spectator, 29 October 2019).

Chapter 2

1. Between 1931 and 1964, support for the Scottish Unionist Party did not fall below 40 per cent at any general election and was as high as 54 per cent in 1931. In the five general elections between 1997 and 2015, support for the party did not exceed 17.5 per cent, before recovering to 28.6 per cent in 2017.

2. In 2015, the Scottish Labour vote fell by 17.7 per cent from 2010, while Liberal Democrat support fell by 11.3 per cent. The SNP's share of the vote rose by 30 per cent at the same election.

3. There are questions every year in the British Social Attitudes Survey which seek to establish whether respondents are inclined to the left or the right (see Evans and Heath 1995).

4. A poll conducted by Panelbase for the Sunday Times in May 2019 showed that 53 per cent of 'No' supporters had voted Conservative in 2017.

5. The same Panelbase poll showed that just 24 per cent of 'No' supporters had voted Labour in 2017.

Chapter 6

1. The title is taken from an article by Katy Balls headlined: 'A lesbian with family values: why Tories love Ruth Davidson' (*Guardian*, 27 April 2018).
2. Several senior Conservatives voted against same-sex marriage, including the future Minister for Women and Equalities Nicky Morgan; a survey of attitudes of the grassroots members of the party in 2018 found that 59 per cent did not support gay marriage (*Business Insider*, 4 January 2018).

Chapter 10

1. It was precisely and specifically this point that Torrance (*Herald*, 9 May 2016) had sought to make.
2. When, during 2019, the Northern Irish journalists Alex Kane and Sam McBride referred to the 'Ulsterisation of British politics' (as a consequence of Brexit), it generated no controversy in Scottish political circles (*News Letter*, 28 September 2019).
3. On the history, make-up and nature of these two parties, see Bean (2008) and Whiting (2017) on Sinn Féin and Tonge et al. (2014) on the DUP.
4. Bonar Law's father was a Free Church of Scotland Minister from Coleraine, Co. Derry. Following the death of his mother, Bonar Law had gone to live with his aunt on the outskirts of Glasgow. He attended the High School of Glasgow and established a name for himself as a successful businessman in the Glasgow iron trade before entering politics (Mansergh 2014: 171).
5. Though as Walker (2010) has demonstrated, the Northern Ireland example exerted some influence on post-Second World War debates about devolution in Scotland, with Stormont variously serving either as a model or as a cautionary tale.
6. This is reflected, for instance, in the growing emphasis on 'Ulster-Scots' heritage, culture and language in Unionist and Loyalist identity politics in Northern Ireland since the late 1990s, which has been less than fully reciprocated and has even been poorly received in Scotland itself (see Gallagher 2007: 53–83).
7. Though, as Aughey (2018: 92) records, Major has himself acknowledged there is something of a tension in the Conservatives' position on Scottish independence, in that if Scotland did leave the Union, then the Conservative Party might stand to benefit 'enormously' in electoral terms. There are also, according to recent polling, some 63 per cent of Tories who would be prepared to sacrifice Scottish membership of the Union in order to guarantee that Brexit goes ahead (BBC News online, 27 June 2019).
8. Brown has insisted that the UK government should maintain a strictly non-partisan position on the constitutional question in Northern Ireland (Brown 2017).
9. A more informal relationship had long existed between the two parties, but as indicated above, this was always lopsided and consistently beset by tension and conflict.

10. The only non-DUP Unionist returned to Westminster in 2010 was the Independent Unionist Lady Sylvia Hermon. She had resigned from the UUP in 2009 in explicit protest at the party's electoral pact with the Conservatives, who she felt had a poor understanding of Northern Ireland (Aughey 2018: 94; Tonge et al. 2019: ch. 3).

11. Despite contemporary claims on the part of some commentators that Ulster Unionists should seek to emulate it (see, e.g., ConservativeHome, 31 July 2019), it is far from clear that deeper integration into 'mainstream' British politics has always served the Scottish Conservatives particularly well, nor, indeed, that Ulster Unionism's separateness has always been a strategic impediment. Attempts to carve out a distinct 'Scottish' identity and programme for the party north of the border have been centrally significant in shaping its recent electoral successes (Simpkins 2018; Former Northern Ireland Conservatives Deputy Chair, interview with author, 2019).

12. Notwithstanding the comparable ways in which 'Britain and the values claimed in its name [constitute] "the invisible empire", an insidious contemporary discourse that continues to legitimate and render a racialized and class-based national identity' (Smith 2017: 56) in both jurisdictions.

13. Power-sharing government at Stormont was restored in January 2020, three years after the collapse of the Northern Ireland Executive and Assembly in 2017, in the wake of the Renewable Heat Incentive (RHI) scandal (see McBride 2019).

14. In 2018, Johnson was the guest speaker at the DUP party conference. He also publicly supported Arlene Foster's calls for the commissioning of a feasibility study for the construction of a bridge between Scotland and Northern Ireland (*Irish Times*, 2 July 2019).

15. It is worth noting that claims about 'kinship' between Northern Ireland and Scotland are not an exclusively Conservative preserve. During a speech to the Northern Ireland Assembly in 2007, then SNP First Minister Alex Salmond referred to the peoples of Ireland – north and south – as 'the blood of our blood and the bone of our bone' (Scottish Government 2007).

16. This argument is contestable and, arguably, essentially false (see Hayward and Phinnemore 2019; Skoutaris 2019).

17. Though, at this stage, this seems an easier issue on which to make an informed call. The SNP, having long and deliberately courted Catholic voters, has come to be seen as something of a 'cold house' for working-class Protestants. Public expressions of pro-Irish Republican and even pro-IRA sentiment by SNP politicians have also played badly in this section of Scottish society. Whether or not Jeremy Corbyn's long-standing associations with Irish Republicanism could yet have consequences for Labour's support among this cohort of voters also remains something of an open question (Graham Walker, interview with author, 2019).

18. Though the EU has agreed to maintain funding for this programme until at least the end of the current programming period in 2020, even in the event of a no-deal Brexit.

BIBLIOGRAPHY

Adcock, C. (2010), 'The politician, the wife, the citizen, and her newspaper', *Feminist Media Studies*, 10:2, 135–59.

Anderson, P. (2016), 'The 2016 Scottish Parliament election: a nationalist minority, a Conservative comeback and a Labour collapse', *Regional & Federal Studies*, 26:4, 555–68.

APSE (2014), *The Future of Elected Members in Scotland*, Association of Public Sector Excellence, <https://www.apse.org.uk/apse/index.cfm/research/current-research-programme/the-future-of-elected-members-in-scotland/the-future-of-elected-members-in-scotland/> (last accessed 29 September 2019).

Arnott, M. and Macdonald, C. M. M. (2012), 'More than a name: the Union and the un-doing of Scottish Conservatism in the twentieth century', in D. Torrance (ed.), *Whatever Happened to Tory Scotland?*, Edinburgh: Edinburgh University Press, pp. 43–61.

Ascherson, N. (2019), 'Scotland, Brexit and the persistence of empire', in S. Ward and A. Rasch (eds), *Embers of Empire in Brexit Britain*, London: Bloomsbury, pp. 71–8.

Ashcroft, Lord (2013), *Cameron's Caledonian Conundrum: Scottish Voters and the Conservative Party*, Lord Ashcroft Polls.com, <https://lordashcroftpolls.com/wp-content/uploads/2013/10/Camerons-Caledonian-Conundrum.pdf> (last accessed 6 December 2019).

Aughey, A. (2018), *The Conservative Party and the Nation: Union, England and Europe*, Manchester: Manchester University Press.

Aughey, A. and Gormley-Heenan, C. (2016), 'The Conservative Party and Ulster Unionism: a case of elective affinity', *Parliamentary Affairs*, 69:2, 430–50.

Bale, T. (2010), *The Conservative Party: From Thatcher to Cameron*, Cambridge: Polity.

Barrett, G (2017), 'The use of referendums in Ireland: an analysis', *Journal of Legislative Studies*, 23:1, 71–92.

BBC Scotland (2019), *Yes/No: Inside the Indyref (part 1) – The Fight for a Question*, BBC Scotland digital channel, 5 March.

Bean, K. (2008), *The New Politics of Sinn Féin*, Liverpool: Liverpool University Press.

Black, S. (1994), 'What's happening to the water and sewerage services in Scotland', *Scottish Affairs*, 6, 25–35.

Bogdanor, V. (2001), *Devolution in the United Kingdom*, Oxford: Oxford University Press.

Bogdanor, V. (2003), 'Asymmetric devolution: toward a quasi-federal constitution', in P. Dunleavy et al. (eds), *Developments in British Politics*, London: Palgrave Macmillan.

Bogdanor, V. (2011), *The New British Constitution*, London: Hart.

Booth, A. and Pugh, K. (2017), 'Kent County council elections for the Isle of Sheppey', Intouch, <https://electionleaflets.org/leaflets/13752/> (last accessed 9 January 2020).

Brack, D. (2000), 'Introduction', in I. Dale (ed.), *Liberal Party General Election Manifestos 1900–1997*, London: Routledge.

Bradbury, J. (2006), 'Territory and power revisited: theorising territorial politics in the United Kingdom after devolution', *Political Studies*, 54:2, 559–82.

Bradley, J. M. (2004), 'Orangeism in Scotland: unionism, identity, politics and football', *Éire-Ireland*, 39:1&2, 237–61.

Brooke, N. (2018), *Terrorism and Nationalism in the United Kingdom: The Absence of Noise*, Basingstoke: Palgrave Macmillan.

Brown, G. (2017), *My Life, Our Times*, London: The Bodley Head.

Budge, L., Robertson, D. and Hearl D. J. (eds) (1987), *Ideology, Strategy and Party Change: Spatial Analyses of Post-War Election Programmes in 19 Democracies*, Cambridge: Cambridge University Press.

Bulpitt, J. (1982), 'Conservatism, unionism and the problem of territorial management', in P. Madgwick and R. Rose (eds), *The Territorial Dimension in United Kingdom Politics*, Basingstoke: Macmillan.

Bulpitt, J. (1983), *Territory and Power in the United Kingdom: An Interpretation*, Manchester: Manchester University Press.

Bulpitt, J. (1986) 'The discipline of the new democracy: Mrs Thatcher's domestic statecraft', *Political Studies*, 34:1, 19–39.

Burgess, M. (1995), *The British Tradition of Federalism*, London: Leicester University Press.

Burness, C. (2003), *'Strange Associations': The Irish Question and the Making of Scottish Unionism, 1886–1918*, East Linton: Tuckwell Press.

Butler, D. and Kavanagh, D. (1980), *The British General Election of 1979*, Basingstoke: Macmillan.

Butler, D. and Kavanagh, D. (2015), *The British General Election of 2015*, London: Palgrave Macmillan.

Calman Commission (2009), *Serving Scotland Better: Scotland and the United Kingdom in the 21st Century*, Edinburgh: Calman Commission.

Cameron, D. (2012), Speech to Scottish Conservative Party conference, 23 March.

Cameron, D. (2014), 'The importance of Scotland to the UK', speech at Glasgow Caledonian University, 7 February.

Cameron, D. (2019), *For the Record*, London: HarperCollins.

Campbell, A. (2011), *The Alastair Campbell Diaries*, Vol. 2: *Power and the People*, London: Hutchinson.

Childs, S. (2001), 'In their own words: New Labour women and the substantive representation of women', *British Journal of Politics and International Relations*, 3:2, 173–90.

Childs, S. and Webb, P. (2012), *Sex, Gender and the Conservative Party: From Iron Lady to Kitten Heels*, Basingstoke: Palgrave Macmillan.

Cochrane, A. (2014), *Alex Salmond: My Part in His Downfall: The Cochrane Diaries*, London: Biteback.

Cochrane, F. (1997), *Unionist Politics and the Politics of Unionism since the Anglo-Irish Agreement*, Cork: Cork University Press.

Convery, A. (2014a), 'Devolution and the limits of Tory statecraft: the Conservative Party in coalition and Scotland and Wales', *Parliamentary Affairs*, 67:1, 25–44.

Convery, A. (2014b), 'The 2011 Scottish Conservative Party leadership election: dilemmas for statewide parties in regional contexts', *Parliamentary Affairs*, 67:2, 306–27.

Convery, A. (2014c), 'A new direction for the Conservatives on devolution?', University of Edinburgh blog, 3 June.

Convery, A. (2016a), *The Territorial Conservative Party: Devolution and Party Change in Scotland and Wales*, Manchester: Manchester University Press.

Convery, A. (ed.) (2016b), *Light Blue: Policy Adventures for Scottish Conservatives*, Edinburgh, <https://www.centreonconstitutionalchange.ac.uk/sites/default/files/migrated/papers/Light%20Blue_Adventures%20in%20Policy%20for%20Scottish%20Conservatives.pdf> (last accessed 9 December 2019).

Cooke, A. B. (2000), 'The Conservative Party and its manifestos: A personal view', in I. Dale (ed.), *Conservative Party General Election Manifestos 1900–1997*, London: Routledge.

Corthorn, P. (2012), 'Enoch Powell, Ulster Unionism, and the British nation', *Journal of British Studies*, 51:4, 967–97.

COSLA (2019), 'Political control', <https://www.cosla.gov.uk//councils/political-control> (last accessed 29 September 2019).

Coulter, C. (2015), 'Not quite as British as Finchley: the failed attempt to bring British Conservatism to Northern Ireland', *Irish Studies Review*, 23:4, 407–23.

Cowley, P. and Kavanagh, D. (eds) (2018), *The British General Election of 2017*, London: Palgrave Macmillan.

Curtice, J. (2007), 'STV goes tartan: a preliminary analysis of its use in the 2007 Scottish local elections', *Representation*, 43:3, 209–16.

Curtice, J. (2012), 'Why no Tory revival in Scotland?', in D. Torrance (ed.), *Whatever Happened to Tory Scotland?*, Edinburgh: Edinburgh University Press, pp. 114–26.

Curtice, J. (2017a), 'The three characteristics of the Scottish Conservative revival', blog, 1 October, <http://blog.whatscotlandthinks.org/2017/10/the-three-characteristics-of-the-scottish-conservative-revival/> (last accessed 22 August 2019).

Curtice, J. (2017b), 'A Tory revival – and a yet more polarised Scotland?', blog, 23 April, <http://blog.whatscotlandthinks.org/2017/04/a-tory-revival-and-a-yet-more-polarised-scotland/> (last accessed 22 August 2019).

Curtice, J. (2017c), *Has Brexit Reshaped British Politics?*, What UK Thinks, <https://whatukthinks.org/eu/analysis/has-brexit-reshaped-british-politics/> (last accessed 22 August 2019).

Curtice. J. (2018a), 'The 2017 election: Scotland re-enters British politics?', *Scottish Geographical Journal*, 134:1–2, 39–44.

Curtice, J. (2018b), *The Emotional Legacy of Brexit: How Britain has Become a Country of 'Remainers' and 'Leavers'*, London: NatCen Social Research.

Curtice, J. (2019), 'Could Brexit yet undermine the future of the British state?', blog, 1 July, <http://blog.whatscotlandthinks.org/2019/07/could-brexit-yet-undermine-the-future-of-the-british-state/> (last accessed 2 October 2019).

Daddow, O. (2019), 'GlobalBritain™: the discursive construction of Britain's post-Brexit world role', *Global Affairs*, 5:1, 5–22.

Dardanelli, P. (2006), *Between Two Unions: Europeanisation and Scottish Devolution*, Manchester: Manchester University Press.

Davidson, R. (2015), 'Ruth Davidson speech to Adam Smith Institute', 25 August, <https://www.adamsmith.org/blog/tax-spending/ruth-davidson-speech-to-adam-smith-institute> (last accessed 9 December 2019).

Davidson, R. (2016), 'Ruth Davidson: keynote speech at Belfast Pride event', 2 August, scottishconservatives.com, <http://www.scottishconservatives.com/2016/08/ruth-davidson-keynote-speech-at-belfast-pride-event/> (last accessed 9 December 2019).

Davidson, R. (2018a), *Yes She Can: Why Women Own the Future*, London: Hodder & Stoughton.

Davidson, R. (2018b), 'Prospects for Scottish unionism', speech, Policy Exchange, 21 May.

Davidson, R. (2019), 'Foreword', in G. Freeman (ed.), *Britain Beyond Brexit*, London: Centre for Policy Studies, pp. xi–xv.

Davidson, R., Wollaston, R. and Fazakerley, D. (2016), *Giving 16 and 17 Year Olds the Vote The Tory Case*, London: Tory Reform Group.

Deschouwer, K. (2003), 'Political parties in multi-layered systems', *European Urban and Regional Studies*, 10, 213–26.

DFA (1993), *Joint Declaration 1993* (Downing Street Declaration), Dublin: Department of Foreign Affairs and Trade.

Edgerton, D. (2018), *The Rise and Fall of the British Nation: A Twentieth Century History*, London: Allen Lane.

Elazar, D. J. (1987), *Exploring Federalism*, Tuscaloosa: University of Alabama Press.

English, R., Hayton, R. and Kenny, M. (2009), 'Englishness and the Union in contemporary Conservative thought', *Government and Opposition*, 4:4, 343–65.

European Commission (2017), *Joint Report from the Negotiators of the European Union and the United Kingdom Government*, 8 December, <https://ec.europa.eu/commission/sites/beta-political/files/joint_report.pdf> (last accessed 9 December 2019).

Evans, A. (2014), 'Federalist in name only? Re-assessing the federal credentials of the Liberal Democrats: an English case study', *British Politics*, 9, 346–58.

Evans, G. and Heath, A. (1995), 'The measurement of left–right and libertarian–authoritarian values: a comparison of balanced and unbalanced scales', *Quality and Quantity*, 29:2, 191–206.

Evison, A. (2019), 'Local government and the Scottish Parliament: parity of esteem?', in J. Johnson and J. Mitchell (eds), *The Scottish Parliament at Twenty*, Edinburgh: Luath Press.

Farrington, C. and Walker, G. (2009), 'Ideological content and institutional frameworks: unionist identities in Northern Ireland and Scotland', *Irish Studies Review*, 17:2, 135–52.

Flinders, M. (2010), 'Constitutional anomie', *Government and Opposition*, 44:4, 383–409.

Flinders, M. and Curry, D. (2008), 'Bi-constitutionalism', *Parliamentary Affairs*, 61:1, 99–121.

Forsyth, M. (1995), 'The governance of Scotland: Richard Stewart Memorial Lecture', in L. Paterson (ed.), *A Diverse Assembly: The Debate on a Scottish Parliament*, Edinburgh: Edinburgh University Press.

Fraser, M. (2014), 'Speech to Visions of Scotland Seminar', University of Glasgow, 26 June.

Fraser, M. (2019), 'From think twice to radical devolution: a Scottish Conservative movement', in G. Hassan (ed.), *The Story of the Scottish Parliament: The First Two Decades Explained*, Edinburgh: Edinburgh University Press, pp. 260–7.

Frymark, K. (2018), 'The Free State of Bavaria and its party: the CSU faces an electoral test', Centre for Eastern Studies, <https://www.osw.waw.pl/en/publikacje/osw-commentary/2018-10-10/free-state-bavaria-and-its-party-csu-faces-electoral-test> (last accessed 22 August 2019).

Gallagher, C. (2007), *After the Peace: Loyalist Paramilitaries in Post-Accord Northern Ireland*, Ithaca, NY: Cornell University Press.

Gallagher, T. (1987), *Glasgow, the Uneasy Peace: Religious Tension in Modern Scotland*, Manchester: Manchester University Press.

Gamble, A. (1995), 'The crisis of Conservatism', *New Left Review*, 214, 3–25.

Gamble, A. (2006) 'The constitutional revolution in the United Kingdom', *Publius*, 36:1, 119–35.

Gamble, A. (2016), 'The Conservatives and the Union: the 'New English Toryism' and the origins of Anglo-Britishness', *Political Studies Review*, 14:3, 359–67.

Geoghegan, P. (2015), *The People's Referendum: Why Scotland Will Never Be the Same Again*, Edinburgh: Luath Press.

Gilmour, I. (1978), *Inside Right*, London: Quartet Books.

Gormley-Heenan, C. and Sandford, M. (2018), '"Taking back control": the UK's constitutional narrative and Schrodinger's devolution', *Parliamentary Affairs*, gsy039.

Graham, L. (2019), 'The modern Briton', in G. Freeman (ed.), *Britain Beyond Brexit*, London: Centre for Policy Studies, pp. 31–8.

Grajewski, J. (2017), 'Intouch with the Hampshire County council division of Chandler's Ford', Intouch, <https://electionleaflets.org/leaflets/13837/> (last accessed 9 January 2020).

Green, J. (2007) 'When voters and parties agree: valence issues and party and party competition' *Political Studies*, 55:3, 629–55.

Hague, W. (1998), 'Change and tradition: thinking creatively about the constitution', speech to the Centre for Policy Studies, 24 February.

Hanretty, C. (2017), 'Area interpolation and the UK's referendum on EU membership', *Journal of Elections, Public Opinion and Parties*, 27:4, 466–83.

Hassan, G. (2012), '"It's only a northern song": The constant smirr of anti-Thatcherism and anti-Toryism', in D. Torrance (ed.), *Whatever Happened to Tory Scotland?*, Edinburgh: Edinburgh University Press, pp. 76–92.

Hassan, G. (2014), *Independence of the Scottish Mind: Elite Narratives, Public Spaces and the Making of a Modern Nation*, London: Palgrave Macmillan.

Hassan, G. (2018), 'Still differently, only slightly less so: Scotland', in P. Cowley and D. Kavanagh (eds), *The British General Election of 2017*, London: Palgrave Macmillan, pp. 125–48.

Hassan, G. and Shaw, E. (2019), *The People's Flag and the Union Jack: An Alternative History of Britain and the Labour Party*, London: Biteback.

Hayton, R. (2010), 'Conservative Party modernisation and David Cameron's politics of the family', *Political Quarterly*, 81:4, 492–500.

Hayton, R. (2012), *Reconstructing Conservatism? The Conservative Party in Opposition, 1997–2010*, Manchester: Manchester University Press.

Hayton, R. (2015), 'The coalition and the politics of the English Question', *Political Quarterly*, 86:1, 125–32.

Hayward, K. and Phinnemore, D. (2019), 'Breached or protected? The "principle" of consent in Northern Ireland and the UK government's Brexit proposals', LSE Brexit blog, <https://blogs.lse.ac.uk/europpblog/2019/01/11/breached-or-protected-the-principle-of-consent-in-northern-ireland-and-the-uk-governments-brexit-proposals/> (last accessed 12 January 2019).

Heffer, S. (1999), *Nor Shall My Sword: The Reinvention of England*, London: Weidenfeld & Nicolson.

Henderson, A. and Mitchell, J. (2018), 'Referendums as critical junctures? Scottish voting in British elections', in J. Tonge et al. (eds), *Britain Votes 2017*, Oxford: Oxford University Press, pp. 109–24.

Henig, S (2007), 'Introduction', in S. Henig (ed.), *Federalism and the British*, London: The Federal Trust.

Heron, E. (2017), 'Hampshire County council elections – Thursday 4th May 2017', Intouch, <https://electionleaflets.org/leaflets/13829/> (last accessed 9 January 2020).

HM Government (1993), *Scotland in the Union: A Partnership for Good*, Cmd 2225, Edinburgh: HMSO.

HM Government (1997), *Scotland's Parliament*, Cmd 3658, Edinburgh: HMSO.

HM Government (2007), *The Governance of Britain*, Cmd 7170, London: HMSO.

HM Government (2018), *EU Exit: Taking Back Control of Our Borders, Money and Laws While Protecting Our Economy, Security and Union*, Cmd 9741, London: HMSO.

HM Treasury (2013a), *Scotland Analysis: Currency and Monetary Policy*, Cmd 8594, London: HMSO.

HM Treasury (2013b), *Scotland Analysis: Business and Microeconomic Framework*, Cmd 8616, London: HMSO.

HM Treasury (2014), *Scotland Analysis: Assessment of a Sterling Currency Union*, Cmd 8815, London: HMSO.

HoCL (2019), *UK Election Statistics: 1918–2019: A Century of Elections*, 18 July, CBP7529, London: House of Commons Library.

Hueglin, T. O. and Fenna, A. (2006), *Comparative Federalism: A Systematic Inquiry*, Toronto: Broadview Press.

ICCFTS (2016), *A Dynamic Scotland: The Role of Competitive and Fair Taxes*, Independent Commission for Competitive and Fair Taxation in Scotland, <http://www.scottishconservatives.com/wordpress/wp-content/uploads/2016/04/A-Dynamic-Scotland-FINAL-1.pdf> (last accessed 9 December 2019).

Institute for Government (2019), 'Irish backstop', <https://www.instituteforgovernment.org.uk/explainers/northern-ireland-backstop> (last accessed 25 July 2019).

Ipsos MORI (2017), 'SNP look set to be biggest party in upcoming election', 31 May, <https://www.ipsos.com/ipsos-mori/en-uk/snp-look-set-be-biggest-party-upcoming-election> (last accessed 4 October 2019).

Jackson, A. (2012a), 'Sociability, status and solidarity: Scottish Unionism in the era of Irish Home Rule, 1886–1920', in D. Torrance (ed.), *Whatever Happened to Tory Scotland?*, Edinburgh: Edinburgh University Press, pp. 14–28.

Jackson, A. (2012b), *The Two Unions: Ireland, Scotland and the Survival of the United Kingdom, 1707–2007*, Oxford: Oxford University Press.

Johns, R. and Mitchell, J. (2016), *Takeover: Explaining the Extraordinary Rise of the SNP*, London: Biteback.

Johnson, B. (2019), 'Boris Johnson's first speech as Prime Minister', 24 July, <https://www.gov.uk/government/speeches/boris-johnsons-first-speech-as-prime-minister-24-july-2019> (last accessed 9 December 2019).

Johnston, J. and Mitchell, J. (eds) (2019), *The Scottish Parliament at Twenty*, Edinburgh: Luath Press.

Kavanagh, D. (2000), 'Labour Party manifestos 1900–1997', in I. Dale (ed.), *Labour Party General Election Manifestos 1900–1997*, London: Routledge.

Keating, M. (2015), 'The European dimension to Scottish constitutional change', *Political Quarterly*, 86:2, 201–8.

Keating, M. (2018), 'The United Kingdom's evolving constitution', in P. Requejo (ed.), *La Evolución de los Modelos Territoriales: Reformulación versus Ruptura* 10, Oviedo: KRK Ediciones, pp. 157–82.

Keating, M. (2019), 'Brexit and the nations', *Political Quarterly*, 90:2, 167–72.

Keen, R. (2016), Oral arguments in *Miller v Secretary of State for Exiting the European Union*, 6 December, https://supreme-court-article-50-appeal.sayit.mysociety.org/hearing-6-december-2016/submissions-by-the-advocate-general-for-scotland (last accessed 2 January 2020).

Kemp, J. (2011), 'The decline of the Scottish Conservative Party', <https://www.jackiekemp.co.uk/2011/03/24/decline-of-the-scottish-conservative-party/> (last accessed 22 August 2019).

Kendle, J. (1997), *Federal Britain: A History*, London: Routledge.

Kendrick, S. and McCrone, D. (1989), 'Politics in a cold climate: the Conservative decline in Scotland', *Political Studies*, 37:4, 589–603.

Kenny, M. and Mackay, F. (2014), 'When is contagion not very contagious? Dynamics of women's political representation in Scotland', *Parliamentary Affairs*, 67:4, 866–86.

Kenny, M. and Sheldon, J. (2019a), *Will a No-Deal Brexit Lead to the Break-up of the UK?*, Cambridge: Bennett Institute.

Kenny, M. and Sheldon, J. (2019b), 'What was Boris up to in Scotland?', blog, Centre on Constitutional Change, 9 September, <https://www.centreonconstitutionalchange.ac.uk/news-and-opinion/what-was-boris-scotland> (last accessed 9 December 2019).

Kerley, R. and McGarvey, N. (2017), *Research Report: Councillors Roles and Workload*, Edinburgh: Local Government Boundary Commission for Scotland.

Kerr, A. (2014), 'The Ulsterisation of Scottish politics', 31 December, <https://aidankerr.com/2014/12/31/the-ulsterisation-of-scottish-politics/> (last accessed 5 September 2019).

Kidd, C. (2008), *Union and Unionisms: Political Thought in Scotland, 1500–2000*, Cambridge: Cambridge University Press.

Kidd, C. (2019), 'Independence and Union revisited: recent interpretations in Scottish history, literature and politics', in G. Hassan (ed.), *The Story of the Scottish Parliament: The First Two Decades Explained*, Edinburgh: Edinburgh University Press, pp. 219–28.

Lamont, J. (2019), 'The Union', in G. Freeman (ed.), *Britain Beyond Brexit*, London: Centre for Policy Studies, pp. 24–30.

Lang, I. (1994) 'Taking stock of taking stock', speech to Conservative Party Conference, Bournemouth, 12 October.

Leith, M. S. (2006), 'Nationalism and national identity in Scottish politics', PhD thesis, University of Glasgow.

Leith, M. S. and Soule, D. (2011), *Political Discourse and National Identity in Scotland*, Edinburgh: Edinburgh University Press.

Letwin, O. (2016), 'Oral evidence to House of Lords Select Committee on the Constitution', 10 February.

Liddle, A. (2018), *Ruth Davidson and the Resurgence of the Scottish Tories*, London: Biteback.

McAngus, C. (2016), 'How Scotland votes; elections and electoral behaviour in Scotland' in McTavish, D. (ed), *Politics in* Scotland, London: Routledge, 24-41.

McAngus, C. (2018), 'A survey of Scottish fishermen ahead of Brexit: political, social and constitutional attitudes', *Maritime Studies* 17:1, 41–54.

McBride, S. (2019), *Burned: The Inside Story of the 'Cash-for-Ash' Scandal and Northern Ireland's Secretive New Elite*, Newbridge: Merrion Press.

McCall, C. (2007), '"Hello stranger": The revival of co-operation between Ireland, Northern Ireland and Scotland', *Journal of Cross Border Studies in Ireland*, 1:2, 7–21.

McCann, D. and McGrattan, C. (eds) (2017), *Sunningdale, the Ulster Workers' Council Strike and the Struggle for Democracy in Northern Ireland*, Manchester: Manchester University Press.

McConnell, A. (2004), *Scottish Local Government*, Edinburgh: Edinburgh University Press.

McCrone, D., Paterson, L. and Brown, A. (1993), 'Reforming local government in Scotland', *Local Government Studies*, 19, 9–15.

McCrone, D. (2001), *Understanding Scotland: The Sociology of a Nation*, 2nd edn, London: Routledge.

McFarland, E. (1990), *Protestants First: Orangeism in Nineteenth-century Scotland*, Edinburgh: Edinburgh University Press.

McGarvey, N. (2002), 'Intergovernmental relations in Scotland post-devolution', *Local Government Studies*, 28:3, 29–48.

McGarvey, N. (2019), 'British political tradition and Scottish local government', in G. Hassan (ed.), *The Story of the Scottish Parliament: The First Two Decades Explained*, Edinburgh: Edinburgh University Press.

McGowan, L. (2018), *Preparing for Brexit: Actors, Negotiations and Consequences*, Switzerland: Springer.

McIntosh, B. (1999), 'Vote Bill McIntosh Scottish Conservative', Scottish Election Ephemera collection, Glasgow: University of Strathclyde Library.

McNally, B. (2003), 'South Ayrshire council elections Dundonald & Loans ward', Scottish Election Ephemera collection, Glasgow: University of Strathclyde Library.

McVicar, M., Jordan, G. and Boyne, G. (1994), 'Ships that pass in the night: Scottish political parties and local government reform', *Scottish Affairs*, 9:1, 80–96.

Macwhirter, I. (2014), *Disunited Kingdom: How Westminster Won a Referendum but Lost Scotland*, Glasgow: Cargo.

Mansergh, M. (2014), 'The role of the leaders: Asquith, Churchill, Balfour, Bonar Law, Carson and Redmond', in G. Doherty (ed.), *The Home Rule Crisis 1912–1914*, Cork: Mercier Press, pp. 167–75.

Marquand, D. (2006), 'Federalism and the British: anatomy of a neurosis', *Political Quarterly*, 77:5, 175–83.

May, T. (2016a), 'Statement from the new Prime Minister Theresa May', 13 July, <https://www.gov.uk/government/speeches/statement-from-the-new-prime-minister-theresa-may> (last accessed 9 December 2019).

May, T. (2016b), 'Britain after Brexit: a vision of a global Britain', speech at the Conservative Party conference, 2 October, <https://www.conservativehome.com/parliament/2016/10/britain-after-brexit-a-vision-of-a-global-britain-theresa-mays-conservative-conference-speech-full-text.html> (last accessed 9 December 2019).

May, T. (2017), 'The government's negotiating objectives for exiting the EU', speech on 17 January, <https://www.gov.uk/government/speeches/the-governments-negoti-ating-objectives-for-exiting-the-eu-pm-speech> (last accessed 9 December 2019).

May, T. (2019), 'PM speech on the Union', Stirling, 4 July, <https://www.gov.uk/government/speeches/pm-speech-on-the-union-4-july-2019> (last accessed 9 December 2019).

Melding, D. (2012), *The Reformed Union: A British Federation*, Cardiff: Institute of Welsh Affairs.

Midwinter, A. F. (1995), *Local Government in Scotland: Reform or Decline?*, Basingstoke: Macmillan.

Midwinter, A. F. and McGarvey, N. (1997), 'Local government reform: managing the transition', *Local Government Studies*, 23:3, 73–89.

Miller, W. (1988), *Irrelevant Elections? The Quality of Local Democracy in Britain*, Oxford: Clarendon Press.

Mitchell, J. (1990), *Conservatives and the Union*, Edinburgh: Edinburgh University Press.

Mitchell, J. (2003), *Governing Scotland: The Invention of Administrative Devolution*, Basingstoke: Palgrave Macmillan.

Mitchell, J. (2014), *The Scottish Question*, Oxford: Oxford University Press.

Mitchell, J. (2015), 'Sea change in Scotland', in A. Geddes and J. Tonge, J. (eds), *Britain Votes 2015*, Oxford: Oxford University Press, pp. 88–100.

Mitchell, J. (2016), 'Tories smiling but challenges ahead', blog, Centre on Constitutional Change, 10 May, <https://centreonconstitutionalchange.ac.uk/opinions/tories-smiling-challenges-ahead> (last accessed 9 December 2019).

Mitchell, J. and Convery, A. (2012), 'Conservative unionism: prisoned in marble', in D. Torrance (ed.), *Whatever Happened to Tory Scotland?*, Edinburgh: Edinburgh University Press.

Monahan, M. (2018), '"Tory-normativity" and gay rights advocacy in the British Conservative party since the 1950s', *British Journal of Politics and International Relations*, 21:1, 132–47.

Moore, C. (2019), *Margaret Thatcher, The Authorised Biography*, Vol. 3: *Herself Alone*, London: Allen Lane.

Moran, M. (2017), *The End of British Politics?* London: Palgrave Macmillan.

Morton, G. (1999), *Unionism–Nationalism: Governing Urban Scotland 1830–1860*, East Linton: Tuckwell Press.

Mulvenna, G. (2016), *Tartan Gangs and Paramilitaries: The Loyalist Backlash*, Liverpool: Liverpool University Press.

NatCen (2017), 'Scotland: How Brexit has created a new divide in the nationalist movement', <https://www.natcen.ac.uk/media/1595212/BSA_35_Scotland.pdf> (last accessed 4 October 2019).

North, L. (2016), 'The gender of "soft" and "hard" news: female journalists' views on story allocations', *Journalism Studies*, 17:3, 356–73.

O'Neill, D., Savigny, H. and Cann, V. (2016), 'Women politicians in the UK press: not seen and not heard?', *Feminist Media Studies*, 16:2, 293–307.

Panelbase (2019), Poll for the *Sunday Times*, <https://www.drg.global/wp-content/uploads/W7181w20-ST-tables-for-publication-170519.pdf> (last accessed 4 October 2019).

Parkinson, A. F. (2012), *Friends in High Places: Ulster's Resistance to Home Rule, 1912–14*, Belfast: Ulster Historical Foundation.

Pedersen, S. (2018), 'Press response to women politicians: a comparative study of suffragettes and contemporary Scottish Parliament leaders', *Journalism Studies*, 19:5, 709–25.

Pike, J. (2015), *Project Fear: How an Unlikely Alliance left a Kingdom United but a Country Divided*, London: Biteback.

Pulzer, P. G. J. (1975), *Political Representation and Elections in* Britain, London: Allen & Unwin.

Randall, N. and Seawright, D. (2012), 'Territorial politics', in T. Heppell and D. Seawright (eds), *Cameron and the Conservatives: The Transition to Coalition Government*, Basingstoke: Palgrave Macmillan.

Rodger, A. (2003), Letter from Alan Rodger to 'Resident', Scottish Election Ephemera collection, Glasgow: University of Strathclyde Library.

Rose, R. (1982), 'Is the United Kingdom a state? Northern Ireland as a test case', in P. Madgwick and R. Rose (eds), *The Territorial Dimension in United Kingdom Politics*, Basingstoke: Macmillan.

Rosie, M. (2004), *The Sectarian Myth in Scotland: Of Bitter Memory and Bigotry*, Basingstoke: Palgrave Macmillan.

Rosie, M. and Hepburn, E. (2015), '"The essence of the Union . . .": Unionism, nationalism and identity on these disconnected islands', *Scottish Affairs*, 24:2, 141–62.

Ross, K. and Carter, C. (2011), 'Women and news: a long and winding road', *Media, Culture & Society*, 33:8, 1148–65.

Royal Commission on the Constitution (1973), *Report of the Commission*, Cmd 5460, London: HMSO.

Salamone, A. (2018a), 'Brexit roundup: uncertain future for Scotland and devolution', Scottish Centre on European Relations, 16 April, <https://www.scer.scot/database/ident-5623> (last accessed 9 December 2019).

Salamone, A. (2018b), 'The Brexit negotiations and the future EU–UK relationship: implications for common frameworks', Evidence to Finance and Constitution Committee: Common UK Frameworks Inquiry, 31 August, <https://www.parliament.scot/S5_Finance/Inquiries/Scottish_Centre_for_European_Relations.pdf> (last accessed 9 December 2019).

Scottish Affairs Committee (2019), 'The relationship between the UK and Scottish Governments', HC 1586, 7 June 2019.

Scottish Conservative Party (1999a), *Scotland First*, Edinburgh: SCUP.

Scottish Conservative Party (1999b), 'The right answers for Renfrewshire from the Renfrewshire Conservatives', Scottish Election Ephemera collection, Glasgow: University of Strathclyde Library.

Scottish Conservative Party (2010), *Invitation to Join the Government of Britain*, Edinburgh: SCUP.

Scottish Conservative Party (2011), *Common Sense for Scotland*, Edinburgh: SCUP.

Scottish Conservative Party (2014a), *European Election Manifesto 2014*, Edinburgh: SCUP.

Scottish Conservative Party (2014b), *Commission on the Future Governance of Scotland*, Edinburgh: SCUP.

Scottish Conservative Party (2015), *Strong Leadership: A Brighter, More Secure Future*, Edinburgh: SCUP.

Scottish Conservative Party (2016), *A Strong Opposition – A Stronger Scotland*, Edinburgh: SCUP.

Scottish Conservative Party (2017a), *Forward, Together: Our Plan for a Stronger Scotland, a Stronger Britain and a Prosperous Future*, Edinburgh: SCUP.

Scottish Conservative Party (2017b), *Localism for Growth*, Edinburgh: SCUP.

Scottish Conservative Party (2018), *Scottish Conservative Unionist*, Edinburgh: SCUP.

Scottish Government (2007), 'First Minister in Belfast' speech, 18 June.

Scottish Government (2011), *Scotland's Census 2011*.

Scottish Government (2019), '"Urgent need" for intergovernmental reform', Joint Scottish Government–Welsh Government letter to the Minister for the Cabinet Office, 4 July.

Seawright, D. (1999), *An Important Matter of Principle: The Decline of the Scottish Conservative and Unionist Party*, Aldershot: Ashgate.

Sheldon, J. and Kenny, M. (2019), 'Unionism and the Conservative Brexit deal rebellion', Constitution Unit, blog, 1 February, <https://constitution-unit.com/2019/02/01/unionism-and-the-conservative-brexit-deal-rebellion/> (last accessed 10 August 2019).

Shipman, T. (2017), *Fall Out: A Year of Political Mayhem*, London: William Collins.

Simpkins, F. (2017), 'The 2016 Scottish Parliament elections: unionist parties and the constitutional divide', *Revue Française de Civilisation Britannique*, 12:4, 1–15.

Simpkins, F. (2018a), 'The 2017 general election in Scotland: a return to multi-party politics?', *Revue Française de Civilisation Britannique*, 23:2.

Simpkins, F. (2018b), 'Challenging Theresa May's vision of Brexit Britain: Ruth Davidson and the 2017 UK general election', *Observatoire de la société britannique*, 21:1, 141–60.

Skoutaris, N. (2019), '"Our precious Union": The backstop and the constitutional integrity of the UK', Verfassungsblog, 29 March, <https://verfassungsblog.de/our-precious-union-the-backstop-and-the-constitutional-integrity-of-the-uk/> (last accessed 29 March 2019).

Smith, A. (2011), *Devolution and the Scottish Conservatives: Banal Activism, Electioneering and the Politics of Irrelevance*, Manchester: Manchester University Press.

Smith, A. (2017), 'Relocating the British subject: ethnographic encounters with identity politics and nationalism during the 2014 Scottish independence referendum', *Sociological Review Monographs*, 65:1, 54–70.

Smith, J. (2001), *The Tories and Ireland, 1910–1914: Conservative Party Politics and the Home Rule Crisis*, Dublin: Irish Academic Press.

Soares, A. (2016), 'Living within and outside unions: the consequences of Brexit for Northern Ireland', *Journal of Contemporary European Research*, 12:4, 835–43.

Stewart, A. T. Q. (1967), *The Ulster Crisis*, London: Faber & Faber.

Stewart, D. (2009), *The Path to Devolution and Change: A Political History of Scotland under Margaret Thatcher*, London: I. B. Tauris.

Thomson, J. (2015), 'Abortion and same-sex marriage: how are non-sectarian controversial issues discussed in Northern Irish politics?', *Irish Political Studies*, 31:4, 483–501.

Thrasher, M., Borisyuk, G., Shears, M. and Rallings, C. (2014), 'Councillors in context: the impact of place upon elected representatives', *Local Government Studies*, 41:5, 713–34.

Todd, J. (2015), 'The vulnerability of the Northern Ireland settlement: British–Irish relations, political crisis and Brexit', *Études Irlandaises*, 40:2, 61–73.

Tonge, J., Braniff, M., Hennessey, T., McAuley, J. W. and Whiting, S. A. (2014), *The Democratic Unionist Party: From Protest to Power*, Oxford: Oxford University Press.

Tonge, J., Braniff, M., Hennessey, T., McAuley, J. W. and Whiting, S. A. (2019), *The Ulster Unionist Party: Country Before Party?*, Oxford: Oxford University Press.

Tonge, J., Leston-Bandeira, C. and Wilks-Heeg, S. (eds) (2018), *Britain Votes 2017*, Oxford: Oxford University Press.

Torrance, D. (2009), *'We in Scotland': Thatcherism in a Cold Climate*, Edinburgh: Birlinn.

Torrance, D. (ed.) (2012), *Whatever Happened to Tory Scotland?*, Edinburgh: Edinburgh University Press.

Torrance, D. (2014), *Britain Rebooted: Scotland in a Federal Union*, Edinburgh: Luath Press.

Torrance, D. (2017), '"Standing up for Scotland": The Scottish Unionist Party and "nationalist unionism", 1912–1968', PhD thesis, University of the West of Scotland.

Waldegrave, W. (2019), *Three Circles into One: Brexit Britain: How Did We Get Here and What Happens Next?*, London: Mensch Press.

Walker, G. (1995), *Intimate Strangers: Political and Cultural Interaction Between Scotland and Ulster in Modern Times*, Edinburgh: John Donald.

Walker, G. (2010), 'Scotland, Northern Ireland and devolution: past and present', *Contemporary British History*, 24:2, 235–56.

Walker, G. (2016), *The Labour Party in Scotland: Religion, the Union, and the Irish Dimension*, New York: Palgrave Macmillan.

Walker, G. and Officer, D. (1998), 'Scottish unionism and the Ulster question', in C. MacDonald (ed.), *Unionist Scotland 1800–1997*, Edinburgh: John Donald, pp. 13–26.

Walsh, C. (2015), 'Media capital or media deficit?', *Feminist Media Studies*, 15:6, 1025–34.

Watts, R. (2007), 'The UK as a federalised or regionalised union', in A. Trench (ed.), *Devolution and Power in the UK*, Manchester: Manchester University Press.

Wellings, B. (2012), *English Nationalism and Euroscepticism: Losing the Peace*, Bern: Peter Lang.

Wellings, B. (2019), *English Nationalism, Brexit and the Anglosphere*, Manchester: Manchester University Press.

Wheatley, Lord (1969), *Report of the Royal Commission on Local Government*, Edinburgh: HMSO.

Whiting, M. (2017), *Sinn Féin and the IRA: From Revolution to Moderation*, Edinburgh: Edinburgh University Press.

Winchester, P. (2017), '6 good reasons to vote Pauline Winchester on 4th May for a strong voice in Midlothian West', Scottish Election Ephemera collection, Glasgow: University of Strathclyde Library. Election leaflets, <https://electionleaflets.org/leaflets/13779/> (last accessed 9 January 2020).

Wright, K. (2017), 'How shifts in Scottish public opinion helped the Conservatives reverse their long-term decline', 26 July, <http://eprints.lse.ac.uk/83964/1/politicsandpolicy-scottish-public-opinion-conservatives.pdf> (last accessed 30 August 2019).

YouGov (2017), 'YouGov survey results', <http://d25d2506sfb94s.cloudfront.net/cumulus_uploads/document/4xpbxy1kyn/InternalResults_170613_Coding_WhyConLab_W.pdf> (last accessed 4 October 2019).

YouGov (2019), 'Most Conservative members would see party destroyed to achieve Brexit', <https://yougov.co.uk/topics/politics/articles-reports/2019/06/18/most-conservative-members-would-see-party-destroye> (last accessed 10 September 2019).

INDEX